Praise for *The Secret c* *Pada*

The Secret of the Yoga Sutra underscores the living appeal of yoga study as a vehicle leading to meditative practice.

—Edwin Bryant, author of *The Yoga Sutras of Patanjali*

The richness, depth, and clarity of *The Secret of the Yoga Sutra* represent the possibility of a sea change for all future generations of seekers to truly appreciate, understand, and practice Patanjali's *Yoga Sutra.* Pandit Rajmani Tigunait's singular vision is informed by his extraordinary knowledge as a scholar, his mastery as a practitioner, and, most vitally, the experiences and secret revelations he received at the feet of living sages, whose timeless wisdom directly connects the reader to Patanjali himself. This book is a gift from the sages, a blessed manual for all of those seeking lasting freedom and the highest fulfillment.

—Rod Stryker, founder of ParaYoga and author of *The Four Desires*

Pandit Tigunait's commentary on the *Yoga Sutra* offers us a true mystical transmission of the inner teachings of this classic text. Writing from his deep understanding of both the text and the tradition behind it, Panditji also shares the fruit of his own meditative practice. The power of his experience and knowledge radiates through these pages. I especially recommend *The Secret of the Yoga Sutra* to any meditator who wants to understand more deeply the higher stages of meditation.

—Sally Kempton, author of *Meditation for the Love of It* and *Awakening Shakti*

I enthusiastically recommend Pandit Tigunait's *The Secret of the Yoga Sutra* for eager yoga students as well as yoga teachers who have already read every translation and the original Sanskrit text. Both are in for a real treat. Panditji's warmth, sincerity, and clear understanding soak every page as he patiently unfolds this deep and profound ancient text step-by-step. Explaining technical terms in precise reference to practical experience, he makes the esoteric seem obvious and even gets us excited to practice. He is careful to ground us in relationship with others, and lets us see them with both intelligence and compassion. As a special treat he introduces us to many specific techniques of pranayama and meditation passed down to him from his teachers. Practitioners from all schools and traditions of yoga will take great delight in finding the endless connections revealed.

—Richard Freeman, founder of the Yoga Workshop
and author of *The Mirror of Yoga*

Of the dozens of translations and explications of this text that exist in English alone, few possess the power and reliability of Pandit Rajmani Tigunait's *The Secret of the Yoga Sutra.* His excellent exploration of the first segment of Patanjali's magnum opus deserves an attentive reading by any serious student of the *Yoga Sutra.*

—Robert Svoboda, ayurvedic physician and author

Pandit Tigunait's brilliant new commentary on the *Yoga Sutra* is destined to become a classic. From its very first pages, the reader can feel the hand of a master—a scholar, a practitioner, a devotee. This commentary is not just about yoga. It *is* yoga. The worldwide yoga community is greatly in debt to Panditji for devoting his life to a work of such luminosity, and we must look forward with great anticipation to the rest of the series.

—Stephen Cope, founder of the Kripalu Institute for Extraordinary
Living and author of *Yoga and the Quest for the True Self*

It is rare to find a teacher who is a true living master and lineage holder, has classical Indian as well as Western academic training, is deeply immersed in the wisdom of the ancients, and is fluent both in English and contemporary Western culture. Pandit Rajmani Tigunait, PhD, is that rare teacher. *The Secret of the Yoga Sutra* will open the hearts and minds of all serious students of yoga to the inner meaning and transformational potential hidden in this great text. This book is a brilliant gem radiating the clear light of yoga to all who open its pages.

—Gary Kraftsow, MA, founder of the American Viniyoga Institute and author of *Yoga for Transformation*

Good news! It is no longer necessary to dumb down the ancient wisdom of the *Yoga Sutra* in an effort to make it accessible. Pandit Tigunait's *The Secret of the Yoga Sutra* reveals with a refreshing clarity the rich and complex implications of the terse verses, which have up to now remained available only to the most sophisticated Sanskrit pundits. This book seems destined to become the standard of reference for a new generation of yogis who are ready for a deeper understanding.

—Rudolph Ballentine, MD, holistic health pioneer and author of *Radical Healing*

Much has been written on the *Yoga Sutra*, which makes evident the dignity, glory, and profound wisdom contained therein. Pandit Tigunait's interpretation has such crystal clarity that a reader can unfold inner joy, bliss, and tranquility in his or her own life. This is an accessible guide to the spiritual discipline of yoga.

—Vasant Lad, MASc, ayurvedic physician and author of *Ayurveda: The Science of Self-Healing*

Simply put, I love this book. It inspires me to return to my study of the *Yoga Sutra* with fresh eyes and an open heart. While there are many translations, this book is one of the best available today. The tone is both scholarly and intensely personal. The translations of the verses and the explanations that follow uniquely echo a spirit of understanding that can only emanate from the wisdom of a long-time practitioner.

—Judith Hanson Lasater, PhD, PT, co-founder of *Yoga Journal* magazine and author of eight books on yoga

I have learned so much from this unique and lucid introduction to the deep yoga tradition of the *Yoga Sutra*. Indeed, it has re-inspired and re-energized my own practice.

—John Kepner, executive director of The International Association of Yoga Therapists

The Secret of the Yoga Sutra is an exploratory adventure, rooted in the insights and experiences of Pandit Rajmani Tigunait, who writes as if he deeply and personally cares about the Divine. And that is infectious. Students of yoga, ayurveda, and life in general are fortunate to receive the benefit of his lively education, background, dedication, and service to life and knowledge.

—Claudia Welch, DOM, author of *Balance Your Hormones, Balance Your Life*

This remarkably readable and accessible translation of Patanjali's *Yoga Sutra* has it all: solid philosophy, practical advice, and a meaningful interpretation. Useful to both novice and scholar, Pandit Rajmani Tigunait's book includes key ideas from Vyasa's commentary, a summary of the theory and practice of Sankhya Yoga, and a beautiful rendering of the Sanskrit that lends itself to ready recitation and chanting. Trained in the tradition of Sri Vidya, Panditji renders this classic work with insightful clarity.

—Christopher Key Chapple, Doshi Professor of Indic and Comparative Theology and director of the Master of Arts in Yoga Studies Program at Loyola Marymount University

It won't be long before this in-depth and insightful contribution—blessedly authentic and delightfully accessible—will rise to the top of the reading and research list for beginners and scholars alike. Panditji's 35 years of experience as a dedicated yogi, teacher, and scholar give him an unparalleled understanding of classical yoga and how this ancient methodology can miraculously serve as a contemporary guide to health, happiness, and wholeness for our world and ourselves.

—Beryl Bender Birch, founder/director of The Hard & The Soft Yoga Institute and author of *Power Yoga* and *Yoga for Warriors*

As a young student, I read and re-read the *Yoga Sutra*. Although I recognized that this essential guide was designed to awaken and usher me toward transcendence, too often the translation was lost on me and I would end up confused. I wish Panditji's book *The Secret of the Yoga Sutra* had been available to me then! This straightforward, easy-to-understand translation lays out traditional concepts in a way that makes them accessible to anyone. I intend to continue using this book for my personal studies, as well as recommend it to all my students as a necessary manual that honors and eloquently interprets this profound practice that we love and yet often crave to understand better.

—Seane Corn, co-founder of Off the Mat, Into the World

The Secret of the Yoga Sutra, the first in a series, is a great gift to yoga practitioners, teachers, and seekers from a modern-day master who brings yoga into action, samadhi into everyday life, and keeps the tradition alive for all beings.

—Shiva Rea, yoga teacher and author of *Tending the Heart Fire*

By devoting an entire book to the first chapter of the *Yoga Sutra*, and including real-life examples, Panditji makes this translation and commentary very easy to read and understandable to the layperson. I look forward to subsequent volumes.

—Nicolai Bachmann, MA, teacher of Sanskrit and Yoga philosophy and author of *The Language of Yoga* and *The Path of the Yoga Sutras*

Pandit Rajmani Tigunait's lifelong commitment to the study and teaching of the *Yoga Sutra* of Patanjali makes him the perfect candidate for this unique publication. *The Secret of the Yoga Sutra* will inevitably be a text all yoga practitioners will refer to for years to come.

—Brenda Feuerstein, director of Traditional Yoga Studies

We think we know yoga. In reality, there are whole dimensions to yoga practice Westerners aren't even aware of. In this superb delineation of the *Yoga Sutra*'s difficult verses, Pandit Tigunait reveals a road map to higher consciousness—and ushers us into that amazing inner universe. His revelation of the hidden dimensions of the yoga tradition is absolutely thrilling.

—Linda Johnsen, MS, author of *The Living Goddess*

The Secret *of the* Yoga Sutra

Upcoming Books in This Series

The Practice of the Yoga Sutra: Sadhana Pada
The Power of the Yoga Sutra: Vibhuti Pada
The Promise of the Yoga Sutra: Kaivalya Pada

Also by Pandit Rajmani Tigunait, PhD

The Pursuit of Power and Freedom: Katha Upanishad
Touched by Fire: The Ongoing Journey of a Spiritual Seeker
Lighting the Flame of Compassion
Inner Quest: Yoga's Answers to Life's Questions
The Himalayan Masters: A Living Tradition
Why We Fight: Practices for Lasting Peace
At the Eleventh Hour: The Biography of Swami Rama
Swami Rama of the Himalayas: His Life and Mission
Tantra Unveiled: Seducing the Forces of Matter and Spirit
Shakti: The Power in Tantra (A Scholarly Approach)
From Death to Birth: Understanding Karma and Reincarnation
The Power of Mantra and the Mystery of Initiation
Shakti Sadhana: Steps to Samadhi
(A Translation of the Tripura Rahasya)
Seven Systems of Indian Philosophy

Video

Living Tantra Series DVD set

Audio

Spirit of the Vedas
Spirit of the Upanishads
Pulsation: Chants of the Maha Kumbha Mela

The Secret *of the* Yoga Sutra

SAMADHI PADA

PANDIT RAJMANI TIGUNAIT, PhD

HIMALAYAN INSTITUTE®

HONESDALE, PENNSYLVANIA USA

Himalayan Institute, Honesdale, PA 18431
HimalayanInstitute.org

Printed in the United States of America

23 22 21 20 19 18 17 16 15 14   1 2 3 4 5

ISBN-13: 978-0-89389-277-7 (paper)

Library of Congress Cataloging-in-Publication Data
Tigunait, Rajmani, 1953- author.
The Secret of the Yoga Sutra : Samadhi pada / Pandit Rajmani Tigunait, PhD.
pages cm
Includes index and glossary.
Includes Sanskrit text, transliteration, and translation into English.
ISBN 978-0-89389-277-7 (alk. paper)
1. Patañjali. Samadhipada. 2. Samadhi. I. Patañjali. Samadhipada. II. Patañjali. Samadhipada. English. III. Title.
BL1238.58.S26T55 2014
181'.452--dc23
2014023467

I. Series

∞ This paper meets the requirements of ANSI/NISO Z39-48-1992 (Permanence of Paper).

Contents

Preface

When I was a teenager I had a vivid experience—from every direction and in every respect I was embraced by a reality bigger than my soul, my mind, and the world of my faith and conviction. This experience freed me from doubt and fear and transported me to a state of joy untainted by want and need. But it did not last. I studied the scriptures, sat at the feet of masters, and undertook spiritual practices in an attempt to reclaim this experience. But only when I practiced what is described in *Yoga Sutra* 1:36 did I find what I had lost.

I grew up steeped in the ideals of the sages. I revered Buddha and Mahatma Gandhi, and was certain I had no animosity and no enemies. I had no reason to fear anything or anyone. But this conviction was shattered early one morning when a gang of bullies knocked me down and threw me into a compost pit. The bullies—my distant uncles—were trying to get a disputed piece of land by terrorizing my family. They slapped my mother and hurled me into the compost pit. Enraged and shouting at the top of my lungs, I climbed out only to be thrown back in. This happened repeatedly.

Very quickly, the people from the village formed a ring around my uncles and me. These were our neighbors—my friends and friends of my family—so when no one came forward to protect me, let alone defend justice, I was overcome by a torrent of anger and sadness. Everyone seemed like my enemy. All I could think of was to destroy everything and everyone, even myself. At this point, my uncles picked me up and hurled me into the pit again.

With this, something shifted. Lying in the bottom of the pit, I thought, "They have bamboo sticks. What is preventing them from beating me and killing me? Why don't I have any broken bones? Who's protecting me from serious injury?" These questions drew me into a state I had never known before. I saw myself—a lonely and helpless fellow hoping for others to protect me. I saw my conviction and my lack of it. I saw the feeling of animosity inside me and the enemies outside. I saw the element of fear, as well as its source. I saw my mind drowning in sorrow. Yet right next to my afflicted mind, I saw a luminous being and instantly recognized it as my own essence—my inner Self. It is the Divinity in me. I looked at my mind through the eyes of this Divinity and found it as pure and bright as the Divinity itself. I was overcome by a joy that had no trace of sorrow. My fear and feelings of animosity vanished. I did not need anyone or anything to protect me. I was not lonely, for I was embraced by the luminous Divinity who spontaneously emitted the light of discernment and profound joy.

I climbed out of the pit. To my surprise, the atmosphere was considerably calmer. My uncles were still loudly claiming the land, but the crowd was now condemning the violence. I could clearly see and hear everything happening around me but my mind was pulled inward, trying to assimilate the experience I'd just had. I was thrilled to realize I had found a new mind. With this new mind, I saw a beautiful world and I also saw it was contaminated by fear and greed. More or less everyone was afflicted by pain. To be born as a human was clearly a gift, yet people didn't seem to know what to do with this gift. A thought swept my being: I must not let this divine gift go in vain. The world run by fear, doubt, and the desire for power and possessions is trivial. Even the biggest achievements are smaller than the life force. My job is to tend this gift and watch it blossom. I can do it and I must do it. I took my mother inside the house, bathed, had my breakfast, and went to school.

As the months went by, the intensity of the experience and the clarity and confidence it engendered faded. The harsh realities of life again claimed my attention. I was back in the same chaotic, unfriendly world, but what bothered me most was my own restless mind. My mother offered a solution—have faith in God and worship him with rituals, as she did. My father told me to recite scriptures. The teachers at my Sanskrit school advised me to meditate on a mantra. I did all these things, but my list of complaints kept growing.

Five years passed. I had recently met Swami Sadananda, a master who embodied the austerity and wisdom of the ancient sages. In his company, I found some solace. Some of my self-confidence and trust in higher reality returned, yet I was still haunted by fear and doubt. I told Swami Sadananda about my experience in the compost pit and asked him to guide me to that experience again. He gave me a mantra and I undertook a long and intense practice of that mantra. I completed the practice, but was utterly disappointed. I had not gotten even a glimpse of the experience that once infused me with inner clarity and love for life.

When I shared my disappointment with Swami Sadananda, he said, "The experience you had in the compost pit was a blessing. You were in the full embrace of the Divinity. You received her protection and guidance. Enlightened by her light, you saw your whole being and you saw both the light and the darkness that had enveloped your inner and outer worlds. You saw life's purpose and realized you had all the tools and means to achieve it. But because the Divinity did not have five heads or a long trunk or ten arms and was not riding on a bull or a lion or sitting on a throne, you did not truly value it. Attachment to the notion of a god outside you is a curse. You must overcome it. Rediscover your luminous Self and embrace it wholeheartedly."

With this, he expounded on the concept of God as described in *Yoga Sutra* 1:23–1:29. His explanation of God was deeply reassuring, but it was only after he taught me the practice of meditation described in sutra 1:36 that I understood the true source of sorrow.

We have all experienced physical and emotional pain and know how to manage it, at least to some extent. But we do not know the nature and the source of our most fundamental pain—the pain of loneliness. This, I came to understand, is the true source of sorrow. The feeling of being isolated, abandoned, and unloved is painful, and the world offers no remedy. This deeply rooted pain manifests as fear and doubt. Most of us are afraid of losing what we have and anxious about what the future may bring. This feeling of disempowerment breeds anger and a sense of hopelessness, and only a few of us conquer it.

As time passed and my study and practice matured, I came to experience vividly what I had been taught to believe: each of us is a pure, self-luminous being. In the light of our inner luminosity, we experience both our essential nature and our eternal relationship with the Divine. Our feeling of loneliness vanishes forever. The feeling of being isolated, abandoned, and unloved no longer has a place in our life. We are free from fear, doubt, anger, and the sense of hopelessness. We are clear and confident. We are grateful for what we have and enthusiastic about achieving what we need to complete our quest.

Looking back now, I realize it was the pristine and straightforward wisdom of the *Yoga Sutra* that helped me reclaim the luminous joy that dawned so spontaneously that day in the compost pit. My intention in writing this commentary is to present the wisdom of the *Yoga Sutra* in the same pristine, straightforward manner it was presented to me. In these pages I have upheld the central precept of the tradition: Yoga is an experiential path, and experience comes from practice. I have treated each sutra as a step toward achieving our ultimate goal—inner fulfillment and freedom. This commentary will guide you on that path. It is a tribute to the teachers of the lineage and is an expression of my gratitude to the Divine Being, whose luminosity infuses our life with meaning and purpose.

Introduction

Patanjali's *Yoga Sutra* is firmly rooted in the insight and experience of the sages: A human being is an island of excellence. We are born to excel. We are surrounded—from every direction and in every respect—by the intrinsic power and creativity of the Divine. Our core is Pure Consciousness; luminosity is our essential nature. Our most distinctive attribute is our ability to know our own essence—our own intrinsic divinity. Life is a priceless gift, for life endows us with everything we need to experience our grandeur. Discovering the intrinsic divinity at our core is the highest achievement; dying without experiencing it is the greatest loss.

The *Yoga Sutra* is a manual for experiencing our intrinsic divinity and becoming firmly established in it. The text opens with an indisputable truth: practice is the key to success, for practice leads to a direct experience of our inherent grandeur. How successful we will be in our practice depends on the quality of our mind. A clear, one-pointed, and confident mind will accelerate our quest and enable us to fulfill life's purpose; a confused and self-doubting mind will block and subvert that purpose. This stark dichotomy emerges because the mind has two sets of attributes—one innate and the other acquired.

The Inherent Power of Mind

Self-luminosity is the mind's innate attribute. It empowers the mind to discern, decide, and act. Because of this virtue, the mind has the capacity to unveil the boundless mysteries of life and become master of the world within and without. This inherent luminosity is the source of all human ingenuity, creativity, and confidence. Our self-contained and self-guided inner radiance manifests as genius and empowers us to excel in life. It has enabled us to unravel the mysteries of the forces of nature and mold the natural world to serve our purposes. Our inner luminosity is also the ground for spiritual revelation, including the revelation of our relationship with the immortal Divine Being. Our self-luminous mind pulled us out of the Stone Age and allowed us to build endlessly diverse civilizations. The torchbearers of the human race have emerged from this luminous mind.

The mind's most significant innate attribute is its ability to know both itself and its creator and guide. It also has the innate ability to know the objective world. The mind can navigate through time and space and comprehend the long chain of cause and effect. When directed outward, the mind unveils the mysteries pertaining to the external world: we become scientists. When directed inward, it unveils its own mysteries and sees the Seer within: we become sages.

The range of our mental abilities is limitless. We begin life totally dependent on others for protection and nourishment. We quickly learn to speak, explore our surroundings, train our senses, and develop a discrete sense of self-identity. When as adults we turn our mind outward, we accomplish marvels: we compose symphonies, splice genes, fuse atoms, build skyscrapers, and observe the universe beyond our galaxy. When as spiritual seekers we turn our mind inward, we discover extraordinary realms of power and intelligence, transcend the linearity of time and space, and see our own Creator.

The Mind's Acquired Limitations

We come into the world with a powerful and illuminating mind. Yet most of us have no clue why we are here because our mind has acquired the tendency to neglect and dismiss its own inherent virtues. This habit causes the mind to create its own little world and then work hard to protect it. It gives rise to distorted self-identity, attachment, aversion, and fear of loss. These acquired attributes veil our inner luminosity, forcing us to grope our way in the darkness of ignorance.

We all are trying to discover the secret of life. We want to know who we are, what our relationship is with the world, what is the true source of happiness, and most importantly, how to live with purpose and without fear. We know the mind has enabled us to master the external world, but we rarely stop to consider that if we master the mind itself, and thereby gain access to its vast pool of power and intelligence, unending joy and eternal freedom will be ours. Instead, we let the mind roam aimlessly. Protecting it from doubt, fear, anger, confusion, and self-incrimination is not among our priorities. As a result, we strive for peace with an agitated mind. We look for clarity with a stupefied mind. We search for our inner self with a mind that knows only how to operate in the external world. We attempt to achieve lasting happiness with a mind accustomed to chasing short-lived pleasure. We yearn for ultimate freedom with a mind enslaved by its own dysfunctional habits. In short, we have set out on the path of conquest with a self-defeating mind. Doubt, fear, uncertainty, sorrow, and grief thus become an integral part of our destiny.

The *Yoga Sutra* tells us step-by-step how to eliminate these acquired and self-defeating properties and reclaim our innate luminosity. In this context, the text explains the dynamics of the mind, its binding and releasing forces, and how to attain mastery over them and thus become established in our self-luminous essential nature.

Another theme concurrent with unlocking the power of the mind is understanding the law of karma. "As you sow, so shall you reap" is a succinct summary of this immutable law. Life is accompanied by a long chain of pleasant and unpleasant experiences, many of which walk into our life unannounced. When we fail to decipher the cause of those events, we call them "destiny." If they are unpleasant, we call them "misfortune." If they are pleasant, we call them "luck." The simple-sounding law—as you sow, so shall you reap—is the key to understanding what propels the events in our lives. This law demands that we become connected to our conscience and conduct ourselves in compliance with it. Only when we are fully connected to our conscience do we see the difference between right and wrong, good and bad. Only then do we decide to perform right actions and avoid wrong ones.

By introducing the concept of karma, Patanjali offers a step-by-step plan to identify the right seeds, sow them, and harvest good and desirable fruits. He explains the dynamics of karma, its association with the mind, and the karmic impact on our memory. He also explains how our past karmic impressions influence our present actions, and how, if not checked in time, our actions lead to the formation of deep karmic impressions, which then impel us to perform similar actions. This vicious cycle veils the innate luminosity of our mind and makes it a slave to its acquired conditions. This entire process is called *karma chakra.* Karma chakra has three distinct components: the thought (*vritti*) that propels the action, the impression (*samskara*) created by that thought and the ensuing action, and the next round (*chakra*) of action propelled by the samskara. Thus, this process is known as *vritti samskara chakra.* This concept is the ground for understanding the law of karma. It is also the ground for understanding the yogic doctrine of ordinary birth and purpose-driven, extraordinary incarnation.

The Concept of Karma Chakra

Each of our actions creates an impression in the mind. These impressions contain the subtle properties of our actions. Our actions are propelled primarily by our desires. Desires are tainted by like or dislike, attachment or aversion, love or hatred. As a result, the subtle impressions stored in our mind are imbued with these properties—the stronger the desire, the more intense the action arising from it. The intensity of the action and the number of times it is repeated determine the strength of the subtle impression.

With the passage of time, the subtle impressions of our actions become strong enough to manifest as habits. When we reinforce our habits through our repeated actions, they become even stronger—veiling our intelligence, dulling our power of discrimination, and heavily influencing our comprehension. As our habits mature, they dominate our decision-making ability. Our actions are then driven by our habits. As this process is repeated, the subtle impressions are strengthened and deepened until they become so powerful that they begin to drive our thoughts, speech, and actions from deep within. At this point, a subtle impression has become a samskara.

Samskaras are habits so deeply embedded in our mind that they shape our inner world. Our personality is molded by our samskaras. For example, as a result of our samskaras, some of us are introverts and others are extroverts; some of us are inclined toward science and technology while others have a natural inclination for art and literature. All of us have numberless samskaras—some are quite strong, some are relatively weak. The strongest samskaras dominate our mind, influencing and shaping our power of discernment from deep within. These defining attributes of our personality influence our judgment, molding our concepts of right and wrong, good and bad. In Yoga, the term for the most powerful samskaras is *vasana,* a potent subtle impression that colors the mind. We see reality through the lens of our vasanas. This lens distorts our perception of others and ourselves. Thus, our mind is no longer in control—we see only what our vasanas allow us to see.

The mind thinks and acts in conformity with our samskaras and vasanas. This kind of mind has little or no mastery over its own thought processes. Our samskaras and vasanas make the decisions about what to think and how to think. Smeared as it is with these powerful subtle impressions, the mind is unaware of what is going on deep inside and has little control over stopping or changing the direction of its thoughts. Agitating thoughts make it agitated. Confusing and stupefying thoughts make it confused and dull. Put simply, the mind has become the slave of its own creation—samskaras that have matured into vasanas. As we have seen, this cycle (*chakra*)—from thought process (*vritti*) to the formation of subtle impressions (*samskara*), and from subtle impressions back to thought process—is known as *vritti samskara chakra* or *karma chakra*. Using the inherent brilliance and power of the mind to change the course of our karmic impression is our birthright. The method that allows us to claim this birthright is Yoga.

Because all karmas are contained in the mind, the mind is known as *karmashaya*, the repository of karmas. Our karmas and our sense of I-am-ness are comingled. We are fully aware of ourselves and of the actions we perform, and we perform our actions with the intention of benefiting from them. In other words, we identify with our actions and their fruit. The stronger the identification, the harder it is to distance ourselves from our actions and their fruit. Our karmas chase us and we chase our karmas—the two are wedded. We are immersed in our karmas and our karmas are immersed in us. As long as this condition persists, we have no ability to see our core being, Pure Consciousness.

To know ourselves as we really are, we must restore the pristine nature of our mind. We must cleanse our mind of its karmic impurities, let the luminosity of Pure Being shine through the mind, let the mind see the objective world in the light of Pure Being, and let the mind rediscover life's purpose as designed by Divine Providence. How to do that is the subject of "Samadhi Pada," the first chapter of the *Yoga Sutra*, and the commentary contained in the present volume.

The *Yoga Sutra* in a Living Tradition

Twenty-two hundred years ago, the great sage and yogi Patanjali gathered the essence of Yoga philosophy and the vast range of yogic practices, distilling them into 196 concise sentences, which in time came to be known as the *Yoga Sutra*. The text is divided into four chapters: "Samadhi Pada," "Sadhana Pada," "Vibhuti Pada," and "Kaivalya Pada." It is so profound, perfect, and well grounded in the direct experience of the long line of sages that it is regarded as *Yoga shastra*, the final authority on Yoga philosophy and practice. The sutra style of writing demands each word be so precisely selected and placed that even the slightest alteration—adding or deleting a word or changing the order—alters the meaning. Sutras are so compact and cryptic that deciphering them requires expert assistance. This has generated a long line of commentarial literature.

Many of the commentaries on the *Yoga Sutra* written in the past thousand years stand out for their distinctive approach to elaborating on the content of this text. My own approach is to view the *Yoga Sutra* as a guide to accomplishing the purpose of life—finding eternal fulfillment and ultimate freedom. I have put the understanding of the sages before my own and have not hesitated to pass on the views and the teachings of the masters who taught me this text in the traditional manner. My teachers made sure I understood that the *Yoga Sutra* is a practice-oriented text. To this end, they taught me the first 36 sutras and fulfilled their promise to teach me the rest only when I had completed the practice set forth in sutra 1:36. This traditional style of learning allowed me to reaffirm for myself what the sages have always known—experience is the best teacher, and experience comes from practice.

The masters I studied with came from various backgrounds and belong to different traditions, but all had a secret identity—they were adherents of the Sri Vidya tradition. From the standpoint of practice, Sri Vidya is a unique blend of three traditions: Yoga, Vedanta, and Tantra. Sankhya philosophy is the backbone of Sri Vidya (see Appendix C).

According to Sri Vidya, the human body is a miniature universe. Although it is mortal and subject to death, decay, and destruction, it is an abode of the Eternal Being. Immortality is our essence. We are truly fulfilled and free only after we experience our self-luminous essential nature. This imperishable luminosity is the source of everything in existence. All of us are innately equipped to experience our inner divinity, for we are born with a mind endowed with limitless power and intelligence. Yoga practice (*sadhana*) is the means for awakening the dormant potentials of our mind, experiencing our inner divinity, and becoming established in our essential nature. Yoga sadhana is the heart of the Sri Vidya tradition, and the *Yoga Sutra* is one of its seminal texts.

Texts dating back approximately 1,000 years list seventy-one masters in the Sri Vidya tradition, beginning with the sage Kapila and ending with the eighth-century master Shankaracharya. Patanjali is the fortieth in this list. The tradition has continued uninterrupted from the time this list was compiled up through the present. These adepts are not confined to a particular geographical region or religious group. Ample evidence that the tradition of Sri Vidya consists of adepts without borders can be found in Vidyaranya's encyclopedic work, *Sri Vidyarnava* (circa eleventh century CE). This volume presents a broad range of practices from different traditions, including Buddhism and Jainism, as integral to Sri Vidya. As you will see in Appendix D, the stature of some of these masters—Kapila, Atri, Vashishtha, Bhrigu, Angira, Vyasa, Patanjali, Shankaracharya, and Gorakhanatha, among them—makes it impossible to confine them to a single tradition. The practices and experiences of these and other masters are documented in the *Yoga Sutra*. One of them, Vyasa, has long been regarded as a sage who reveals and brings forward knowledge, even that which had fallen into obscurity. For centuries, his commentary on the *Yoga Sutra* has been recognized as the final authority on both the intent and the content of this text.

Following in the footsteps of the tradition, I have treated Patanjali's *Yoga Sutra* and Vyasa's commentary as one. I have also occasionally turned to *Patanjala-Yoga-Pradipa* by Swami Omananda Tirtha, a twentieth-century adept. But first and foremost, I have made a sincere effort to present the practices in the *Yoga Sutra* exactly the way my two most beloved masters, Swami Sadananda and Swami Rama, taught them to me. They made sure I understood that the *Yoga Sutra* is more than a book of Yoga philosophy, psychology, ethics, and metaphysics. It is more than a book listing *siddhis*—extraordinary powers—and a series of practices designed to unlock those powers. The *Yoga Sutra* embodies the very spirit of Yoga sadhana, grounded in the direct experience of a long line of masters.

In this commentary I have done my best to delineate the practice of Yoga in its fullness. In writing this commentary, my loyalty has been to Patanjali and Vyasa, which means I am presenting their teachings and practices without coming between these masters and their students. I have made a deliberate effort not to burden my readers, friends, and students with the conflicting opinions of commentators and translators. I have strictly followed the guidelines Patanjali himself set forth in the first and last sutras—*atha* and *iti.* With *atha,* as you will see in the first sutra, Patanjali tells his students—me, you, and everyone reading the text—to dive into the primordial pool of intelligence located deep within us and see the truth of our practice through our own inner eye. In the last sutra, with *iti,* he tells us that Chiti Shakti, unalloyed Pure Consciousness, is our core being.

The message of Patanjali in the *Yoga Sutra* is simple and straightforward: Remove the veil of darkness and allow your intrinsic luminosity to illuminate both your inner and outer worlds. Be free here and now, and experience your everlasting, self-luminous joy. The goal of Yoga is nothing less than that. In this light, I present this commentary to you.

SAMADHI PADA

SUTRA 1:1

अथ योगानुशासनम् ॥१॥

atha yogānuśāsanam ॥1॥

atha, now; *yoga*, union, balance; *anuśāsanam*, instruction

Now begins the instruction on the practice of Yoga.

Patanjali begins his discourse on Yoga with the long-held conviction of the sages that a human being is an island of excellence. To be born as a human is the greatest achievement, and to die without knowing the essence of life is the greatest loss. The immense wisdom and power buried in our body and mind is clear evidence that nothing is beyond our reach. No other creature has a brain and nervous system as evolved as ours. The retentive power of our mind is unmatched. Our ability to comprehend time, space, and the law of cause and effect, as well as our ability to store our experiences non-sequentially and retrieve them both sequentially and non-sequentially, places us above all other living beings. Our boundless intelligence and power of discernment give us access to the infinitely vast universe inside us and outside us. Nothing is impossible for us. We are extraordinary beings—individual islands of excellence.

The key to discovering the full scope of our excellence lies in understanding our mind and attaining mastery over it. The mind is the greatest of all mysteries. A clear, calm, one-pointed, friendly mind puts all the treasures of the world at our disposal. But a mind that has become dense, agitated, scattered, confused, and unfriendly robs us of our most fundamental privilege—our indomitable will to excel and achieve what only humans have the capacity to achieve. Unveiling the mystery of the mind is the core of Yoga philosophy and practice.

Unveiling this mystery is the most fulfilling and auspicious of all human endeavors—a fact Patanjali expresses with the first word of this sutra, *atha.* In Sanskrit literature, *atha* indicates an auspicious beginning. It conveys a feeling of sanctity and is used as an invocation. In our tradition, *atha* embodies this and much more. Ours is a tradition of Shakti Sadhana—more precisely, the esoteric path of Shakti Sadhana known as the tradition of Sri Vidya. The *Yoga Sutra* is one of the most significant texts in the Sri Vidya tradition, and Patanjali is one of the cardinal masters. Teachers in our tradition take pride in elaborating on the unique meaning of *atha* both in conjunction with the next word, *yoga*, and with *chiti-shaktih* and *iti,* which are the last two words in the *Yoga Sutra.*

In the tradition of Sri Vidya, *atha* is expressive of the self-luminous guiding intelligence residing in all of us. This inner luminosity constitutes the core of our island of excellence. It is the Divine in us—Ishvara (YS 1:24–1:26). Eternal and all-pervading, it is the principle of immortality, which awakens us from the slumber of death, brings us back to life, and guides us on the path of complete fulfillment and ultimate freedom. It is the vibrant, ever-awakened Power of Consciousness (*Chiti Shakti*), our final destination (*iti*). It is the beginning of our quest (*atha*) as well as its culmination.

From the standpoint of Yoga sadhana, *atha* denotes the intrinsic power of the guru chakra, represented by the letters *a* (अ), *ka*

(क), and *tha* (थ). These three letters form the triangle of the guru chakra, which corresponds to a space in the center of our forehead. Patanjali captures the essence of the guru chakra represented by *a*, *ka*, and *tha* in one word—*atha*—by applying the grammatical rule of *pratyahara* established by his predecessor, Panini.

According to the Sri Vidya tradition, the guru chakra is the primordial pool of intuitive wisdom. Here past, present, and future shine non-sequentially. Upon gaining access to this primordial pool, we are able to comprehend both the reality that corresponds to the world of time, space, and the law of cause and effect, and the reality that transcends it. In other words, the wisdom represented by *atha* gives us access to transcendental reality. Only when we are bathed in the luminosity of this inner wisdom can we cut asunder the knots of ignorance, false identification, attachment, aversion, and fear of death and become fully established in our true self. The purpose of undertaking Yoga sadhana is to immerse ourselves in this self-luminous inner wisdom and attain freedom from our karmic bonds once and for all—a fact Patanjali expresses here with the second word, *yoga*.

In his commentary on this sutra, Vyasa equates *yoga* with *samadhi*. Put simply, samadhi is a perfectly still, clear, tranquil state of mind. Vyasa goes on to say that samadhi is the mind's natural attribute. In other words, our intrinsically radiant mind is a conduit for enlightenment. Endowed as it is with the power of discernment, the mind has the ability to distinguish the real from the unreal. In its innate pristine state, it is crystal clear and as illuminating and revealing as the transcendental Divine Being itself. Nothing stands between the mind and Inner Divinity.

The mind's discerning power declines only when it falls from its pristine state. With that, it loses its confidence. It becomes prey to doubt and fear and begins to seek validation outside itself. Yoga sadhana enables us to restore the pristine nature of our mind and recapture its immense power and wisdom. Consisting of step-by-step methodical practice, Yoga sadhana requires us to commit ourselves to a system of discipline (*anushasanam*). This discipline begins with knowing the dynamics of our mind and discovering what causes it to slip from its pristine, radiant state. That is the subject of the next sutra.

SUTRA 1:2

योगश्चित्तवृत्तिनिरोधः ॥२॥

yogaścittavṛttinirodhaḥ ॥2॥

yogaḥ, union, balance; *citta*, mind; *vṛtti*, the mind's roaming tendencies; *nirodhaḥ*, mastery

Complete mastery over the roaming tendencies of the mind is Yoga.

Patanjali describes the dynamics and power of the mind by selecting a precise term, *chitta. Chitta* is derived from the verb root *chiti,* "to comprehend, understand, realize, or experience completely (*chiti kiti sanjnane*)." The fact that the word for mind—*chitta*—is derived from *chiti* tells us the mind is both the means of, and the conduit for, understanding truth in its fullness. Through the mind we become aware of reality within and without.

The mind is the repository of all our thoughts, feelings, and memories. It is a storehouse of our likes and dislikes. We see the world—and ourselves—through the eye of our mind. When the mind is clear and peaceful, we see the world as bright and peaceful. When the mind is convoluted, our understanding of the world and our relationship with it becomes equally convoluted. Our concepts of good and bad, right and wrong, depend on the quality of our mind, as do our likes and dislikes. The quality of our mind, in turn, shapes our thoughts, speech, and actions.

Both the sage and the demon within us are the products of our mind. A luminous mind enables us to see and embrace the immortal Omniscient Being within, while a mind darkened by ignorance entangles us in the long chain of birth and death, with its incessant experiences of pleasure and pain. In other words, we shrink when the mind shrinks and expand when the mind expands. But in all circumstances, the mind's inherent virtue—self-awareness—remains intact. No force can rob the mind of its capacity to know and experience the reality within and without. Patanjali expresses this intrinsic ability by choosing *chitta* over the many other words for mind in the Sanskrit language.

The mind has the ability to comprehend the object of cognition, the process of cognition, and itself as the cognizant force. Because it has the ability to know its own essence—its powers and privileges—it is known as *buddhi*, the force and conduit of illumination. Because the mind is aware of the object of thought, the process of thinking, and itself as the agent of thought, it is known as *manas,* that which thinks. Because the mind has the ability to take on the qualities and characteristics of the object of its thought, it is known as *ahamkara,* the faculty of self-identification. The mind's most distinctive attribute, however, is its ability to know its own essence—its pure, pristine nature. The mind is intrinsically as pure and luminous as Pure Consciousness itself (YS 3:54 and 3:55). Its discerning power is limitless. It can flow inward or outward.

Despite this innate capacity to rule the objective world and to explore and master the vast universe within, the mind suffers from lack of confidence in its own abilities. This is because in the course of our personal evolution the mind has become heavily influenced by the subtle impressions of our past deeds and experiences. Those deeds and experiences are contaminated by likes and dislikes.

They carry feelings of anger, hatred, jealousy, greed, love, lust, pity, compassion, and cruelty. Every deed and every experience contains traces of doubt, fear, regret, and guilt, and these feelings accompany every segment of our memory.

Memories pertaining to our deeds and experiences are deposited deep in our mind. These memories—subtle mental impressions—agitate our mind from deep within. Propelled by these impressions, the mind thinks and acts. Impressions and the thoughts and actions propelled by them are endless. That is why we find our mind constantly chasing one object after another. It has almost forgotten how to be still and be aware of its thoughts and actions. When awake, the mind is in the service of the senses, busily collecting pleasant sensory experiences and avoiding painful ones. During the dreaming state, it busies itself with its own fabrications. When it is asleep, the mind casts a blanket of unawareness over its intelligence and busies itself holding on to that blanket. These incessant mental activities further reinforce the subtle impressions. Thus, the wheel of subtle impressions and mental operations gains an ever-increasing momentum, and the mind becomes ever more deeply entangled.

Patanjali calls these mental operations *vrittis*, mental tendencies in motion. These roaming tendencies affect the mind in various ways. They can be disturbing, stupefying, or distracting. They can make the mind one-pointed and can lead it to a point where it is free of all thought constructs. In this context Vyasa identifies five distinct states of mind: disturbed (*kshipta*), stupefied (*mudha*), distracted (*vikshipta*), one-pointed (*ekagra*), and perfectly controlled (*niruddha*) (YS 1:1). Each of these states causes the mind to function differently.

The mind is disturbed because deep within the elements of attachment, desire, anger, fear, and doubt are active and the mind is operating under their influence. The mind is stupefied—dark, dense, and dull—because deep inside the elements of worry, grief, dejection, and hopelessness are active and have rendered the mind inert. The mind is distracted because disturbance and stupefaction are mingled with enthusiasm, courage, motivation, clarity, and purposefulness—and all these elements are randomly active. As a result, the mind is partly focused and partly dissipated.

A mind caught in any of these three states lacks clarity. It has no confidence in its own powers and privileges. It is indecisive and is only halfheartedly willing to act on its thoughts and ideas. It seeks validation from external sources. When propelled by a disturbed, stupefied, or distracted mind, our endeavors, no matter how noble, bear little fruit. The fruit they do bear is invariably tainted by doubt, uncertainty, and fear. It is a vicious circle: the actions and their fruits reinforce the subtle impressions that caused the mind to be disturbed, stupefied, and distracted. As Vyasa states in his commentary on the first sutra, these dysfunctional operations must be arrested. This is where the quest for samadhi begins—with arresting the disturbed, stupefied, and distracted mind and by acquiring a mind that is one-pointed (*ekagra*) and perfectly controlled (*niruddha*).

The mind becomes one-pointed when the elements of purity, clarity, and peacefulness are active deep within. Acting under the influence of these elements, the mind regains its power of illumination (*sattva*). It glimpses its own inner luminosity. As its attention focuses on its luminous nature, it regains confidence in its unique powers and privileges. A one-pointed mind is stable. It no longer grieves over the past nor worries about the future. The elements of disturbance, stupefaction, and distraction have been put to rest. The mind is serenely active and flowing peacefully inward.

Now the practice of Yoga, in its truest sense, has begun. As

Yoga practice deepens, the experience arising from it becomes increasingly refined and profound. As we will see in sutras 1:42 through 1:50, this inward journey has four distinct stages, all of which are accomplished by a one-pointed mind. Finally, the mind acquires such a high degree of purity, clarity, and perfection that it is as brilliant as Pure Consciousness itself (YS 3:55). In this state, all subtle impressions are reabsorbed into Primordial Nature (*Prakriti*) and we are absolutely free of the mind's roaming tendencies. According to Patanjali, this state is Yoga.

When we attain this level of yogic realization, what happens to our core being? That is the subject of the next sutra.

SUTRA 1:3

तदा द्रष्टुः स्वरूपेऽवस्थानम् ॥३॥

tadā draṣṭuḥ svarūpe'vasthānam ॥3॥

tadā, then; *draṣṭuḥ*, of the seer; *svarūpe*, one's own form; *avasthānam*, establishment, residence

Then the Seer becomes established in its essential nature.

Our core being is Consciousness—pure, eternal, and unchanging. Consciousness is luminous and all-pervading. Yoga philosophy calls it Purusha, "that which resides in the city of the body." The body is finite, but the Consciousness residing in it is infinite, for it is unconfined by space. The body is mortal, but the Consciousness pervading the body is immortal, for it is unconfined by time. Consciousness knows life and death, for its intelligence is not dependent on the conduits of body, mind, and senses for knowledge. It is the Seer, the Seeing Power itself. It is the fundamental principle of pure awareness. Consciousness is an infinite and eternal field of intelligence, devoid of differentiation between subject-object. It is pure existence. Nothing—not even the sharpest mind—can fully comprehend this indivisible, self-luminous intelligence. It is untouched by decay or decline and beyond want and need. It is perfect in every respect. This is the great and glorious truth of our core being. And yet, from where we stand today in the journey of life, we are completely at the mercy of our mind.

At this stage in our journey, the luminosity of our consciousness has become so subdued it is unable to comprehend its own essential nature—Consciousness itself. Its capacities are so dormant it must seek help from the body, mind, and senses for its own self-realization. Its intelligence is so thickly veiled it feels its presence only within the confines of the body, and that only vaguely. Its power of comprehension has become so limited it is unable to see it existed before birth and will continue to exist after death—it has fallen victim to the conditioning of time and space. Our core being, although all-pervading, omniscient, and beyond want and need, can move only with the help of the body, can perceive only with the help of the senses, and can cognize only with the help of the mind.

The Seer can no longer see itself. It has lost its capacity to experience its pure being directly and now depends on the mind to show it its reflection. Before it can perceive its true identity, it must see and recognize its own image—a process mediated by the mind. The validity of this recognition depends on how accurately the image is reflected in the mind and how accurately the mind presents that image to Consciousness. In other words, Consciousness—our core being—can see only what the mind shows it. Practically speaking, it no longer has an independent existence. Consciousness is so intermingled with the mind that it knows and feels only what the mind knows and feels. The mind's fear and doubt have become its own. The craving for pleasure and the aversion to pain now haunt our core being as strongly as they haunt our mind.

The question of when and how self-luminous Consciousness became intermingled with the mind, and so strongly identified with it, has long captured the imagination of philosophers and thinkers. According to Patanjali, the cause is ignorance (*avidya*). According to Vyasa, ignorance is our strong attachment to what is contrary to truth. The discussion of when, how, and why ignorance threw its veil over Consciousness leads us nowhere when we are already deeply entangled. But it is important for us to understand that Consciousness has fallen into the domain of the mind, and the mind has appropriated the role of Consciousness. As a result, the mind is accompanied by the properties of both Consciousness and the objective world. Although it is imbued with Consciousness, it remains unaware of its conscious nature. The mind has assumed the form of its perception yet behaves like the perceiver. Everything—object and subject, the perceived and the perceiver—has become its object (YS 4:23). This painful condition must be reversed. Consciousness must regain freedom from the slavery of the mind, and the mind must serve the purpose of Consciousness.

We can reverse this painful condition by purifying our mind and making it one-pointed, clear, and tranquil, so it can begin to flow peacefully inward. Eventually, we reach the point in our inward journey where the mind's roaming tendencies subside and the subtle impressions lose their grip. There is no longer anything in the mind that can distort or contaminate the light of Pure Consciousness reflecting in it. As soon as Consciousness sees its reflection and recognizes its true nature, the mind's purpose is accomplished. The curiosity to know who I am, how I came to be here, and what will happen to me in the future vanishes (Vyasa on YS 4:25). The mind is no longer tossed by its wandering habits. Figuratively speaking, the mind and our core being remain next to each other, but our core being is no longer touched by memories and mental cognitions, for there are none. This is what is meant by "the Seer becomes established in its essential nature."

With the exception of those established in the highest state of samadhi, none of us know ourselves apart from our mind. The concept of pure being (as opposed to impure being) makes no sense to us. For most of us, the idea of a higher and a lower self has no real meaning. But we do know we have a mind. Experience tells us the mind enables us to succeed in both worldly and spiritual endeavors. As soon as we gain mastery over our mind, the door to all achievement swings open.

A pristine mind is our best friend. It enables us to explore external and internal reality. However, when the mind becomes entangled in its own fluctuations, it has neither the time nor the energy to discover its own immense power. It no longer sees any reason to undertake the quest for inner fulfillment and ultimate freedom. It is so busy shifting among the disturbed, stupefied, and distracted states that it has neither the energy nor the wisdom to lift the veil of ignorance. The mind is essentially groping in darkness. Only when its roaming tendencies are arrested, its field of memory is purified, and it regains its pristine nature can it recognize and communicate with the immortal, self-luminous Pure Being. With this experience, the intuitive understanding of our core being dawns. And this is when the mind's purpose is accomplished.

What happens when we do not arrest the roaming tendencies of the mind is the subject of the next sutra.

SUTRA 1:4

वृत्तिसारूप्यमितरत्र ॥४॥

vṛttisārūpyamitaratra ॥4॥

vṛtti, the mind's roaming tendencies; *sārūpyam*, becoming one with form; *itaratra*, elsewhere

Elsewhere [the Seer] conforms to the roaming tendencies of the mind.

Our mental conditioning shapes our reality. It is an outgrowth of the subtle impressions deposited in the mind. These subtle mental impressions shape our mind and add their unique color to it—we see the world in their light. The shape and color of our mind determines the shape and color of the world we see. Our trust in ourselves, in our family, friends, society, religious practices, and ethical and moral values, is determined by our inner conditioning. In other words, the mind defines truth in light of its subtle impressions; we then use all our resources to find truth as we have defined it.

As explained by the previous sutra, if the building blocks of our inner conditioning are eliminated and the roaming tendencies of the mind come to an end, we regain our pristine state of mind. We see our essential nature—Pure Consciousness—and become fully established in it. Our experience of fulfillment and freedom no longer depends on whether we are rich, poor, young, old, religious, or non-religious. We have found our soul and know it is neither male or female, human or non-human, virtuous or non-virtuous. It is pure being—nothing more and nothing less.

As long as the subtle impressions persist, the roaming tendencies they engender dominate the mind. The mind is unstable and its perception of both Pure Consciousness and the objective world is distorted. We mistake our distorted perception for reality. A scattered and confused mind cannot see how elements such as fear, doubt, attachment, desire, anger, hatred, grief, love, compassion, happiness, piety, and pride shape our outer world. Nor does it see how these feelings, which are mingled with the subtle impressions, shape our inner world. Rooted in our subtle mental impressions, our feelings and emotions grip our conscience—the light of our core being—as firmly as they grip our mind.

Practically speaking, our core being is established in these inner tendencies and they are established in it. All the problems of our mind are now the problems of our core being. It suffers from the changing conditions of the body, mind, and senses—disease, old age, and death. We—a composite of Pure Consciousness and a mind encumbered with numberless impressions—are perpetually fearful. Our power of discernment is so subdued that the question of whether these feelings are arising from our core being or from the mind is meaningless. We experience ourselves as thinking and feeling beings, nothing more. We are happy when our actions yield desirable fruits and miserable when they do not. We do not see ourselves as a witness, or our body and mind as agents of our actions. We know ourselves only as doers, fully responsible for our actions and their fruits.

As long as the mind is dominated by its roaming tendencies, Pure Consciousness is only a metaphysical category. Our comprehension of reality stretches only as far as our mind. That is why our mind has to be refined and restored to its pristine state, a process that begins with understanding and analyzing our mental operations (*vritti*). That is the subject of the next seven sutras.

SUTRA 1:5

वृत्तयः पञ्चतय्यः क्लिष्टाक्लिष्टाः ।।५।।

vṛttayaḥ pañcatayyaḥ kliṣṭākliṣṭāḥ ॥5॥

vṛttayaḥ, tendencies that cause the mind to rotate; *pañca-tayyaḥ*, fivefold; *kliṣṭa*, afflicting; *akliṣṭāḥ*, non-afflicting

The tendencies that cause the mind to rotate are fivefold. They are either afflicting or non-afflicting.

When was the mind created? Who created it? Because the mind is timeless, the answers are beyond our ken. When did the mind and Consciousness become indistinguishably intermingled? That is also beyond our comprehension. Sometimes the mind thinks in a rational manner, other times irrationally. Sometimes it ponders with purpose, other times aimlessly. Sometimes it thinks randomly, other times with intention. Some thoughts are accompanied by love, others by hatred. Some are compelling and meaningful, others vague and useless. And the mind never stops—thought after thought rolls through it. Every thought, every mental movement, makes an impression on the mind, and each impression contains the qualities and characteristics of the thought construct that created it. With each repetition, the impression becomes deeper and more pronounced. In Yoga, these deeply imbedded subtle impressions are known as *samskaras*.

Samskaras are the products of our thoughts, and our thoughts are the products of our mind. Thoughts and samskaras are born in the mind and live in the mind. As we continually reinforce these subtle mental impressions, they become so potent they dictate how and what the mind thinks. This cycle—from thoughts to subtle impressions and from subtle impressions to thoughts—is called *vritti samskara chakra,* the wheel of thoughts and subtle impressions. It has been revolving from time immemorial. In the case of a careless soul, it revolves with an ever-increasing velocity. The purpose of Yoga is to understand the nature of this wheel (*chakra*)—its direction and speed—and bring it to a halt. The state in which it comes to a complete stop is samadhi, the perfectly still, well-controlled state of mind.

Most of our thoughts emerge in our mind without our being aware of where they come from and why. We brood without knowing why we are brooding. A scattered, untamed mind has no access to the vast field of samskaras from which our thoughts emerge. Samskaras influence how our mind functions, even though they are themselves products of our previous thoughts. With willful determination, we can choose to entertain a thought conducive to our purpose and protect it from the influence of undesirable samskaras. Freedom of choice is our innate virtue, but it is up to us whether or not we exercise it. Although the mind is caught in the *vritti samskara chakra*—the cycle of thoughts to subtle impressions back to thoughts—we have the ability to slow its momentum and eventually bring it to a complete halt.

The mind is in constant motion. Now it is here; the next moment it is likely to be somewhere else. It is addicted to surfing the wave of thoughts. These waves fall into five broad categories, as detailed in sutras 1:7 through 1:11. Some thoughts are associated with the objects of the external world and are accompanied by right understanding of those objects, while others are accompanied by false understanding of them. Some thoughts are purely imaginative. Some emerge when we are in dreamless sleep and we are unaware of them. Some emerge from the field of memory. All are the product of a disturbed mind, a stupefied mind, a distracted mind, a one-pointed mind, or a relatively still mind. Except when it is perfectly still, the mind continues rotating.

Regardless of the category to which they belong, all thoughts have a common characteristic: they agitate and spin the mind. That is why they are called *vrittis,* the principle of spinning. They take the mind for a ride. Thoughts manufactured by a disturbed mind spin the mind violently. Thoughts emerging from a disturbed mind have the qualities and characteristics of the object that created the disturbance. Some thoughts emerge from a one-pointed, relatively peaceful mind and are accompanied by an aura of peacefulness. In other words, some thought constructs are easier on the mind than others. Some are pleasant; others are unpleasant. Some are conducive to our overall growth and development while others are destructive.

In this sutra, Patanjali divides our thought constructs into two broad categories based on how they affect us: constructive, pleasant thoughts and destructive, painful thoughts. Understanding exactly what is meant by constructive and destructive requires that we examine the words Patanjali uses: *klishta* and *aklishta.* Both are derived from *klesha*, translated as "affliction." The thoughts that afflict us physically, mentally, and spiritually are *klishta* thoughts—in layman's language, "bad" thoughts. They block our growth and disturb us internally and externally. No matter how committed we are to a spiritual path, if we fail to pay attention to the effect of our thoughts, we will make no progress. To a large extent, spiritual practice involves removing these painful thoughts and replacing them with constructive, auspicious (*aklishta*) thoughts.

The word *klesha* is more profound than the translation "affliction" conveys. *Klesha* encompasses ignorance, mistaken self-identity, attachment, aversion, and fear (YS 2:3). Thoughts that contain any of these disturbing, painful conditions or that have a tendency to lead to them are *klishta* thoughts. Those that do not are *aklishta* thoughts. We call them "painful" and "non-painful" thoughts for the sake of simplicity. The systematic practice of Yoga leading to samadhi begins with eliminating painful thoughts and replacing them with non-painful ones. At the final stage, all thought constructs are brought to a complete halt, and we find ourselves fully established in our pure being.

Yoga practice often begins with asana and pranayama, but the ultimate goal is to attain mastery over the mind's roaming tendencies and elevate the mind to its pristine state, allowing it to bathe in the unalloyed light of Pure Consciousness. This is what Patanjali calls *yoga* and Vyasa calls *samadhi*—a state where our core being is established in its essential nature. In samadhi, we know exactly who we are, in isolation from our mind as well as in association with it. We know our relationship both with the external world and with our inner world. Thus, the mind plays a crucial role in Yoga. The better we understand our mind, the greater our chances of succeeding in our inner quest. Understanding the mind includes understanding the dynamics of our thoughts, as well as the subtle nuances of where and how thoughts originate. Patanjali devotes the next six sutras to enhancing our understanding of thought constructs, a clear indication of how important they are in our self-discovery.

SUTRA 1:6

प्रमाणविपर्ययविकल्पनिद्रास्मृतयः ॥६॥

pramāṇaviparyayavikalpanidrāsmṛtayaḥ ॥6॥

pramāṇa, correct or valid; *viparyaya*, incorrect or invalid; *vikalpa*, imaginary; *nidrā*, dreamless sleep; *smṛtayaḥ*, memory

The five mental functions are correct understanding, false understanding, imagination, dreamless sleep, and memory.

The entire range of our mental activities falls into five categories: correct understanding, false understanding, imagination, dreamless sleep, and memory.

An undisciplined mind is the victim of the information brought to it by the senses. It is in the habit of involving itself in everything it sees, hears, tastes, and smells. It registers and reacts to every form of touch it perceives. Regardless of how correct or incorrect the sensory information, the mind is spun by it. Furthermore, because the mind has its own unique tastes, interests, likes, dislikes, and preferences, it adds its own input to the information the senses bring. Its roaming tendencies force the mind to brood over what it perceives. Lack of self-mastery causes us to be mentally scattered and outwardly oriented. From the standpoint of reaching the still space within and seeing the core of our being, all sensory perception—correct or incorrect—is equally useless. The purpose of Yoga sadhana is to enable us to attain mastery over sensory perceptions and the mind's reaction to them so that our awareness moves inward one-pointedly.

The first of the five categories of mental activities is correct understanding (*pramana*). Correct understanding of the objective world contributes to our success in worldly matters, but has little bearing on our spiritual growth. That is why Patanjali classifies it as a *vritti,* a mental condition that makes the mind spin.

Brooding over our lack of comprehension and miscomprehension is the second category of mental activity. Hidden deep in the mind, our powerful subtle impressions (*samskaras*) wait for an opportunity to manifest. For example, fear is one of the most deeply ingrained mental impressions. When we step on a rope while walking in the dark, we panic, thinking we have stepped on a snake. There is no comprehension of the rope, only the miscomprehension of a snake. This miscomprehension (*viparyaya*) arises from lack of comprehension, quickly followed by a chain of reactions, thoughts, and feelings. The mind is caught in a train of thought that does not have truth as its object. In order to restore its inner luminosity, the mind must arrest this and all other thought constructs that do not have truth as their object.

Imagination (*vikalpa*) is the third category of mental activity. Imagination is a mental fabrication. It is completely different from the miscomprehension arising from lack of comprehension. It is the clear comprehension of an object existing only in our imagination. Even though it does not correspond to an actual substance, it can be communicated through language. For example, there is no cow with seven horns teaching scriptures to a group of doctoral candidates, yet there are corresponding words: "cow," "seven," "horns," "scriptures," "doctoral students." Arranged in proper order, these words make sense. We can communicate using these words and the notions conjured up by them; we can also stretch our imagination and turn them into an interesting story. From the standpoint of reaching samadhi, however, imaginary thoughts pose a barrier and are to be arrested.

Dreamless sleep (*nidra*), the fourth category of mental activity, has a unique effect on the activity and behavior of the mind. During dreamless sleep the mind throws a veil over all its experiences, thus putting its activities, concerns, and preoccupations out of view as actively as it attends to them in the waking state. The process of distancing itself from its previous involvements makes the mind revolve at almost the same velocity as when it yokes itself with those involvements when awake. However, the nature of this process of distancing—dreamless sleep—is such that the mind does not register it. Dreamless sleep lasts only 90 to 120 minutes before the mind resorts to dreaming. Dreamless sleep is another source of mental activity and is relaxing only in the sense that it disconnects us from the concerns of the reality belonging to the waking state. Spiritually speaking, dreamless sleep is as detrimental to samadhi as any thought construct. Sutra 1:38 describes a dimension of sleep that is spiritually uplifting. This is also a vritti, but it arises in an exceptionally purified and spiritually cultivated mind. It is a highly technical form of meditation, requiring precise instructions from a competent teacher.

The fifth category of mental activity is memory (*smriti*). Uncontrolled retrieval of the experiences deposited in our memory prevents us from turning our mind inward and reaching our core. Attaining mastery over the flow of memory, which includes voluntarily recalling a memory when it is needed and remaining oblivious to it when it is not, is the key to remaining focused on the object we have chosen for meditation. As we see in sutras 1:11, 1:20, 1:43, 1:47, and 1:48, memory plays an important role in our journey toward samadhi—both as an obstacle and as a means of removing obstacles. To reach samadhi, we must purify our memory field. Half of Yoga sadhana, as we will see in sutra 1:12, consists of removing these colorings (*vairagya*). Until then, memories continue churning the mind.

The five categories of mental function are described in detail in the following sutras.

SUTRA 1:7

प्रत्यक्षानुमानागमाः प्रमाणानि ॥७॥

pratyakṣānumānāgamāḥ pramāṇāni ॥7॥

pratyakṣa, sense perception; *anumāna*, inference; *āgamāḥ*, revelation; *pramāṇa*, correct understanding

Correct understanding is threefold: sense perception, inference, and revelation documented in the scriptures.

This and the next four sutras describe the five categories of mental activity and how they disturb, stupefy, and distract the mind. The purpose of all five sutras is to help us understand both the causes of these mental activities and their consequences.

The first mental activity, correct understanding (*pramana*), has three sources: sense perception, inference, and scriptural revelation. Scholars have debated the validity of these three categories at length. According to the Sri Vidya tradition in which I was trained, however, these scholarly debates are irrelevant from the standpoint of practice. By classifying correct understanding as a revolving behavior of the mind (*vritti*), Patanjali is making a clear point: an aspirant committed to inner discovery must bring all roaming tendencies of the mind to a halt, even those originating from a valid source of knowledge.

Each of Patanjali's three sources of correct understanding—sense perception, inference, and scriptural revelation—enables us to understand the nature and dynamics of objective reality correctly, but they all cause our mind to spin and thus destroy the inner tranquility we are seeking. From a spiritual perspective, therefore, these three sources of correct understanding are vrittis, conditions that make our mind unstable.

Sense perception (*pratyaksha*) is the source of correct understanding. According to Yoga philosophy, the mind uses the senses as vehicles for going into the external world, gathering information, and presenting it to the ego (*ahamkara*) and intellect (*buddhi*). Perceptual knowledge comes from a valid source and embodies correct understanding. It is indisputable for it reflects the reality of the object being perceived. Our ego confidently identifies it, and our intellect gives it the stamp of approval.

As students of the inner dimension of life, we must pay attention to how this so-called correct understanding of the objective world influences our mind. We are in the habit of perceiving objects and experiences as good or bad, right or wrong, useful or useless, friendly or unfriendly. As a result, we are inclined to accept one thing as desirable and reject another as undesirable. We put a tag of right or wrong, vice or virtue on almost everything. Thus, we perceive experiences brought by the senses, acknowledged by the mind, and analyzed by the intellect as pleasant or unpleasant. If they are pleasant, we develop an attachment to them, and if they are unpleasant, we have an aversion to them. Either way, these experiences agitate the mind and we lose the neutral ground from which to see and enjoy things the way they are. How to regain that neutrality and retain tranquility and transparency of mind while interacting with the external world is the subject of sutra 1:12.

The second category of correct understanding is inference (*anumana*). Inference depends on perception. For example, experience has taught us that where there is smoke there is fire—when we see smoke we conclude there is a fire. With the assistance of logic and reason, inference helps us comprehend what lies beyond the domain of perception. However, a negative mind, bent on entertaining its prejudices and preoccupations, can distort this source of correct understanding and entangle itself in a self-created net of mental constructs. We rarely realize that such mental constructs are by and large our own projections. Instead, we work hard to convince others (and ourselves) that our understanding is correct by constructing a detailed trail of logic and reason. This throws our mind into a useless revolving mode. Even a perfectly correct process of inference attended by a clear, calm, and tranquil mind is an obstacle to reaching samadhi. Therefore, Patanjali classifies inference as a vritti, a mental construct that deters us from reaching the still space within.

Revealed scripture (*agama*) is the third category of correct understanding. Many great souls have received knowledge pertaining to a reality far beyond the comprehension of an ordinary mind. Some of these revelations are documented in scriptures or sacred texts. While there is great merit in studying scriptures and putting them into practice, using them to clutter our mind with conflicting thoughts and ideas is damaging.

In the final analysis, any form of information or knowledge on the material plane, even perfectly valid knowledge, is a vritti. It is to be quieted. To reach samadhi, the mind must be free from all vrittis, brought to a single focus, and turned inward.

SUTRA 1:8

विपर्ययो मिथ्याज्ञानमतद्रूपप्रतिष्ठम् ॥८॥

viparyayo mithyājñānamatadrūpapratiṣṭham ॥ 8 ॥

viparyayaḥ, false comprehension; *mithyā*, false or unreal; *jñānam*, knowledge; *atadrūpapratiṣṭham*, corresponding to that which has no ground

Mistaking the unreal for the real is false understanding. False understanding is not grounded in reality; instead it corresponds to that which has no ground.

The mind has a tendency to brood over things that are baseless and to entertain things that are contrary to reality. It sees only what it wishes to see, hears only what it wishes to hear, respects only what it wants to respect, loves only what it wants to love. It does this by first blocking what is in view, then projecting what it wishes to see. What the mind now sees is non-apprehension and misapprehension (*viparyaya*). Viparyaya is actively embracing that which is contrary to reality. It refers to a false understanding so potent and formidable that it creates a seemingly insurmountable commotion in the mind. False understanding is the source of our most fundamental affliction, ignorance (*avidya*), for it blocks the view of reality regarding ourselves, then projects a distorted sense of self-identity (*asmita*) in its place. It leads us to become attached (*raga*) to that distorted identity. Attachment matures into strong dislike or hatred (*dvesha*) toward those who do not confirm the identity so dear to us. Fear of losing that identity is as painful as dying (*abhinivesha*).

Under the influence of false understanding, we brood over our health, wealth, power, and possessions; we project our honor and dignity into the world around us; we proclaim our rights and discharge our duties; and we plan our spiritual quest. We see nothing wrong in our understanding until we approach a state of stillness in meditation and become somewhat established within. Then we begin to realize how false understanding of ourselves and others has created its own self-propelled atmosphere and sucked our mind into spinning endlessly—more confusion, more misunderstanding, more prejudice, more misconceptions, and a never-ending blame game. According to Patanjali, to reach samadhi a student of Yoga must master this powerful vritti.

SUTRA 1:9

शब्दज्ञानानुपाती वस्तुशून्यो विकल्पः ॥९॥

śabdajñānānupātī vastuśūnyo vikalpaḥ ॥ 9 ॥

śabda, word; *jñāna*, knowledge; *anupātī*, that which follows; *vastu*, content or substance; *śūnyaḥ*, devoid of; *vikalpaḥ*, imagination

Imagination is knowledge, which due to the use of words appears to have content, but in reality is devoid of content.

Imagination is a unique category of mental activity. It arises neither from lack of comprehension nor from miscomprehension (*viparyaya*). Unlike *viparyaya*, the content of imagination is not rooted in untruth but is the product of the mind—a thought without substance as an object. It is an idea that can be communicated through words, but the content denoted by these words does not exist. A rabbit with horns is the classic example.

Imagination distracts the mind just as effectively as thought constructs belonging to the categories of correct understanding—sense perception, inference, and scriptural revelation—and false understanding. During meditation, imaginative thoughts block the peaceful and inward flow of mind. Even though they lack substance of their own, they are powerful enough to derail the mind from its spiritual course. To acquire a one-pointed mind and restore its innate luminosity, we must arrest this seductive mental tendency.

SUTRA 1:10

अभावप्रत्ययालम्बना वृत्तिर्निद्रा ॥१०॥

abhāvapratyayālambanā vṛttirnidrā ॥10॥

abhāva, non-existence; *pratyaya*, cognition; *ālambanā*, support; *vṛttiḥ*, tendencies that cause the mind to rotate; *nidrā*, dreamless sleep

Swirling of the mind around the cognition of non-being is dreamless sleep.

Sleep is a mental construct—or rather a broad and complex range of mental constructs. All thought constructs have one thing in common—an object. Every thought has an object, and the thought construct of dreamless sleep (*nidra*) is no exception. The difference is that in dreamless sleep the mind is not aware of what it is cognizing.

To understand this, think of the mind as a camera that records images on film. The senses are the lens. To take a picture, open the lens and click, exposing the film to the light, creating a picture. This is how the mind works when we are awake. Through the lens of our eyes, the light illuminates a tiger, for example, and the image is imprinted on the film of our mind. This imprint evokes a feeling: awe, fear, curiosity, or joy. Through the medium of these feelings, the construct (in this case, the tiger) spins our mind.

Sleep is a unique thought construct—its object is non-being. In dreamless sleep, we are taking pictures without opening the lens. The mind goes on clicking, but nothing emerges on the film. As far as the mental impressions and the cognition of them are concerned, the process and the effect are the same as if the lens was open. But because it is not, no light is entering, so the "click" exposes the film to the lack of light. The film is as exposed to the interior of the lens as when it was exposed to the light illuminating the tiger. This exposure results in a picture of the lens' interior, which is immersed in darkness. For all intents and purposes, the interior of the lens and the cognition of it is the same as non-being, non-existence. This non-being constantly emerging on the film of the mind is dreamless sleep.

During the waking state, our senses are active. They go into the external world, interact with their corresponding objects, return to their home base—the mind—with cognition of those objects, and then go into the external world again. Sleep begins when the senses withdraw to their home base and remain there. Nature pulls the curtain of inertia, confirming that the senses can now rest. The *Mandukya Upanishad* describes how consciousness rests during dreamless sleep while the mind continues spinning. As we sleep, the mind continues producing thought constructs with non-being as their objects. Thought constructs are still accumulating in the mind, but the sleepy mind is not fully aware of what is accumulating. The mind is not completely asleep, which is why we wake up with the recollection of sleeping well or having disturbed sleep.

Disturbed sleep drains our vitality as much as disturbed thought constructs do when we are awake. The quality of sleep depends on the quality of the sleeping mind. When we sleep with a disturbed mind, we will have disturbed sleep. Upon awakening from disturbed or shallow sleep we find ourselves exhausted, sluggish, and drained. This is proof that sleep is a powerful modification of the mind and that we must master our sleep patterns to acquire a clear, tranquil mind. Because we are unaware of what is happening in our inner world while we are asleep, it is imperative that in our waking state we practice techniques for sleeping in a healthy and enlightening manner. The subject of yogic sleep (*yoga nidra*) is addressed in chapter 3 of the *Yoga Sutra.*

Sleep poses a hurdle on our way to samadhi during meditation. When due to consistent practice and willful determination, the disturbances and distractions caused by the correct understanding of sensory experiences, incorrect understanding, and imagination have been somewhat attenuated, the body and mind move toward inertia. Our limbs, organs, brain, and nervous system interpret this relatively disturbance-free state as an opportunity to rest, relax, and sleep. Sleep occupies our mind in the form of drowsiness and we begin dozing instead of meditating. Sleep, spinning around inertia, is deceptive. It fools a meditator by inducing a feeling of pseudo-joy while drowning the mind in stupor. Stupor is the opposite of enlightenment. To reach samadhi we need to be alert.

SUTRA 1:11

अनुभूतविषयासम्प्रमोषः स्मृतिः ॥११॥

anubhūtaviṣayāsampramoṣaḥ smṛtiḥ ॥11॥

anubhūta, previous experience; *viṣaya*, objects; *asampramoṣaḥ*, not completely disconnected; *smṛtiḥ*, memory

Not being completely disconnected from the objects of previous experiences is memory.

As we have seen, every action—physical, mental, or verbal—creates an impression in the mind. Repeating an action reinforces those impressions. Once they have created deep grooves, they become samskaras, impressions so firmly deposited they cannot be easily erased. From deep within the mind they demand their right to manifest. In this way, samskaras motivate us to undertake actions similar to those already completed. The past is never lost, but our preoccupation with the present and our anticipation of the future crowds it out of awareness. Our total engagement with the present disconnects us from past experiences, so we remain unaware of what is in the back of our mind. When this disconnection is removed, we remember our past. In other words, we "re-collect" what we have previously collected, which is why another term for memory is *recollection.*

Recollection depends on two conditions: a significant degree of disengagement from present and future concerns, and the strength of the samskara pertaining to the event being recalled.

The strength of past mental impressions depends on how attached we were to our actions and their fruits at the time we performed them. The greater our attachment, the stronger the impression it creates. The scope of attachment determines how much space a particular samskara occupies in our mind; the degree of attachment determines how compelling this impression of our past actions will be. When we are significantly disengaged from present and future concerns, and the impressions of a past event are strong, the past comes to life and occupies our mind more clearly and powerfully than the present and future.

An example may be helpful. When fully engaged in playing soccer, watching a movie, analyzing stock prices, or solving a complex equation, we are not recollecting the past because the mind is fully absorbed in the present. Then we decide to meditate. We bring the mind to a focal point—an image of Krishna, the cross, or a mantra. We are fully aware of this object of meditation, and our strong engagement with it keeps us well anchored in the present, thereby blocking awareness of the past. But after a few minutes, the mind becomes distracted and drops the object of meditation. Now that the mind is no longer fully engaged with the meditative object, a powerful impression pushes its way into our awareness from deep within. We become cognizant of what already exists in our mind. This recollection begins to occupy and churn the mind. This thought construct—memory—turns and tosses the mind as effectively as thoughts having their objects in the realm of the senses, false understanding, and imagination.

In the final analysis, memory and samskaras are the same (YS 4:9). Memories are the building blocks of our personality. Our collective pool of memories constitutes our psyche. Sitting in the background of our conscious awareness, memories influence all our mental activities. To a large extent, they dictate how we perceive, infer, postulate, and comprehend what we study. They also influence our imagination, dreams, and sleep. Anything arising from the depths of our mind is colored by memory. To reach samadhi, we must purify our memory field.

Not all forms of memory deter us from our inner quest. Only unwanted memories, which capture our mind and force it to drop the object of meditation, act as impediments. Deleting memories or attempting to make the mind blank will not ensure that we reach samadhi. Instead, we must master the art of selecting only one train of thought, depositing that train of thought in our memory field, and staying focused on it so well that other memories have no opportunity to surface. This requires training our mind to attend to its meditative focus and refrain from engaging in thoughts that lie outside the domain of its current pursuit.

How to fully engage with the task at hand and free ourselves from disturbing, stupefying, and distracting mental activities is the subject of the next sutra.

SUTRA 1:12

अभ्यासवैराग्याभ्यां तन्निरोधः ॥१२॥

abhyāsavairāgyābhyāṁ tannirodhaḥ ॥12॥

abhyāsa, practice; *vairāgya*, non-attachment or dispassion; *tat*, that or those; *nirodhaḥ*, mastery or restraint

That can be controlled through practice and non-attachment.

By telling us that ardent practice (*abhyasa*) and non-attachment (*vairagya*) bring the roaming tendencies of the mind to a halt, Patanjali is making a powerful and conclusive statement: we have the capacity to arrest our thoughts and attain mastery over our mind. By training the mind to be clear, calm, and one-pointed, we can change the nature of our thoughts and emotions and achieve mastery over our body, senses, speech, actions, and the world around us. We can be confident in our decisions and pursue our goals fearlessly. The formula for transforming our mind is simple and straightforward: abhyasa and vairagya.

The literal meaning of *abhyasa* is "practice"; *vairagya* means "non-attachment." These terms are the backbone of Yoga sadhana and should not be taken lightly. Together, they constitute a time-tested technique for removing the causes and conditions of inner unrest and creating conditions leading to samadhi. Vyasa states, "Arresting the roaming tendencies of the mind is dependent on a twofold technique." This twofold technique is abhyasa and vairagya.

This commentary will use the original Sanskrit terms because the literal translations, "practice" and "non-attachment," do not convey the precise meaning intended by Patanjali and Vyasa. As we will see in the following sutras, *abhyasa* means "making an ardent effort to retain an inward peaceful flow of mind, free from roaming tendencies." *Vairagya* means "cultivating a mind free from the coloring of deeply imbedded mental impressions (*vasanas*)." Abhyasa and vairagya are not two separate practices, but two intersecting parts of one practice. They are integral to a well-defined system of sadhana, the aim of which is to acquire a peaceful mind endowed with the power of discernment. It is with this peaceful and discerning mind that we reach samadhi. Understanding how abhyasa and vairagya form a complete system of Yoga sadhana and how they infuse other systems of spirituality with life is crucial to understanding the essence of spirituality itself.

We all want to be happy, but two inseparable problems block our happiness: we are unable to stop being negative, and we do not know how to start thinking and acting positively. We want to remain unperturbed, but become upset instead. We do not want to drown in remorse, yet we cannot let go of self-incrimination. The same is true of anger, grief, and the desire for revenge. We know fear and insecurity are crippling, but we cannot quell these feelings. We know peaceful, positive thoughts are the foundation for a happy, healthy life, but we are not motivated to actively seek and embrace peaceful and positive strategies. Why? The answer lies in the link between our deep-rooted habits and our current mental behavior.

According to Yoga philosophy, the causes of our thought patterns have a much deeper source than we normally realize. Our inner world is propelled by our habits, which in turn govern and determine the nature of our emotions, thoughts, speech, and actions. Our habits form our personality. They have a powerful influence on our unconscious behavior, as well as on our conscious decisions.

Samskaras are strong habits deeply embedded in our mind. They shape our inner world. The strongest samskaras are known as *vasanas. Vasana* means "coloring." A vasana is a samskara that has become so strong and irresistible that in the normal course of life its influence is inescapable. Vasanas color the mind, giving it no opportunity to see the truth independently. The mind's comprehension is molded by the attributes and characteristics of our vasanas—we see what our vasanas allow us to see. Our sense of pleasure and pain, good and bad, right and wrong is largely dependent on the nature of our vasanas. So how are samskaras and vasanas created? How do they gather so much power? How do they exert such an irresistible influence over our mind?

Every action we perform—physical, mental, or verbal—creates an impression in our mind. Each time an action is repeated, these impressions become stronger. This is how habits are born. Habits can be erased when they are new and relatively weak. But if we continue repeating them, the groove they make in the mind deepens and they become samskaras, which then motivate us to perform similar actions. This well-defined process is known as *vritti samskara chakra.* As it gathers momentum, it further reinforces our subtle impressions—our samskaras—until they become self-sustaining. At this stage, they are vasanas.

Figuratively speaking, vasanas color the mind so completely it loses its pure, pristine, transparent qualities. It no longer sees things as they are, but instead perceives the world through the lens of its vasanas. Our desires, feelings, thoughts, intentions, and ambitions are all affected by our vasanas. We become their product and thus have little control over our thoughts, speech, and actions.

Attenuating and ultimately eliminating our vasanas is difficult. We have not yet purified our mind, so it is operating under the influence of the prejudices and conditioning established by our vasanas. Attempting to identify and delete our vasanas with the help of a mind overwhelmed by vasanas is like one drowning man attempting to rescue another. The only solution is to cultivate a mind endowed with the ability to stop itself from drowning, and then employ this transformed mind to encounter and eventually conquer the dimensions of the mind that are still smeared with negative vasanas. This is accomplished with abhyasa. In other words, with vairagya we rid ourselves of old mental habits, and with abhyasa we create new ones.

Abhyasa enables us to tap the wellspring of the power of discernment (*viveka*). With abhyasa we create samskaras that help the mind cultivate a taste for peace, stability, and introspection. As we continue nurturing our practice of abhyasa, the samskaras it engenders become stronger. Eventually, the grooves created by sincere and prolonged abhyasa become so ingrained they begin to influence the mind from deep within. These new deeply ingrained impressions are also vasanas, but because they are generated by abhyasa and imbued with its properties, they are endowed with the power to neutralize negative vasanas. These new vasanas are the result of a well-designed Yoga sadhana, which is accompanied from the outset by *viveka,* the power of discernment. Abhyasa and the deep mental grooves it creates embody the intention that propelled us to undertake the practice in the first place.

In summary, abhyasa helps us create a new cast of mind, one that enables us to clearly see the negative vasanas and the aspect of mind propelled by them. This new mind-set helps us see without fear and doubt: we are able to decide what type of samskaras and vasanas must be deleted and are confident in our ability to delete them. In this way, abhyasa assists vairagya in deleting the negative vasanas, thus freeing us from the unwanted aspects of our past.

By itself, however, abhyasa has a potential weakness: if we are not careful, we may become attached to the process of making an ardent effort to retain the mind's peaceful flow and to the fruit that flows from it. Attachment undermines the purity of abhyasa and may have negative consequences. This is where vairagya assists abhyasa, allowing us to make a deep commitment to our practice of abhyasa while keeping us free from anxiety about its fruit.

This twofold technique leading to the cessation of the mind's roaming tendencies does not refer to a particular spiritual discipline or path, but to the fundamental principle that makes a spiritual discipline valid and effective. The principles of abhyasa and vairagya make a path perfect. Only a perfect path can lead us to perfection.

In the next four sutras, Patanjali explains the exact nature of abhyasa and vairagya, how they are mastered, and how they can lead us to the experience of samadhi.

SUTRA 1:13

तत्र स्थितौ यत्नोऽभ्यासः ॥१३॥

tatra sthitau yatno'bhyāsaḥ ॥13॥

tatra, there; *sthitau*, in a stable condition of mind, or in a peaceful flow of mind free from roaming tendencies; *yatnaḥ*, ardent effort; *abhyāsaḥ*, practice

Ardent effort to retain the peaceful flow of mind free of roaming tendencies is *abhyasa*.

Samadhi is the mind's natural state. Illumination and stability are its intrinsic virtues. The power to move and the power to flow are the mind's inherent capacities. Its basic function is to illuminate the objects of the senses and present sensory experiences to fulfill the purpose of Consciousness within. A stable, transparent mind perceives without distortion and presents objective experience to Consciousness without adding its own interpretation.

The problem most of us face is that layers of highly potent samskaras, also known as vasanas, are blocking the mind's transparency and suppressing its stability, causing it to seek reasons to be disturbed and distracted. Due to these vasanas, the mind has acquired a taste for these mental states and is thus drawn to disturbing, stupefying, and distracting thoughts and objects. For example, our acquired taste for disturbance and distraction causes us to find violent movies pleasurable. Because of this acquired taste, we cannot live without thrills, which churn our mind, keeping it engaged in a whirlpool of *vrittis*, thought constructs. Abhyasa reverses this condition, restoring and maintaining the mind's natural state of stability and groundedness.

To understand why abhyasa has the power to restore and maintain the mind's natural state, it is helpful to examine the terms Patanjali uses in this sutra to define it: *sthiti* and *yatna*. Sthiti is the peaceful flow of the mind, free from all roaming tendencies. Yatna is investing energy and enthusiasm in a system of discipline. In other words, sthiti is a state free from thought constructs. Yatna is enthusiastically investing everything it takes to achieve sthiti. Commitment to yatna is abhyasa. Thus, abhyasa entails making an ardent effort to identify a particular time and space where the mind is no longer agitated and is moving peacefully within a well-defined domain of awareness.

Abhyasa begins with the assumption that there is a time when the mind is free of its wandering habits and a space in which it can move peacefully and purposefully. Most of us find it hard to identify that time and space. Even when we do, the opportunity to stay there slips away due to the mind's unstable habits. We need to reach a stable state within, and we need a clear, tranquil mind to attend that state. We also need to attend that state wholeheartedly and one-pointedly. For most of us, finding the starting point is a delicate process.

The best way to begin is by learning to unite the mind with the breath. The Yoga tradition tells us the mind and breath are twin laws of life. They travel together. When the mind is calm and clear, the breath flows smoothly. Conversely, when the breath flows smoothly, the mind calms and clears. The condition of one determines the condition of the other. This fundamental law governs life on the material plane.

To free the mind from disturbance, stupefaction, and distraction and allow it to flow inward one-pointedly requires understanding the dynamics of our breath and attaining mastery over it. And this in turn requires freeing our mind from its roaming tendencies and making it flow peacefully. The tradition of the Himalayan masters in which I am trained advises us to first attain mastery over our breath; this leads naturally to freedom from the mind's habit of wandering aimlessly.

According to the sages, the mind is the greatest mystery for it contains the mystery of the entire universe, the mystery of past, present, and future, and the mystery of life here and hereafter. Attempting to understand the dynamics of the mind, unveil all its mysteries, and attain mastery over it in the initial stages of our inner quest is like an atom trying to conquer a star. But if we begin our quest by understanding the dynamics of our breath and practicing the time-tested techniques of pranayama, we can see the underpinnings of our mind and the thoughts, feelings, sentiments, and emotions that agitate it. We also experience the boundless joy deposited in the mind itself, which manifests when a peaceful mind begins to plumb its own depths. The practice of pranayama enables us to see that the mind is our friend. The mind is benevolent and trainable. Its guiding ability is unfailing; it has a natural tendency to be clear and tranquil, and to reflect the total truth of the reality within.

We can begin practicing pranayama without knowing much about the dynamics of the *pranic* force we are attempting to bring under control. Just as we breathe without knowing much about the mysteries of our breath, we can manipulate our breathing without knowing much about it. But as soon as we become aware of the flow of our breath, the mind rediscovers its best friend. The two resume their perennial task—flowing together peacefully and joyfully.

When the mind and breath begin to flow together, all the conditions of abhyasa are met. We find ourselves spontaneously investing our attention and energy in retaining the peaceful flow of the mind. We are enthralled by the realization that the mind is fully with us rather than with the charms and temptations of the world. The mind is neither brooding over the past nor anxious about the future—all causes of disturbance have vanished. The mind is free to focus on whatever it wishes and is fully prepared to enter and retain the state of samadhi.

Yogis in the Himalayan tradition call the science of breath *prana vidya*. Prana is the force of pulsation, the power that animates us. It is the fundamental force of movement. Unlike the numberless forms of energy operating in the material world, prana is a self-guided, intelligent force. It is conscious of its own flow. It is aware of the intention behind its flow. Prana is the basis for respiration, including the cellular level of respiration. It regulates our heart rate and the heart's electrical impulses. It guides our body. This pranically charged atmosphere enables our limbs and organs to move and maintain a mutually supportive relationship.

According to Sankhya Yoga, prana is the first and foremost manifestation of the intention of Pure Consciousness (*Purusha*) to awaken the primordial cause of matter (*Prakriti*). Prana, the intelligent power of pulsation, contains the primordial benevolence of the Divine Being, ever intent on helping individual souls caught in the cycle of worldly transmigration (*samsara*). The subtle dimensions of prana include inspiration, aspiration, enthusiasm, and the fundamental desire to live, grow, move with purpose, and find the perennial source of dynamism itself. The Divine Being enters and pervades creation in the form of prana. Through prana—its flawless and infallible intention—the Divine Being breathes life into matter. Prana manifests in us as breath.

Breath is the most visible function of prana. Breath is innate, so we take it for granted. Although we know we will die if we stop breathing, we are not aware of the transforming power of the breath nor of the gift of ultimate freedom and lasting peace that prana is capable of granting us. Breath is the access point to the kingdom of immortality within. Aligning the mind with the breath means aligning the mind with the intention of Consciousness itself, which is invariably auspicious and benevolent. The greater our lack of awareness of the benevolent intention of the Inner Divinity, the more reason for the mind to become disturbed, stupefied, and distracted. As soon as we become aware of the primordial intention flowing in us in the form of breath, the underlying causes of our mental disturbances begin to lose their power. In other words, conscious awareness of the flow of breath automatically creates a condition for the mind to become clear and calm.

A clear, calm mind can easily be made one-pointed, and a one-pointed mind can easily be turned inward. An inwardly flowing mind eventually reaches samadhi, where we see ourselves in the light of truth. The more clearly we see ourselves in the light of truth, the easier it is to understand our relationship with the all-pervading Divinity.

Without a clear, tranquil, and inwardly flowing mind, we cannot successfully undertake the practice of Yoga. Without such a mind, we will waste our time fighting with our own thoughts. Freedom from our thought constructs is essential. The enthusiastic commitment (*yatna*) to doing whatever is necessary to achieve a state free from thoughts (*sthiti*) is Patanjali's definition of abhyasa. Abhyasa is both unique and general: unique in that it takes us all the way to samadhi, where we are able to see the Seer within; and general in that it endows us with a peacefully flowing mind free of all thoughts.

We engage in abhyasa to reach and eventually sustain this peaceful thought-free mental state. The first step is to consciously unite the mind and the breath. To accomplish this, we do our utmost to become fully aware of the flow of our breath. We employ the faculties of the mind to feel where and how the breath begins; how it touches the opening of the nostrils; how it travels upward; how it feels when it reaches the bridge of the nose and the corners of the eyes; and finally, how the subtle energy of the breath reaches the center between the eyebrows, then moves to the forehead and beyond (see YS 1:34 and 1:35).

By using yogic tools and means, we remind the mind and breath of their loving and mutually supportive bond. We introduce the mind to the sweetness of prana, which is contained in the pranic pool at the eyebrow center. Once the mind tastes that sweetness, it begins to lose interest in associating itself with disturbing, stupefying, and distracting experiences. It pays no heed to memories of the past and no longer entertains anxieties about the future. The charms and temptations of the world start to lose their power to distract. The mind is free to accompany the flow of the breath. The more it does, the more it gathers the strength to enjoy its pristine state, rather than being tossed by sensory experiences. Thus, the mind begins to attain freedom from its habit of churning out thought constructs and being churned and tossed by them in turn.

When the mind acquires the direct experience of happiness, free from dependence on the objects of the senses, it begins to enjoy its own peaceful flow. As time passes, this peaceful flow creates peaceful habits. As the grooves deepen, habits turn into samskaras. With further reinforcement, these samskaras turn into vasanas. Vasanas of peacefulness prevent us from creating disturbing thought constructs. After that, the quest to become established in our core being becomes natural and exhilarating.

However, we must not forget that from time immemorial we have been generating disquieting thoughts, and in the process, creating and reinforcing disturbing samskaras and vasanas. Therefore, we must not underestimate their influence while we are in the process of cultivating a mind that flows peacefully. How to gain maturity in our current practice and ensure that the ground for our practice becomes so firm that we will never slide backward is the subject of the next sutra.

SUTRA 1:14

स तु दीर्घकालनैरन्तर्यसत्कारासेवितो दृढभूमिः ॥१४॥

sa tu dīrghakālanairantaryasatkārāsevito
dṛḍha-bhūmiḥ ॥14॥

sa, that; *tu*, verily or definitely; *dīrgha*, long; *kāla*, time; *nairantarya*, continuously or without interruption; *satkārāsevito*, fully attended or attended with reverence; *dṛḍha*, firm or unshakeable; *bhūmiḥ*, ground

That becomes firm only when done for a long period of time, with no interruption, and with reverence.

From a practical standpoint, abhyasa—the ardent effort to cultivate a peacefully flowing mind free of all its roaming tendencies—can be divided into two parts: the process of withdrawing the mind from the objective world and turning it inward, and the process of focusing the mind inward and preventing it from running back to the objective world.

Withdrawing the mind from the external world and turning it inward is difficult. There are two reasons for this. The first is our deep familiarity with the external world. This is what we know. This is where we were born. We live here and we will die here. Our concepts of loss and gain, failure and success, are defined by the external world and confined to it. We experience it as complete, solid. Our belief in the reality of this world is unshakeable. In short, it is extremely difficult to let go of the external world.

The second reason we find it so hard to turn the mind inward is that we know very little about the inner dimension of life. The little we do know is based on momentary intuitive flashes or on what others have said. Because we have no direct experience of inner reality, we are not fully convinced it exists. For most of us, the inner world has no substance. Our belief in it is undermined by doubt. We are curious about the inner world, but the idea of becoming established in it seems far-fetched.

As a result, we have never made it a priority to explore the inner world and stay there for any length of time. Unless we are convinced of the importance of knowing our inner world, we will never invest significant time and energy in exploring it. And unless we practice persistently over a long period of time, the habits created by our practice will never become strong enough to overcome the habits that distract, stupefy, and disturb our mind.

Most of us have the same complaint—we don't have enough time. But curiously enough this complaint applies only to our practice. We have plenty of time for eating, sleeping, traveling, working, shopping, socializing, and entertaining ourselves. We have no shortage of time for worry, fear, anger, insecurity, and anxiety. Smartphones, iPads, and Facebook devour substantial chunks of our time and we have no problem with that. But when it comes to practice, we feel pressed for time. Why?

While busily embroiled in our lives, we rarely pause to reflect that the mind gives us the ability to engage in all these activities that seem so pressing. If we lose our mind, what are we? The world is organized only when we have an organized mind. It is a wonderful place only when we have a positive mind. For someone with a confused, negative mind, the world is chaotic and ugly.

Worldly objects and achievements are meaningful only when our mind is tranquil and clear. Our professional skills depend on the mind's retentive power. We excel only because we have a mind with the power of sharp, linear thinking. We are humans—and above all other species—only because we have a powerful mind.

What is more important than understanding the dynamics of this powerful mind and keeping it healthy, organized, and sharp? What is more urgent than protecting it from inner unrest and stupor? What takes precedence over preventing our mind from being consumed by fear, anger, jealousy, greed, and endless cravings? If we ever stop and actually reflect on how crucial it is to restore our mind to a clear, peaceful state, we will find plenty of time for practice. Our practice becomes firm only when we do it, and only a firm practice can guarantee that we will conquer the mind's roaming tendencies.

In this sutra, Patanjali outlines three golden rules for making our practice firm: (1) *dirgha kala asevitah,* (2) *nirantara asevitah,* and (3) *satkara asevitah.* The first one, *dirgha kala asevitah,* means "tending" (*asevitah*) the practice of abhyasa for a long period of time. *Asevitah* is a significant word. It demands that we offer ourselves in service of our practice. To serve our practice well, we must have specific qualifications. We have to be sincere and mindful. We must cultivate the attitude that practice is our master and being in the service of this master is our prime duty. We have to find pleasure in attending our practice and to develop a sense of gratitude that we have an opportunity to be in the service of the practice. The prefix *a* in *asevitah* tells us to arrange the elements conducive to our practice properly. This includes creating an inspiring environment, cleansing the body, relaxing the nervous system, calming the mind, sitting in a comfortable posture, and renewing our intention to practice abhyasa. Doing the practice with these supporting elements and with a sense of responsibility, and resolving to do it for a long time (*dirgha kala*) without counting the days, months, or years, is the first golden rule for ensuring our practice becomes firm.

Establishing a practice is like establishing an orchard. First you prepare the land—till the soil, remove the rocks, add fertilizer, and sow the seeds. Once the seeds have been sown, you cannot see what is happening inside them but you trust they will germinate. You trust because you have a basic knowledge of the seed, the soil, and the season. You trust because you have seen other seeds sprouting and growing into trees. Once the sapling pushes its way to the surface, you tend it by watering, weeding, pruning, and protecting it from insects and animals. When it will blossom and how much fruit it will bear is not in your hands. The harvest depends on a variety of factors, most of which are beyond your control, but that does not stop you from tending the plant. You must be in the service of the plant from beginning to end. Only then will you reap the fruits of your endeavor. The same is true with abhyasa.

We must cultivate trust in the outcome of our practice. We must be patient when we do not see it bearing fruit for a long time. We must remind ourselves that many people in the past have done their practice and were rewarded with delightful results. The same will be true for us. Doing the practice is in our hands, but the exact time it will yield its fruit and the precise fruit it will yield is not. The factors determining the yield are numerous; a few are known but many are not. And except for the actual process of doing the practice, none of these factors are under our control. With this understanding, we must be determined to do our practice until it comes to fruition—no matter how long it takes. This is what is required to make our practice firm.

The second golden rule for making our practice of abhyasa firm is to serve it without interruption (*nirantara asevitah*). To clarify this point, let us return to the example of establishing an orchard. A fruit tree requires a certain level of water, heat, light, and range of nutrients if it is to blossom. If we expect the tree to blossom, we cannot drench it with gallons of water for a month and then not give it a drop for the next eleven months. We cannot dump all the nutrients into its root system at once and let it starve the rest of the year. The tree cannot be exposed to scorching temperatures for a month and freezing temperatures for the rest of the year. And it will never blossom if we uproot and replant it repeatedly.

Interruption and sustainability are not compatible. It is only a sustained practice that one day becomes firm. In addition to doing our practice for a long period of time, the major elements of sustainability include doing it regularly, on time, and in a gradual, progressive manner. Doing several hours of practice one day and none for the next several days is like overeating one day and fasting the next. It is unhealthy, and an unhealthy practice cannot yield a healthy result. When we do our practice every day, without interruption (*nairantarya*), it bears fruit.

The third golden rule is to serve our practice of abhyasa with reverence (*satkara*). If we fail to cultivate reverence for our practice it becomes dry and mechanical. According to Vyasa, to infuse it with reverence our practice must be accompanied by *tapas*, *brahmacharya*, *vidya*, and *shraddha*.

In general usage, *tapas* means "penance or austerity." However, according to Patanjali (YS 2:43), tapas refers to a practice or a set of practices that detoxify the body and purify the mind and senses. According to Vyasa (YS 2:1 and 2:32), tapas is the ability to conquer resistance to practice. No matter where we stand in our spiritual evolution, there is resistance to going beyond our current state. All of us, regardless of how strong and knowledgeable we are, have our own unique level of inertia. A certain amount of energy is required to nullify that inertia before we can move forward. In a spiritual context, the subtlest form of inertia is resistance to the practice itself. Overcoming this resistance is tapas. Conquering resistance involves pain. Our natural tendency is to be comfortable, and staying under the pain threshold preserves our sense of comfort. Renouncing comfort, tolerating a degree of pain, thus increasing our endurance and fortitude, and eventually breaking through our resistance, is tapas.

The result of tapas is invariably delightful. Take exercise, for example. Exercise requires shaking off inertia. There is resistance to exercising, but once we have done it, we feel good. Exercise detoxifies the body, energizes the nervous system, increases lung capacity, strengthens the heart, clears the brain, and, in time, purifies the mind and sharpens the intellect. Similarly, dieting, practicing silence, and refraining from indulgence are all forms of tapas. Unless we embrace tapas, our practice remains vulnerable to our inherent weaknesses. Identifying our principal weaknesses and preventing them from impeding our progress is an essential component of fruitful practice.

The second element that breathes reverence into our practice of abhyasa is brahmacharya. Generally, *brahmacharya* is defined as "celibacy," but here the meaning is broader. According to Patanjali (YS 2:37), that which helps us cultivate an indomitable will, attain vigor, and acquire the power to retain and impart knowledge is brahmacharya. Brahmacharya refers to the degree of achievement that prepares the ground so virtues can grow unimpeded.

The problem is that in the process of experiencing the world and worldly objects, the mind has become dependent on the senses. Further, the senses contact objects indiscriminately and the mind attends them indiscriminately, running busily from one sensory experience to another. Running aimlessly after sensory pleasures depletes our physical vitality and mental clarity. With a weak body and a tired, disoriented mind, we cannot accomplish much of anything. The heart of brahmacharya is self-discipline, leading to mastery over the senses so that the mind participates purposefully in sensory experiences.

Brahma means "supreme consciousness"; *charya* means "daily routine." Thus, brahmacharya is a daily routine that by its intrinsic virtue reminds us of the higher purpose and meaning of life. Practicing brahmacharya involves living a balanced life: eating the right food at the right time in the right proportion with the right attitude; doing the right kind of exercise in the right proportion at the right time; complying with a code of conduct designed to regulate day-to-day activities and interactions with others; and finally, going to bed on time and waking up on time. Living a balanced life helps us conserve our energy, stay focused, and attend our main objective with few distractions. A lifestyle where all our physical and mental activities are geared toward reaching and serving our core being is brahmacharya.

The practice of brahmacharya also has a subtle aspect—preserving and expanding the field of inner vitality, strength, stamina, and endurance. At the practical level, this involves awakening the vast dormant energy (*kundalini shakti*) at the navel center and channeling it to flow upward. According to the yogis, when this dormant energy awakens, the lower tendencies of our mind—and the range of negative emotions springing from our primitive urges—come under our control. The awakening of kundalini shakti infuses us with the vigor, enthusiasm, willpower, and self-confidence we need to shake off the inertia hidden deep in our mind and senses. Then the power of our mind and senses flows upward spontaneously. Consequently, this level of brahmacharya is also known as the upward flow (*urdhva-retas*). Once urdhva-retas begins, our fight with the senses and mind is over. We enjoy the activities of our senses, but pleasure is no longer an impediment because contact with worldly objects no longer dissipates our energy. Our biological and emotional energies are at our disposal, and we have the strength and insight to invest them to undertake our practice successfully.

The third element that breathes reverence into our practice of abhyasa is knowledge (*vidya*). In the present context, knowledge is comprised of understanding three things: the nature of the world and worldly objects; the vastness of the inner dimension of life and how little we know about it; and the urgent need for us to become citizens of both the inner and outer worlds.

We first need clear knowledge of the nature of the world and worldly objects and the power they exert on us, because this enables us to clearly see how much physical, mental, and spiritual energy we are spending on worldly concerns. We need to examine the toll our relationship with worldly objects is exacting and to recognize how much importance we are giving these short-lived sensory experiences. Second, we need to understand how vast the inner dimension of life is and how little we know of it. In this connection, we also need to realize the extent to which our lack of knowledge of the inner world makes life seem empty. And finally, we need to recognize how urgent it is to direct all our worldly resources to gaining access to the inner world, to creating a bridge between our outer and inner worlds, and ultimately, to becoming a citizen of both. This threefold knowledge prompts us to invest ourselves wholly in our practice of abhyasa and to have a profound appreciation and reverence for it.

In our tradition, knowledge has yet another dimension, one that lights the flame of reverence in our heart. This is the knowledge of *parampara*, the lineage of the masters who discovered Yoga sadhana, refined it, documented the pitfalls, and delineated a precise sequence of practices. The greater our understanding of the spiritual depth of these masters and the transforming power of the practices they have shared with us, the greater our reverence. That is why particularly potent practices are transmitted along with general knowledge of the lineage, precise knowledge regarding the seer (*rishi*) who serves as a conduit, and finally, the right understanding of the power (*shakti*) a particular practice awakens. This unique knowledge helps us forge a connection with the practice, its seer, and its shakti. The sense of nearness it engenders makes us cherish the practice with reverence.

The fourth and final element that breathes reverence into our practice of abhyasa is faith (*shraddha*). According to Vyasa, faith is a joyful state of mind (*samprasada*) (YS 1:20). Doubt and fear are contrary to joy. Doubt about the effectiveness of the practice takes away the joy in doing it, and fear pertaining to the change it will bring makes it difficult to do the practice joyfully. In the absence of joy, practice becomes a chore. By embracing knowledge (*vidya*), we cultivate faith in our practice and faith in ourselves. Knowledge pertaining to the lineage, the sages, the revealing and transforming power of the practice, and our connection with it fills us with confidence and a profound sense of gratitude. We recognize that our practice is a privilege and look forward to doing it. When we are occasionally confronted with doubtful, fearful, or conflicting thoughts, we remain steadfast, confident in the efficacy of the practice and in our ability to do it. This unshakeable conviction is an outgrowth of knowledge.

In summary, abhyasa is the ardent effort to retain the peaceful flow of mind, free of all roaming tendencies. This definition reminds us that the mind is a dynamic force—its nature is to move, illumine, and become still. These three properties—movement, illumination, and stillness—co-exist. One sometimes dominates the others but never nullifies them. With ardent effort, it is possible to discover a moment when the mind is moving peacefully inward. Identifying that moment and extending its scope is the essence of abhyasa. This must be done for a long period of time, uninterrupted, and with reverence.

The practice of retaining the peaceful flow of mind for a prolonged period without interruption and with reverence creates the subtle impressions (*samskaras*) of tranquility. As they mature, these samskaras influence the functions and behavior of our mind in a peaceful and illuminating manner. They guide us by training our mind from deep within. In this way, the subtle mental impressions created by abhyasa transform the mind, awakening the power of discernment and eventually guiding the mind to reach samadhi.

There is a complication, however. Our efforts to identify and retain the peaceful flow of mind are heavily influenced by deeply ingrained karmic impressions formed in the past. These powerful impressions (*vasanas*), residing in the deepest recesses of our mind, heavily influence our thoughts, speech, and actions, as well as our determination to undertake the practice of abhyasa. The key to erasing these vasanas and to protecting our current course of practice lies in integrating the principle of vairagya. That is the subject of the next sutra.

SUTRA 1:15

दृष्टानुश्रविकविषयवितृष्णस्य वशीकारसंज्ञा वैराग्यम् ॥१५॥

dṛṣṭānuśravikaviṣayavitṛṣṇasya vaśīkārasaṃjñā vairāgyam ॥15॥

dṛṣṭa, seen or perceived; *ānuśravika*, that which has been heard; *viṣaya*, object; *vitṛṣṇasya*, free of craving; *vaśīkāra-saṃjñā*, a state characterized by the ability to grant complete self-mastery, or a state that enables the mind to remain free of craving for sensory objects and objects mentioned in the scriptures; *vairāgyam*, non-attachment

Non-attachment, known as *vashikara samjna*, belongs to the one who is free from the craving for sense objects and objects mentioned in the scriptures.

In sutra 1:12, Patanjali prescribes a two-part method—abhyasa and vairagya—for arresting the roaming tendencies of the mind and yoking it to samadhi. By practicing abhyasa, we train our mind to retain its peaceful flow and clearly discern what is real and what is not real. By practicing vairagya, we cultivate a mind free from the coloring of vasanas. Vairagya is non-attachment in the sense that it enables us to detach ourselves from the binding forces of the vasanas stored in our mind. This is a lengthy process—how lengthy depends on the number and complexity of our vasanas. But once they are cleared, few if any obstacles remain on our inner journey.

A mind free from vasanas reflects the true nature of the inner self. At this point, vairagya as a process of decolorizing the mind comes to an end because the mind's illuminating power is no longer veiled. The truth pertaining to our inner self reflects in the mind in its purity and fullness. This clear and complete understanding of reality is the highest state of vairagya. In other words, the preliminary stages of vairagya are a process, but the final step is a state of pure understanding (Vyasa on sutra 1:16).

In the Yoga tradition, these two stages are known as lower vairagya (*apara vairagya*) and higher vairagya (*para vairagya*). Lower vairagya, the process aimed at clearing the mind of vasanas, unfolds in a series of four well-delineated steps. Patanjali and Vyasa both assume their students have a general knowledge of all four. For this reason, Patanjali begins his discussion with *vashikara samjna,* the fourth and final step of lower vairagya.

Because most contemporary students are not familiar with these steps, we will examine all four in some detail. However, because the practice of vairagya focuses directly on clearing the mind of vasanas, we will first take a closer look at how vasanas influence our current thoughts, speech, and actions, and how we can erase or transform them.

As we have seen, the mind is the repository of innumerable habits, samskaras, and vasanas, which are constantly influencing us from deep within. When we do our practice well, we create new habits, and as we continue practicing for a long time, these new grooves turn into samskaras. As these new samskaras are continually reinforced, they become vasanas. At this stage, the well-defined, extremely focused vasana of our practice has gathered enough strength and momentum to withstand the storm of vasanas arising from deep within and to eventually neutralize them.

This inner accomplishment, engendered by the practice of abhyasa, emerges when we are extremely fortunate. It arises from an unshakeable determination to stay with the practice, in conjunction with factors Patanjali addresses later, including the grace of God, the blessings of accomplished masters, and vairagya. Vairagya is prominent among these factors, for it leads to the attenuation and ultimate elimination of the vasanas that agitate our mind. Patanjali elaborates on this last factor in this sutra.

The negative samskaras and vasanas deposited in our mind perform two functions: they agitate the mind, causing it to fluctuate aimlessly, and they take up so much space that they afford little room for the newly created samskaras of our practice. Evicting these agitating samskaras, making room for those that are spiritually illuminating, and ultimately, cultivating a mind that is perfectly clear and still and thus constantly aware of the reality within is vairagya.

Vairagya is derived from *viraga.* The prefix *vi* means "devoid of; free from; above and beyond; very special; unique"; *raga* means "coloring; smearing; influencing; attachment." *Viraga* means "devoid of any coloring, influence, or attachment." Thus, viraga refers both to the process of decolorizing the mind and to the state where the mind is no longer affected by our thoughts, speech, or deeds.

The essence of viraga is vairagya. Vairagya refers to our ability to live in the world and yet remain above it—to perform our actions and yet remain unaffected by both the process of action and its fruit. Vairagya is a state of mind in which our current thought constructs are no longer influenced by previous karmas, habits, samskaras, and vasanas. In other words, vairagya is a highly transparent, stable state of mind. In this state, we can see the reality of both our inner and outer worlds clearly while remaining unaffected by what we see. It is the highest state of knowledge and the ground for perfect freedom.

Vairagya is both the contemplative process that enables us to reach this highest state of knowledge and the state itself. It is both the unsmeared state and the process of unsmearing. Embracing vairagya in daily life means retaining a highly perceptive, clear, and enlightened state of mind. Such a state of mind is not agitated by what it perceives or by what it learns from any source. Attaining and retaining this perceptive, clear, and enlightened state of mind is para vairagya, and the process leading to it is apara vairagya. Here, in sutra 1:15, Patanjali elaborates on apara vairagya—the process of purifying the mind.

What defines *apara vairagya* (literally, "not-the-highest non-attachment") is conclusive knowledge derived from a broad range of self-reflection. At maturity, this knowledge becomes the ground for our conviction regarding the precise nature of reality in both the inner and outer worlds. This conviction is free of doubt and affords no room for fear. Furthermore, its brilliance and power nullify the influence of all contrary experiences, both past and present. This powerful conviction rids the mind of its old stains and prevents it from being stained again.

Apara vairagya is a long, progressive unveiling process. According to Patanjali, attaining this high level of self-mastery requires that we eliminate the craving arising from two sources: *drishta* and *anushravika*. Drishta refers to objects known to us through our senses, anushravika to objects we have only heard about from outside sources, such as the scriptures and our teachers. The complete range of the lower level of vairagya eliminates cravings arising from both sources. It is traditionally divided into four steps: *yatamana, vyatireka, ekendriya,* and *vashikara samjna.*

We remove the cravings pertaining to sense objects (*drishta*) and the mental agitation they cause by practicing the first three steps. The final step—vashikara samjna—enables us to free ourselves from the cravings arising from objects we have heard about from external sources, such as revealed scriptures.

As noted earlier, Patanjali assumes aspirants are familiar with the first three steps and so describes only the nature of the final step, vashikara samjna. Here, following the approach of the traditional commentaries, I will explain the full range of lower vairagya, beginning with yatamana.

Yatamana means "the process or the force behind making an effort." Nothing can be done without making an effort. Inertia is a formidable obstacle to inner growth. Reflecting on the nature of inertia and the importance of overcoming it is the first step toward attaining freedom.

To begin, we need to make a realistic assessment of where we stand and how happy we are with the lifestyle and values we hold so dear. How content are we? How important is it to transform ourselves and become better, healthier, and happier? When we reflect on how many of our actions are driven by custom, superstition, and dogma, we see that we allow others to define our values and that our priorities are often set by them. This self-reflection brings us to the realization that we are victims of our conditioning. Our thinking process is molded by the viewpoints and opinions of others. Further, our concepts of right and wrong, virtue and vice, good and bad are contaminated by prejudices and preoccupations. Our views on the meaning and purpose of life are shaped by the likes and dislikes, opinions, and preferences of others. In short, we have adapted ourselves to live in a box created by other people. Self-reflection allows us to see that our life is governed by cultural and personal habits, leading us to seek happiness in the wrong places, using the wrong tools. Self-reflection also gives us the strength and insight to have faith in our own self-effort. It gives us the courage to seek independently. We are no longer afraid of seeing our weaknesses. And along with recognizing our weaknesses, we identify our strengths.

Knowledge born of self-reflection awakens us from our long-cherished habits of procrastinating and of expecting someone else to give us salvation. We become self-motivated. We regain our trust in ourselves and lose our anxiety about the results of our actions. Problems and concerns may persist, but the mind is not disturbed and distracted by them as easily as before. Our desire to experience the fullness of life becomes stronger than our habit of staying within our comfort zone. Our resistance to practice weakens. Our joy in doing the practice becomes stronger than our anxiety about when and how it will show a result. Self-reflection has yoked us to the practice of abhyasa so meaningfully that we find no reason to avoid doing it. This form of self-reflection—*yatamana,* "the process or the force behind making an effort"—is the first step in lower vairagya. Thus, even in its most initial stage, vairagya merges with abhyasa to form a complete path, with the goal of attaining victory over the roaming tendencies of the mind.

As we continue our practice under the watchful eye of self-reflection, we begin to see more clearly the deeper causes of our problems, disturbances, distractions, and resistances. Our strengths and weaknesses become more vivid and our habits more identifiable. We become more aware of our internal tendencies—our samskaras and vasanas. At the same time, our intellect becomes sharper and our resolve firmer. Our power of discernment increases. As a result, we are able to distinguish among various sets of habits, samskaras, and vasanas, and to see which are the most pressing and how to isolate them. This process of identifying and isolating is *vyatireka*, the second step in lower vairagya.

Vyatireka, "isolating one from the other," is a natural outgrowth of yatamana. In the course of self-examination and self-reflection, we begin to see that some of our strengths and weaknesses are more significant than others. We isolate those that are the most significant and work on them skillfully. For example, if we have a number of negative habits, we identify those that are most damaging. Using our power of discernment, we assess their strength. Some negative habits can be dealt with easily, while breaking others requires skill, wisdom, and determination. Some can be renounced, whereas others must be transformed. Some can be put to positive use, while others must be rejected altogether.

Eventually, we see that a particular habit, samaskara, or vasana—or a group of them—is irresistible. It influences our thoughts, speech, and actions so subtly and potently that we are unable to avert it. Such strong samskaras and vasanas are usually associated with the cravings of one of the senses. Thus, we come to the next stage of vairagya, *ekendriya,* "belonging to one sense." At this stage, we cleanse our mind of the potent samskaras that are associated with our sense cravings.

As we continue neutralizing the unwanted karmic accumulations stored in our mind and our practice becomes firmer, we become more perceptive and intuitive. We measure our progress with greater precision and confidence. We are happy to have attained a significant degree of freedom from our disturbing thoughts and feelings, but we are also aware of where we consistently stumble. We can clearly see that although hardly any disturbing and distracting thoughts are left, those that remain grip our mind firmly. They are so powerful, subtle, and slippery that only after they have exerted their influence on the mind, and our sense organs have been employed to satisfy the craving, do we become aware of their adverse consequences.

The remedy for minimizing and eventually abolishing these powerful sense cravings is to remind ourselves that life is precious, and to reflect deeply on the short-lived nature of worldly objects and the sensory pleasures associated with them. This brings us to the realization that not even the most pleasing object and experience the world has to offer is as precious and important as life itself and the opportunity it affords us to find complete fulfillment and ultimate freedom.

As our reflection deepens, we come face-to-face with the fear of losing our life and the intense desire to preserve it. We notice that not only do worldly possessions, which seem to promise security, inevitably slip away, but so does life. This is so terrifying that we become intensely interested in life hereafter. We may start exploring our spiritual roots, consulting religious texts, visiting holy men and women, or listening to sermons and discourses. Often we are motivated less by a sincere desire to discover the mysteries of spiritual life than by the desire to secure a place in the hereafter. In short, our fear of dying causes us to seek God with the hope of earning a place in heaven. If we are to attain samadhi, we must transcend this fear- and desire-based form of spirituality. This is where the practice of the fourth and final step of lower vairagya comes in: *vashikara samjna*, "a state characterized by the ability to grant complete self-mastery."

Spiritual practice undertaken out of desire and fear undermines our trust in ourselves. It fills our mind and heart with doubt, making us dependent on others. This type of spirituality not only pulls the mind outward, it makes God seem petty. It blocks divine grace, and our growth stops. Vashikara samjna remedies this subtlest of spiritual diseases, allowing the mind to flow peacefully toward the center of Consciousness.

The samskaras of desire and fear are extremely powerful. They are like the proverbial carrot and stick and exert their power in both worldly and spiritual matters. The craving for objects we desire and the fear of losing them cause us to act blindly. Greed and fear are incompatible with spirituality, but they become intertwined with it when we confuse spirituality with religion.

According to Patanjali, this is a great bondage for spiritual seekers. We undertake a spiritual practice not because we sincerely love God but because we covet his favor or fear his wrath. Patanjali repeatedly states that the grace of God is the most crucial factor in the experience of true fulfillment and ultimate freedom. He emphasizes the importance of God and the role of grace in shaping both our worldly and spiritual destinies. However, God and liberation as described by Patanjali are quite different from God and liberation as described by most institutional religions. Patanjali's God takes away all our fears, for it is an exalted state of consciousness—pure, pristine, all-pervading, and eternal. God is our inner guide, the source of inspiration. Even the prospect of experiencing this divine presence fills our mind with indescribable peace. The God of religion, on the other hand, evokes fear, and the religious concept of heaven kindles greed. Fear and greed fuel inner unrest; they agitate the mind and can never be the ground for peace. A fearful, agitated mind is incapable of comprehending and experiencing reality as it is. Only a mind flowing peacefully inward has that capacity. The purpose of Yoga sadhana is to cultivate this inwardly flowing, peaceful mind.

Many of us are eventually able to renounce our desire for worldly power, possessions, honor, and even sense pleasures, but we find it much harder to renounce our desire for spiritual power, possession, honor, and celestial pleasures. The craving for power, possession, honor, and dignity—and the pleasure derived from them—is subtler than we normally realize. Religious and spiritual leaders compete among themselves, just as corporate and political leaders do. In the realms of commerce and politics, recognition flows from wealth and from the influence we exert over others. In the world of religion and spirituality, piety and nearness to God constitute wealth. There is tremendous satisfaction in having this wealth, and an even deeper satisfaction when people recognize us as having it. The desire for recognition is an extremely subtle desire, and Patanjali warns us against falling prey to it.

There is another subtle desire that poses a powerful impediment to samadhi—the craving for experiences we have read about in the scriptures or heard about from spiritual teachers or fellow seekers. This obstacle has two sources: our spiritual ambition and our lack of trust in our conscience. We want to be spiritually advanced, but we do not want to examine the defining elements of spirituality. We rely on books to tell us what practice is spiritual and gravitate toward practices compatible with our ambitions.

Since the dawn of civilization, millions of books have been written and thousands of them are considered scriptures. The theories and practices described in these voluminous scriptures are said to flow from revelation, and we are told not to question revealed scriptures. When there is a conflict between what the scriptures say and what our conscience tells us, we usually ignore our conscience. We rarely stop to remember that scriptures are supposed to guide us in the direction of true fulfillment and ultimate freedom, and if this basic objective is missing, it is better to look elsewhere. Instead, we force ourselves to believe that what is written in the scriptures must be honored and our conscience must not be allowed to stand in the way. However, cultivating right understanding of the scriptures while honoring our conscience will enable us to overcome the deep-rooted cravings that impel us to seek rewards and avoid punishment. Then we will clearly see the shallow nature of the concepts of vice and virtue, hell and heaven, and realize that, without exception, all are contradicted by opposing religious faiths.

To free ourselves from this subtle form of craving, it is important to ponder how the desire for objects we have never seen arises and the profound influence this desire exerts on our thought processes. When we reflect on this, we come to see that we have a habit of relying on others rather than on our own conscience. This habit leads us to believe anything written in the scriptures, especially if they are ancient. Fear prevents us from examining the validity of those concepts and precepts. Centuries pass as we strive to measure up to the standards of spirituality the scriptures set forth. Patanjali is not averse to scriptures—in sutra 1:7, he confirms that scriptures are a valid source of knowledge. They are the final authority regarding the reality imperceptible to the senses. What Patanjali does oppose is both blind belief in scriptural proclamations and blind rejection of them. He discourages us from embracing or denouncing scriptures mindlessly. He also advises us to avoid anything that engenders fear and greed, for this becomes the ground for deep-seated inner agitation.

The final level of lower vairagya, therefore, is a contemplative process that helps us understand the true meaning of what is written in the scriptures. Only after we sidestep scriptural traps rooted in fear and greed can we bring purity to the process of our inner search and become high-grade seekers. That is why this final level of lower vairagya is called *vashikara samjna,* "a state defined by its ability to grant self-mastery."

According to Vyasa, embracing vairagya at the level of vashikara samjna means maintaining awareness that no achievement—worldly or spiritual—is absolute, including the extraordinary powers (*siddhis*) we can achieve through our yogic practices. These siddhis include the experience of celestial fragrance, sweetness, touch, form, and sound (YS 1:35); the ability to diagnose our body intuitively (YS 3:29); a vision of unembodied sages and siddha masters (YS 3:32); clairvoyance (YS 3:33); and the ability to leave our body voluntarily and enter another body (YS 3:38). But even these extraordinary powers are temporary and subject to decay. They must not be allowed to feed our ego. Patanjali stresses that these yogic achievements become obstacles if we are attached to them (YS 3:37). Further, if a vision of God, for example, makes us feel we have become purer than others, or if we feel degraded by a vision of the devil, we are attached to one and averse to the other. Attachment and aversion are afflictions (YS 2:3). These afflictions feed the mind's roaming tendencies and these tendencies must be arrested.

Being vigilant regarding this form of attachment is vashikara samjna. Once we achieve this level of mental clarity, we have the natural ability to comprehend the total range of truth pertaining to both manifest and unmanifest reality. At this stage, we automatically move toward the highest level of vairagya—para vairagya. This is the subject of the next sutra.

SUTRA 1:16

तत्परं पुरुषख्यातेर्गुणवैतृष्ण्यम् ॥१६॥

tatparaṁ puruṣakhyātergunavaitrsnyam ॥16॥

tat, that; *paraṁ*, beyond; *puruṣa*, consciousness; *khyāteḥ*, to self-realization; *guṇa*, attributes of nature; *vaitṛṣṇyam*, free of all forms of desire

The highest level of non-attachment, leading to self-realization, takes place when the aspirant is free from all forms of desire, including desires resulting from the interplay of *sattvic*, *rajasic*, and *tamasic* forces of nature.

P*ara vairagya* is the highest form of non-attachment, a state of consciousness in which we are fully established in our core being. In this state, the mind is so clear and tranquil that we see ourselves without distortion. Our self-understanding is so firm and bright that there is no need to remind ourselves that we are Consciousness itself. We know—with absolute certainty—that we are pure Seer, the very power of seeing itself.

When, as the Seer, we see the world of Primordial Nature, we are affected neither by the process of seeing nor by what we see. Material loss and gain no longer affect us for we know we are immortal. Even as we see ourselves aging, we know these changes are occurring in the body, not in Consciousness itself. We know we are beyond destruction, decay, and death, for these affect only the mortal part of us, which is a temporary acquisition. We do what we wish to do, in full knowledge that our deeds are not motivated by unfulfilled desires. We perform our actions as a natural expression of what we are, rather than out of compulsion. We seek no reward, yet when—following the law of nature—rewards walk into our life, we welcome them. When our actions do not bear fruit, or bear fruit contrary to what we anticipated, we accept it as a gift from Providence. Peace is our spontaneous virtue. We do not reach this state of consciousness by running after it, however. It is a natural outgrowth of the final state of lower vairagya (*vashikara samjna*) described in the previous sutra.

The more tightly we embrace vairagya at the level of vashikara samjna, the more intense our desire to see the Seer within. This growing interest creates an internal environment in which the mind finds no reason to manufacture thought constructs aimlessly. It becomes quiet, one-pointed, and begins to flow inward. Our ego stops identifying with its virtues and follies. The intellect becomes so sharp and penetrating it comprehends objects presented to it through the senses at lightning speed. No time or effort is required to differentiate real from unreal, good from bad. Spontaneity becomes the hallmark of our being. We become so aware of ourselves that the external world is like a reflection in a mirror. This is the dawning of the highest level of vairagya, para vairagya. As Vyasa explains, para vairagya is identical to the highest state of knowledge. Nothing lies between it and ultimate liberation. It is this state of knowledge, not the practice of abhyasa, that is the direct cause of final liberation (*moksha*).

Our practice of abhyasa is itself an action. Every action we perform creates an impression in the mind. Those impressions form ever-deepening grooves as we repeat our actions, creating habits, samskaras, and ultimately, vasanas. From deep within, vasanas influence our thoughts, speech, and actions. Like other actions, abhyasa creates ever-deepening impressions. In order to acquire an absolutely clear, perfectly tranquil mind and to ensure that the peaceful flow of mind will not be disrupted by inner tendencies, we must ultimately delete even the impressions created by our practice of abhyasa.

In the lower stages, vairagya also creates its own samskaras. We become attached to the process of embracing non-attachment. We develop a strong liking for contemplative strategies that help us loosen our attachment to worldly possessions and increase our desire for self-discovery. Such contemplative strategies traditionally begin by censuring sense pleasure, worldly possessions, name, fame, honor, and dignity. These approaches also emphasize the fleeting nature of our physical beauty, vitality, strength, and stamina. As part of our contemplation, we are led to reflect on the dirtiness and ugliness of our body, filled as it is with bile, mucus, urine, and feces. This traditional approach to contemplation is designed to encourage us to withdraw our mind from the charms and temptations of the world, to help us attain freedom from our cravings, and to minimize our identification with the body.

However, in the course of this contemplative process, we create a samskara of negativity about our body, mind, senses, the world in which we live, and ultimately, about life itself. Many monastic orders discredit worldly achievement as a means of emphasizing renunciation. They become judgmental, opinionated, self-righteous, angry, and sometimes even abusive. So we must take care when using the contemplative tools of self-reflection, self-observation, and self-examination to acquire a clear, calm, and tranquil mind. Forming an attachment to these tools, or using them improperly, carries the potential for inner agitation. However, even contemplative samskaras that are tainted with agitation are transcended when we become established in the highest state of non-attachment (*para vairagya*).

In summary, sutras 1:12 through 1:16 show us that abhyasa and vairagya form one complete whole. Practiced together, they enable us to arrest the roaming tendencies of the mind. As its wandering habits weaken, the mind is increasingly less prone to disturbed, stupefied, and distracted states. In the same proportion, it becomes clearer and more tranquil. It takes less effort to make the mind one-pointed and to confine it to a defined space for a longer time. Training the mind to stay in a defined space for an extended period of time is the basic criterion for entering samadhi, the state in which Consciousness experiences its essential nature.

The mind is not a static field of energy but a continuous flow, accompanied by objective awareness. As long as the mind is functioning, we will be aware of the objects it carries. If the current of the mind is too tumultuous, we fail to perceive the objects correctly. If we are to correctly comprehend what the mind is carrying, the current of the mind must flow peacefully. Altogether eliminating objects from the current of the mind is neither possible nor necessary in the initial stages of sadhana. The mind passes through different stages of peaceful flow before it dissolves into the oceanic and absolutely peaceful existence of Primordial Nature (*Prakriti*). Similarly, as the mind becomes increasingly peaceful, it drops the grosser and heavier objects and carries only the subtler and lighter ones, dropping even these when it is fully embraced by the Seeing Power of the Seer (*Purusha*).

This is enlightenment, the state in which the mind and everything it contains is fully lit by the light of the Seer. There are a variety of Sanskrit terms for this state. Because we now clearly discern the difference between the source of illumination and what it is illuminating, this state is called unshakeable discernment (*viveka khyati*). For all intents and purposes we are free from the mind's binding and releasing forces, so it is called freedom from mind (*chitta vimukti*). Because all the roaming tendencies of the mind cease absolutely and the mind is perfectly at peace, this state is called samadhi.

Patanjali favors this latter term over all the others. Samadhi emerges as a result of a long process, the entire sweep of which is Yoga sadhana. Before samadhi emerges, the grosser and heavier objects are dropped from the current of the mind; then, as the current of the mind becomes more peaceful, it drops even the subtler and lighter objects; finally, even the subtlest are filtered out. Patanjali traces the progressive development of samadhi in four lower stages, culminating in the purest and highest state of samadhi. That is the subject of the next two sutras.

SUTRA 1:17

वितर्कविचारानन्दास्मितारूपानुगमात्
सम्प्रज्ञातः ॥१७॥

vitarkavichārānandāsmitārūpānugamāt
samprajñātaḥ ॥17॥

vitarka, a perceptible object; *vicāra*, a subtle object or thought; *ānanda*, joy; *asmitā*, the feeling of I-am-ness; *rūpa*, form; *anugamāt*, accompanied by; *samprajñātaḥ*, state of samadhi in which the meditator is aware of the meditative object, the process of attending it, and oneself as a witness

***Samprajnata samadhi* is accompanied by a gross object, a subtle object, joy, or the feeling of I-am-ness.**

These next two sutras briefly describe the full range of samadhi. Samadhi is a state as well as a process leading to that state. An analogy will be helpful in explaining these two aspects. Let's say we are driving from New York City to Los Angeles. Every evening we check into a motel for the night; perhaps we do a little sightseeing before continuing our journey. Eventually, we reach Los Angeles. Once there, we enjoy the city. Depending on our goal, we stay for a week or two, a month, or perhaps permanently.

Los Angeles represents samadhi as a final state. The journey represents samadhi as a process. How long it takes us to reach Los Angeles depends on our starting point, the vehicle we use, the condition of the vehicle, how often we stop and for how long.

Patanjali calls the process portion of samadhi *samprajnata*, and the final state, *asamprajnata*. In layman's terms, the process portion can be called lower samadhi, and samadhi as a final state, higher samadhi. This sutra describes lower samadhi.

In any journey we pass landmarks that tell us if we are headed in the right direction. Signs along the road help us decide whether we should continue our journey or stop for a while. In the course of most long journeys, we take breaks either to avoid exhaustion or to enjoy the sights. From the perspective of each discrete portion of the journey, the places we stop are destinations. Thus, the process leading to our main destination is comprised of a series of interim destinations.

Lower samadhi is the journey leading to higher samadhi. It consists of a series of interim destinations, which are largely determined by the quality of the objects employed in meditation and by the quality of the mind using those objects. If we walk from New York City to Los Angeles, our final destination is the same as if we drive, but there will be many more interim destinations—and the distance between them will be much shorter. The number of interim destinations and the distance between them change drastically if we travel by bicycle or plane. In the same way, in Yoga sadhana each of us has our own starting point, a uniquely trained mind, and a particular object we use to remain one-pointed. In an external journey, how fast we travel and how often we stop and where depend on the nature and quality of the vehicle. In terms of our inward journey, the vehicles are the objects we use to make our mind flow peacefully. Therefore, the nature and quality of the objects determine where and how often we stop on our way to higher samadhi. Based on the quality of the objects and the mind's relationship with them, Patanjali divides lower samadhi into four categories: *vitarka, vichara, ananda,* and *asmita.*

Vitarka means "perceptible object." When the process of samadhi occurs by focusing on a perceptible object, it is called *vitarka anugata samadhi*. *Anugata* means "accompanied by; followed by." A mind not established in the state of samadhi always seeks the company of an object and must therefore be accompanied or supported by a thought construct (*vritti*). Some thought constructs make the mind fluctuate aimlessly, robbing it of the experience of its natural state of samadhi. Others help the mind rediscover and restore its natural state. When a thought construct enabling the mind to restore its natural state corresponds to concrete, perceptible sensory objects, that state is called *vitarka anugata samadhi*. It is accompanied (*anugata*) by a perceptible object (*vitarka*) that helped the mind become peaceful and inward. Using the sun, the moon, the polar star, the face of an anthropomorphic god or goddess, a lotus, a yantra, or a mandala as an object of concentration to bring the mind to a perfectly still, well-controlled state is an example of vitarka anugata samadhi.

The brain demands a name for each object it perceives. A word is assigned to each experience. Sensory experiences are discretely embodied in words and stored in the brain in that form. The meaning of the word contains the entire range of all the qualities, properties, and attributes of the object it denotes. When we provide the mind with a perceptible object to make it become one-pointed and flow peacefully, the entire meaning comes forward and infuses the mind with all the qualities, properties, and attributes contained in that object. That is why some objects and the words denoting them lead the mind toward samadhi faster and with fewer interim destinations than others. And that is why we must select a concrete, perceptible object for concentration wisely. As we use that object for a focus of concentration, it progressively drops its grosser qualities and subtler ones emerge.

Eventually, only the sheer essence of the object and its subtle meaning remain. The essence accompanies the mind without disturbing its peaceful flow. Even so, the inward flow of awareness is split into three parts: the mind is aware of the object; it is aware of the process of flowing inward; and it is aware of itself as an observer.

The next category in the process of samadhi is *vichara anugata samadhi. Vichara* means "subtle object; pure thought." This category of samadhi is characterized by meditation on a subtle object, such as sound, fragrance, touch, or taste. The clearest example is meditation on a mantra. As we will see in sutra 1:44, as we meditate on a mantra, our mind becomes absorbed in the mantra and its subtle meaning occupies our mind. As meditation on the mantra deepens, the essence of the mantra alone remains. The mind and the essence of the mantra merge. The state where the essence of the mantra and the mind merge is vichara anugata samadhi.

When the joy (*ananda*) buried deep in our body and senses is used as an object to arrest the roaming tendencies of our mind, the quietude engendered is *ananda anugata samadhi.* However, this practice requires that we first awaken the joy lying dormant within us. Vyasa describes practices for awakening this joy in his commentary on sutras 1:35 and 1:36.

The fourth category, *asmita anugata samadhi,* occurs when we use the sense of I-am-ness, the feeling of our own self-existence, as an object of concentration. This is possible only when we have access to the cave of our heart, where the sense of I-am-ness resides in its most concentrated form. Sutras 1:36, 3:34, and 3:49 describe the techniques for gaining access to our own heart, thereby acquiring the ability to meditate on our own I-am-ness (*asmita*).

In each of these four categories of samadhi, we are fully aware (*samprajnata*) of the object of meditation, the process of meditation, and ourselves as a meditator; hence the name *samprajnata samadhi.* Furthermore, because these four process-driven samadhis have an object of some sort as their focal point (*alambana*), they are also known as *salambana samadhi. Sa* means "with"; *alambana* means "resting ground; supporting element; focal point." The process of using an alambana as a support in samadhi is like using a thorn to extract another thorn from our foot. We use one thought to eliminate other thoughts. Ultimately, we must eliminate even the potential for our foot to be pierced by a thorn, and we do that by disposing of all thorns. Similarly, any object we use during this process-driven samadhi eventually must be discarded because any object, regardless of its illuminating properties, is a source of vrittis and thus has the potential to create samskaras.

As long as there are samskaras, the mind will be the victim of its fluctuating tendencies. How to reach the state in which there is no longer a possibility for the mind to associate itself with its own vrittis is the subject of the next sutra.

SUTRA 1:18

विरामप्रत्ययाभ्यासपूर्वः संस्कारशेषोऽन्यः ॥१८॥

virāmapratyayābhyāsapūrvaḥ saṁskāraśeṣo'nyaḥ ॥18॥

virāma, cessation; *pratyaya*, cognition; *abhyāsa*, practice; *pūrvaḥ*, preceded by; *saṁskāra*, subtle impressions of past deeds; *śeṣaḥ*, residue; *anyaḥ*, the other

The other [higher samadhi] is preceded by *abhyasa*, which brought all cognitions to a complete halt. What remains is the *samskara* [of abhyasa itself].

As we have seen, samadhi is both a process and a state. Samadhi as a process is often called lower samadhi, and as a state, higher samadhi. Lower samadhi is what we know as meditation today. Higher samadhi is a state of being—a state of awareness where the distinction between subject and object no longer exists. Lower samadhi occurs only when we make an effort, but in higher samadhi all effort ceases.

The most distinctive attribute of lower samadhi is that we are creating and accumulating subtle impressions through our practice. These meditative samskaras nullify non-meditative samskaras, which disturb, stupefy, and distract the mind. Meditative samskaras engender vrittis, just as other samskaras do. The only difference is that thought constructs engendered by meditative samskaras carry meditative qualities, whereas other thoughts carry distracting qualities. Even though meditative samskaras are transformative, they nonetheless have the potential to prevent us from reaching higher samadhi and so must ultimately be eliminated. Higher samadhi dawns only when all samskaras have been eliminated.

Lower samadhi is an object-driven process. From beginning to end, the peaceful flow of the mind is accompanied and supported by an object in one of four categories: gross and perceptible; subtle and thus imperceptible in a physical sense; reflective of an extraordinary joy springing from the depths of our senses and mind; or pure I-am-ness, the well-defined feeling of self-existence. As explained in the previous sutra, the fourfold nature of lower samadhi arises from these four different classes of objects. Regardless of the focal point, however, we are aware of a trinity: the object of meditation, the process of meditation, and ourselves as the meditator. In this state of samadhi, therefore, we are not perfectly one-pointed. In higher samadhi, this trinity is left behind. All mental operations cease, and the mind stands so still that even subtle impressions of the past, including the impressions created by our meditative practice, no longer have any influence.

In higher samadhi, time and space are left behind, and the law of cause and effect no longer applies. In this state of realization, we are free from all karmas and all the fruits of karmas. We see the truth in all its purity and perfection. We are master of our destiny and live with the confidence that after death we will have the ability to decide whether or not to return. We live in the world while remaining above it.

This highly sought level of samadhi emerges when abhyasa comes to an end. Technically, abhyasa is not the immediate cause of the highest samadhi. Rather, the immediate cause is the highest level of vairagya, including non-attachment to the samskaras created by abhyasa. However, it is a mistake to expect to attain higher samadhi without committing ourselves to a methodical and sincere practice. Some commentaries give the impression that lower samadhi is inferior to higher samadhi, but in truth, higher samadhi is the fruit of the hard work we put into our earlier practice. Higher samadhi brings the process of lower samadhi to completion. Practice-driven samadhi is so important that later, in sutras 3:51 and 4:26–4:30, Patanjali reminds us that we must always continue our practice lest we fall backward, for there is always a possibility that undetectable samskaras remain.

Practically speaking, the four stages of lower samadhi are abhyasa. Refinement in abhyasa comes through vairagya. Together, abhyasa and vairagya lead to higher samadhi. Lower samadhi is a process; higher samadhi is the experiential state we attain when our practice is completed. One describes the journey; the other, the place where the journey ends. Reaching our destination without making the journey is an enticing idea, but it is only a fantasy. The reality is that most of us have a mind that has not been thoroughly trained. We need a system of discipline to gain mastery over our thought patterns and then to turn the mind inward. Once it turns inward we have to provide the mind with a suitable object for meditation. We also have to make an effort to rest our attention in that object. This is easier when the object is spiritually illuminating and uplifting by its own intrinsic virtue. When the consistent practice of concentrating on the meditative object has led to absorption in the object, its intrinsic virtue induces a qualitative change in our mind. The mind sees what it could not have seen before: reality without attributes—reality that transcends name, form, shape, size, and color. Meditation on nameless, formless reality begins only when the mind has become clear and sharp enough to comprehend it. This comprehension comes through the process of lower samadhi.

The Yoga tradition tells us that the subtlest dimension of sadhana lies in understanding the dynamics of the transition from lower to higher samadhi. Comprehending the mystery of this transitional state requires attention to the precise terms Patanjali uses for lower and higher samadhi: *samprajnata* and *asamprajnata.* A little later in the text, he uses two parallel terms: *sabija* and *nirbija* (YS 1:46, 1:49, and 1:51). These two sets of terms illumine the mystery of the transitional state—of how to walk through it and enter the higher state of samadhi, leaving the lower one behind. In lower samadhi, we are fully aware of the object we are meditating on, the process of meditation, and ourselves as a meditator. This condition gives lower samadhi its name, *samprajnata. Samprajnata* means "to be fully aware of everything going on in the mind: what the mind is thinking; how it is thinking; and how we observe the object, the process, and the mind itself." Transcending this awareness or dissolving it enables us to enter higher samadhi (*asamprajnata*). *A* means "not; absence of"; *samprajnata* means "conscious awareness." Thus, *asamprajnata* means "renouncing the conscious awareness of lower samadhi and entering a state of consciousness devoid of subject-object divisions." Patanjali's use of these two terms gives us a clue about how to enter and retain the higher state of samadhi.

Again, an analogy is helpful. When we are learning to drive, we are taught to be aware of details: engage the clutch before shifting gears, look both ways before turning, check the rearview mirror before changing lanes, slow down when approaching an intersection. Being aware of details requires us to be vigilant and conscious of everything going on around us. We are aware of the car, we are aware that we are driving the car, we are aware of the road conditions, and we are careful to keep the car centered in our lane. We make a conscious effort to monitor our speed, and we become even more alert when approaching our exit on the freeway.

The less experienced we are, the more conscious we are of our driving. As time passes, the car begins to seem like an extension of our body, and coordinating the different elements of driving no longer requires a conscious effort. Our feet move between the clutch, gas pedal, and brake almost automatically. We confidently change lanes, overtaking and passing an 18-wheeler at 75 mph with ease. It doesn't seem like much is going on in our mind, but everything that was going on when we were learning to drive is still happening now that we have become expert drivers. The only difference is that, earlier, the various elements of driving appeared to be complete tasks in themselves. Those different tasks were somewhat disjointed and we were somewhat anxious about doing them correctly. Linking and coordinating those disparate tasks required considerable effort. Many things were going on at once. The mind was attending each task separately, and this was causing the mind to fluctuate. As we continue practicing, these discrete tasks begin to blend. Eventually, the mind begins to perceive driving as a single process, with little awareness that dozens of actions together constitute this process.

As experienced drivers we are not inattentive to the myriad processes involved in driving but have become expert at stringing them together smoothly and coordinating our mind to attend to them without anxiety. If we keep all the details driving entails in the forefront of our mind and continue remembering each of them separately, we will never be able to drive skillfully. Similarly, keeping all the details of our meditation in the forefront of our mind—remembering the object, anticipating a disturbing thought, planning not to be disturbed, vigorously trying to capture the perfectly still state of mind, and working hard to dis-identify from the role of being a meditator—prevents us from embracing the peaceful flow of mind free from thought constructs (*vrittis*).

The other two terms Patanjali uses to refer to lower and higher samadhi are *sabija* and *nirbija*. *Sabija* means "with seed," and *nirbija* means "without seed." Here, "seed" refers to subtle karmic impressions. Samskaras are seeds—our vrittis germinate from them. With the help of meditation, we attenuate and eventually eliminate our negative samskaras. But the process of meditation creates its own impressions in the mind. These meditative impressions are a necessary step in eliminating negative mental impressions, yet from a higher perspective, they pose an obstacle to reaching the highest state of samadhi. As long as the seeds of meditative samskaras accompany our meditation, we remain in lower samadhi. Sooner or later we must wash away even these positive meditative impressions. This is accomplished by embracing the highest level of vairagya.

In other words, reaching higher samadhi requires eliminating the exertion involved in maintaining conscious awareness of all the details of meditation, and further, resolving to detach ourselves from the samskaras created by our meditation. These two factors help us avoid becoming entangled in the transitional state between lower and higher samadhi. The first factor requires us to refine our practice, pay attention to its subtle components, and make sure that we are free of anxiety regarding when and how we will reap the fruits.

During this transitional phase, refining practice means identifying the exact nature of the meditative experience that dawns when the mind is not discretely aware of what it is experiencing. In other words, refining our practice means cultivating sensitivity to what the mind is experiencing and skillfully staying with that experience for a prolonged period, without interruption, and with reverence. This refinement sharpens our intelligence and we begin to comprehend the subtle component of the practice—the observer observing itself. At this stage, both the object of observation and the process of observation have dissolved. The mind and Pure Consciousness (*Purusha*) have become indistinguishable. Paying attention to this indistinguishability pulls us out of the transitional state and places us in higher samadhi, where there is no objective awareness and no meditative seeds. Refinement at this level of practice is the second factor and comes by infusing our practice with the light of higher non-attachment (*para vairagya*).

The journey from lower to higher samadhi comes easily to some and not so easily to others. The reason for this difference in the result of our sadhana is the subject of the next sutra.

SUTRA 1:19

भवप्रत्ययो विदेहप्रकृतिलयानाम् ॥१९॥

bhavapratyayo videhaprakṛtilayānām ॥19॥

bhava-pratyayaḥ, innately present at birth; *videha,* a yogi who has transcended body consciousness; *prakṛti-layānām,* of a yogi whose consciousness rests in the primordial matrix *(prakṛti)*

The experience of the higher level of samadhi is innate to [extraordinary yogis technically known as] ***videha*** **and** ***prakritilaya.***

There are two kinds of yogis—*bhava pratyaya* and *upaya pratyaya.* Bhava pratyaya yogis—*videha* and *prakritilaya*—are innately equipped with all the tools, means, powers, and privileges required to reach the highest state of samadhi. Upaya pratyaya yogis reach the highest samadhi only if they have a plan for doing so and a strategy for implementing that plan. Bhava pratyaya yogis are born with extraordinary capacity; upaya pratyaya yogis with ordinary human qualities. Here Patanjali explains the difference in capacities, the type of practices and experiences natural to these two categories of yogis, and how we can join the league of the extraordinary.

In the two preceding sutras, the range of self-realization has been measured and divided into two broad categories: the realization gained in lower samadhi (*samprajnata*) and the realization gained in higher samadhi (*asamprajnata*). The realization gained in lower samadhi lies in the domain of a mind still confined to the world of subtle karmic impressions (*samskaras*). The realization that dawns during higher samadhi lies in the domain of a mind that is perfectly still, fully lit by Pure Consciousness (*Purusha*), and no longer confined to the world of samskaras.

In lower samadhi, the mind is relatively active, its habit of goal-driven action remains intact, and it is still influenced by its samskaras. In other words, the mind is clinging to its karmic impressions and finds pleasure in consuming them. In higher samadhi, the mind is perfectly still. The samskaras have lost their motivating power. The mind is fully lit by Pure Consciousness; thus, its actions are propelled by Ishvara, our inner and eternal guide in whom lies the unsurpassed seed of omniscience. From the vantage point of our life and work in the world, the mind is "dead." Actions performed by such a mind create no impressions, have no karmic consequences, and thus support no mental activity (*vritti*). Attaining this level of mastery over the mind is the hallmark of higher samadhi.

The longer we stay in higher samadhi, the firmer it becomes. The more firmly we are established in it, the easier it is to maintain the constant awareness of our true essence (*Purusha*). The less effort it requires to maintain this constant awareness, the easier it is to remain unaffected by fear and commotion, which often become overwhelming at the time of death. The more unaffected we are by fear at the time of death, the greater freedom we have to suspend the mind in higher samadhi.

Suspending the mind in higher samadhi means returning it to Ishvara, who gave it to us as a tool. No more mind, no more vrittis, no more samskaras, no more bondage, no more liberation, no more coming and going—in other words, perfect freedom.

Living in Pure Consciousness and abiding with its will becomes our nature. One who has reached this far is known as a *brahma rishi,* the Seer of all-pervading Pure Consciousness (*Brahman*). Omniscience and eternity define the being of a brahma rishi, who now shares the pervasiveness of all-pervading Consciousness. The experience of fullness constitutes his core. Spirituality as a journey has come to an end—he and the destination have become one. In that height of experience, the entire world and all worldly experiences are inside him, and he remains untouched by them. He is far above the forces that govern time, space, and the laws of cause and effect. The guidelines laid down in spiritual and yogic texts, including the *Yoga Sutra,* no longer apply.

The rest of us, however, are subject to the laws of cause and effect. Our inner growth is dependent on the clarity, tranquility, and one-pointedness of our mind. Our spiritual aspirations are strongly influenced by our samskaras. We must recognize, face, and conquer our weaknesses. We must gather all the tools and means needed for our self-discovery. For us the path consisting of abhyasa and vairagya is the only way. When and how our practice of abhyasa and application of vairagya will bear fruit depends on our level of preparedness.

The desire to progress spiritually is the most important factor in our inner growth, and this desire must be both genuine and intense. To a significant degree, the intensity of this desire is dependent on our samskaras—the stronger the spiritually illuminating samskaras, the greater our desire for enlightenment. These subtle mental impressions are created by the practices we have done in the past. Their strength and motivating effect depends on the strength and maturity of our past practices. To those less than perfectly established in the highest truth, the past is never dead—it continually reemerges in the form of the present. We are innately equipped to know ourselves only to the extent we knew ourselves before. The samskaras in our mind compel us to revisit our previous experiences. In other words, our current tastes, interests, spiritual aspirations, and experiences are dependent on what we have done before and to what extent. That is why the spiritual journey appears short, straightforward, and smooth for some of us, while for others it is lengthy, bumpy, and somewhat convoluted.

As ordinary seekers we are not innately equipped to experience higher samadhi, and so must work hard to gather the necessary tools and means (*upaya*) and use them appropriately. Dependence on Providence may lead to self-deception and inertia. To be effective in our practice, we must commit ourselves to self-effort. For this reason, ordinary seekers are called *upaya pratyaya yogis*—yogis whose experience (*pratyaya*) depends on tools and means (*upaya*).

The upaya required by extraordinary souls in this lifetime is too subtle to be comprehended by those of us who have not yet reached their level of realization. Divine Providence itself is their tool. The abundant fruits of their abhyasa and vairagya are stored in the domain of Providence and manifest when they need them. Thus, these highly accomplished yogis are called *bhava pratyaya yogis*, yogis innately equipped to experience higher samadhi. In this sutra, Patanjali describes what it takes to be born as a bhava pratyaya yogi. According to him, this privilege is the exclusive domain of *videha* and *prakritilaya yogis*.

Videha means "without body; beyond body; or with a special body." Videha yogis have risen beyond body consciousness through their sadhana. They have attained such a high level of self-mastery that they no longer depend on their physical body and worldly objects for inner fulfillment. They have discovered a unique world within themselves by penetrating the very core of the senses, a core comprised of a unique joy not available in the objective world. Their senses are no longer tools for experiencing objects outside themselves but instead are the locus of experience.

These accomplished yogis have come to realize that the ears, skin, eyes, tongue, and nostrils are not senses but sense organs. A subtle, non-physical power infuses the sense organs with the capacity to apprehend objects. This capacity is a direct extension of the mind's inherent luminosity. As we will see in sutra 1:36, this inner luminosity (*jyotishmati*) is invariably accompanied by sorrowless joy (*vishoka*). Yogis who have gained access to this subtle self-luminous field of sorrowless joy experience inner joy without being dependent on sense organs or sense objects. This extraordinary joy is the fundamental power of the senses, the power from which the senses derive their ability to contact objects and project their joy onto them. The joy inherent in this power is what makes objects appear so pleasant. This extraordinary joy is essentially independent of the sense organs and the objects they contact; yogis of this caliber use this joy as their locus.

Videha yogis have penetrated and entered the subtle realm of the senses and use this unique joy as an object of their meditation. Through their prolonged practice of abhyasa and vairagya, they stay with this joy for long periods without interruption. As they continue their practice, their meditation matures into lower samadhi (*samprajnata samadhi*). Because this form of samadhi is accompanied by the inner joy of the senses, it is called *ananda anugata samadhi.*

In addition to unique joy, ananda anugata samadhi is characterized by illumination. During meditation, videha yogis rise above body consciousness, which is replaced by the awareness of pure illumination. While in samadhi, they have no feeling of their physical body, but instead are aware of pure light. This awareness serves as the locus for their consciousness. In other words, effulgence itself is their body. Thus, a videha yogi is also known as *deva,* "shining being; bright being." *Deva* is often translated as "god" or "celestial being." In the Yoga tradition, however, videha yogis are devas because they embody and emit light. If they die before reaching the highest state of samadhi, they dissolve into the light and joy of the subtle senses. They return to this world guided by Divine Providence. Their return is technically reincarnation, not rebirth. They reincarnate with their knowledge and memory intact.

A person who is reborn has only limited power of memory. His thoughts, speech, and actions are propelled by samskaras. He is subject to the consequences of his karma and so finds himself caught in the cycle of consuming his karmic fruits and being consumed by them. His comprehension of the inner dimension of life is quite faint; doubt, fear, confusion, and inertia obstruct his spiritual practices. In contrast, a reincarnated soul is accompanied by a sharp memory. Her past experience, wisdom, and accomplishments manifest spontaneously. Her thoughts, speech, and actions are governed by the wisdom attained in her previous life. Contentment is her inner virtue. The charms and temptations of the world have no effect on her. She resumes her journey at the point she left it when she died. That is why videha yogis are drawn to spiritual practices for no apparent reason. Their practice seems to be effortless, their experiences startling, their non-attachment firm, their conviction unwavering, and their spiritual progress rapid.

The other category of bhava pratyaya yogis, who reincarnate fully accompanied by the experiences and wisdom they gathered in their previous lifetime, is that of *prakritilaya yogis. Prakritilaya* means "dissolved in Primordial Nature." Through their sadhana, prakritilaya yogis discovered the essence of their personal existence, the fundamental ground for the sense of I-am-ness. They used this natural, clear, and crisp sense of I-am-ness as a focal point for their meditation. Through prolonged and sincere practice, they penetrated the world made of individuated consciousness. By using the combined forces of abhyasa and vairagya, they were able to withdraw themselves entirely from the objective world and were able to stay with the peaceful flow of one awareness—the very essence of "I am" (*asmita*). In this state of *asmita anugata samadhi*, they were free of the karmic consequences corresponding to the material world, the world made of senses and sensory pleasures, and all the samskaras that make the mind flow outwardly.

Yogis of this caliber use their mind as their locus without being affected by the samskaras deposited there. They have complete mastery over their mind. They have risen beyond awareness of their physical body, senses, thoughts, feelings, and sentiments during their meditation. This awareness is replaced by the sheer sense of I-am-ness, which is using the mind as its locus.

When yogis of this caliber die before reaching the highest level of asamprajnata samadhi, they dissolve into the mind (*chitta*). It is important to understand, however, that this dissolution is completely at their command. Theirs is not an ordinary death but an extraordinary, yogic method of voluntarily leaving the physical body and entering the kingdom of the mind. There they remain until Providence brings them back to this world to complete their journey. Like videha yogis, prakritilaya yogis reincarnate, bringing their wisdom and spiritual accomplishments with them. Like videhas, they are drawn to spirituality spontaneously, resume their sadhana effortlessly, and appear to achieve the highest level of realization miraculously.

Those of us not yet at the level of videha and prakritilaya must awaken our human prowess and privileges and employ them to experience the higher reality we embody. How to awaken this prowess and attain what adepts have attained is the subject of the next sutra.

SUTRA 1:20

श्रद्धावीर्यस्मृतिसमाधिप्रज्ञापूर्वक इतरेषाम्
॥२०॥

śraddhāvīryasmṛtisamādhiprajñāpūrvaka itareṣām ॥ 20 ॥

śraddhā, faith; *vīrya,* vigor; *smṛti,* retentive power; *samādhi,* completely still, pristine state of mind; *prajñā,* intuitive wisdom; *pūrvakaḥ,* preceded by or accompanied by; *itareṣām,* in the case of others

In the case of others, it [samadhi] is preceded by faith, vigor, retentive power, stillness of mind, and intuitive wisdom.

For most of us, acquiring a peaceful mind and becoming established in our core being is not a priority. The world's objects are more charming than all the world's bibles combined. Spirituality is rarely our primary focus—our days are occupied in the pursuit of possessions and power. We have no time to work with the roaming tendencies of our mind, and we feel little need to acquire spiritual insight.

When we do seek spiritual wisdom, it is usually out of curiosity or because our convictions have been shaken by circumstances beyond our control. For example, we may read a biography of a holy man. Part of us admires his spiritual achievements, another part questions them, while still another part is curious to see if we can have such experiences. So we begin our spiritual search motivated by curiosity. Or we may begin the search for our spiritual identity after a calamitous loss. For example, when someone we depend on dies we may wonder: Why did this calamity befall me? Where has my loved one gone? Is he at peace? Is she with God? Can I communicate with her? Does he sense my pain? These and other questions pertaining to life here and hereafter haunt our mind. But they vanish quickly and we again immerse ourselves in the old familiar world of loss and gain, honor and insult. Practices undertaken under these two conditions—curiosity or calamitous events—are too weak to lead to a fruitful engagement in spiritual exploration. We need a more constructive and positive reason to begin our search—one that comes from reflecting on life's purpose and becoming determined to achieve it.

Life is not merely a long string of pleasant and unpleasant events. Life is a powerful force. It is intelligent—it knows its destination and its zeal for reaching it is inexorable. Further, the life force has the ability to discover and collect what it needs to reach its goal. When our practice is grounded in mindful reflection on the immense power and wisdom inherent in the life force, the other ingredients we need to successfully complete our practice come on their own. The scriptures call this mindful reflection *vichara.* Properly guided, vichara helps us understand and cultivate five ingredients essential to spiritual practice: faith (*shraddha*), vigor (*virya*), retentive power (*smriti*), stillness of mind (*samadhi*), and intuition (*prajna*).

Patanjali tells us that to be effective a practice must be accompanied by *shraddha.* Although *shraddha* is loosely translated as "faith," Vyasa defines it as "a completely clear and joyful state of mind" (*samprasada*). For many of us, filling a segment of our day with a prescribed set of disciplines is practice. This type of practice is comprised of a list of techniques and injunctions, and we undertake it because we have been told it will bring us a specific result. It is a recipe for solving a problem. As a result, the value of the practice is dependent on when and to what extent it meets our expectations. If it does not meet our expectations, we dump it without hesitation.

When we engage in spiritual practice on a trial basis, we are not fully committed to it. Our practice is fruitful only when we do it wholeheartedly, and we do it wholeheartedly only when we love it. Love for practice comes from knowing its importance. It must be the center of our lives. We must be convinced that without practice we are living in vain. This conviction cannot be based on sectarian belief. Our faith in our practice needs to be supported by a clear understanding that life is precious and we must not waste it running after fleeting material achievements. We have been given our body, breath, and mind so that we can use them to find life's purpose and meaning. Dying without finding it is the greatest loss.

The more convinced we are about the key role of our practice in enabling us to live a purposeful and meaningful life, the more we love and respect it. Love and respect springing from a true understanding of our practice is shraddha. We are joyful at the prospect of doing our practice. The reasons for delaying or dispensing with it become meaningless. We no longer care whether our practice lowers our blood pressure or relaxes our nervous system—we do it for the simple joy of doing it. According to Vyasa, shraddha is the joy that accompanies a practice. It is more than faith—it is the thrill of realizing that we are fortunate to have a practice that helps restore the pristine nature of our mind, takes us inward, and gives us a vision of life's purpose.

According to the scriptures, shraddha is the fruit of valuing our practice and recognizing its connection to the purpose of life. This knowledge comes from interaction with enlightened souls (*satsanga*), but such encounters are rare. Studying the scriptures (*svadhyaya*) also enlightens us regarding our practice. The more we reflect on the deeper meaning of the scriptures, the clearer our understanding becomes. The clearer our understanding, the greater our love for the practice and the greater our motivation to do it. And that, in turn, leads us to take pleasure in our practice and infuses our mind and heart with faith and joy in it.

Faith leads to *virya*. *Virya* means "strength, vitality, and virility." Our inner strength, stamina, and endurance depend on our access to the innate wisdom of our body and the immense power of our mind. Our faith in ourselves, in our practice, and in the goodness that life embodies awakens both our body and mind and introduces them to a previously unknown dimension. As our conviction matures and our joyful state of mind expands, the body's innate wisdom heals past emotional injuries. Our limbs and organs are energized. Our senses begin receiving nourishment from within. The mind begins taking satisfaction from a pool of inner elixir—contentment. Consequently, the fulfillment we seek through the senses begins to flow from within. Fulfillment from within enables our mind and senses to conserve our virya—our vitality, strength, stamina, endurance, and agility—for higher pursuits. The richer we are in virya, the greater the manifestation of our retentive power (*smriti*).

When we resolve to start a practice on the spur of the moment, our resolution fades as time passes; our zeal for practice wanes, and eventually the practice peters out. This is not necessarily because we lack willpower but because we lack strong, stable retentive power. In worldly endeavors we are much better at adhering to our resolutions. Our will to succeed in worldly matters is unbending. But when it comes to our spiritual practice, we have to be reminded of its importance and to continually be inspired by others. Our retentive power is weak in relation to our spiritual goals and objectives because we have not trained our mind to remember that life has a higher purpose and meaning.

Once we tap into the pool of inner elixir, and our body, mind, and senses are receiving nourishment from inside, our retentive power becomes sharper and more stable. As a result, our resolve to do our practice remains firmly in the forefront of our mind. Sloth, inertia, and carelessness have no power to block the flow of our inner inspiration. Our enthusiasm for the practice keeps anxiety and impatience at bay. Practice becomes as effortless as eating, sleeping, and breathing. Practice flows effortlessly when we are constantly aware that life has a purpose and that we will find this purpose through practice. Patanjali calls this constant awareness smriti. In time, smriti, accompanied by vigor (*virya*) and faith (*shraddha*) engenders another essential ingredient—samadhi.

Here the word *samadhi* has a different meaning than it has in the previous sutras. In his commentary on this sutra, Vyasa clarifies the precise meaning of *samadhi* in this context: "Upon the acquisition of memory, the unperturbed mind settles down." In the context of this sutra, the well-settled state of an unperturbed mind is samadhi.

Normally, the mind is turned and tossed by the charms and temptations of the world. Constant awareness of life's purpose and the role of practice in attaining it renders worldly charms and temptations lifeless. Issues and concerns that previously galvanized our attention now appear insignificant. Similarly, concerns pertaining to our safety and security, which pulled our mind into an unending whirlpool of anxious thoughts, lose their power. Constant awareness of life's purpose keeps our vision clear and our priorities straight. This enables us to remain unperturbed in the face of the demands life makes on us. We also know that if we miss our practice, we will not be able to erase the gap, for time waits for no one. This realization makes us resolute, and we attend our practice with a steady and peaceful mind.

A person with a settled mind is like an ocean. Countless rivers and streams pour their waters into the ocean, yet it is never overwhelmed. Similarly, pleasant and unpleasant sensory experiences, loss and gain, success and failure, and honor and insult do not overwhelm a yogi whose mind is unperturbed. Such a state of mind automatically engenders intuitive wisdom (*prajna*). Intuitive wisdom is special (*pra*) knowledge (*jna*), a clear understanding that needs no verification. Its discerning power is unfailing. All of us are endowed with intuitive wisdom, but a disturbed mind blocks its flow. As soon as the mind is free from inner unrest and is settled, intuitive wisdom begins to flow incessantly.

In the light of intuition, we are able to see the difference between right and wrong, good and bad. We are free of the forces of logic and reason that normally bind us with an unending chain of doubt, fear, and confusion. Intuition becomes our guide and protector. We do our practice joyfully. Our practice may or may not comply with the norms and standards of the religions and cultures of our time, but we intuitively know that it is grounded in the direct experience of truth and will lead us only to truth. This intuitive understanding enables us to remain focused and protects us from doubt, fear, and contradictions. That is why intuitive wisdom, along with the other four essential ingredients of sadhana, empowers us—the ordinary yogis—to achieve the lofty goal of Yoga, which extraordinary yogis achieve seemingly without effort.

In the next two sutras, Patanjali tells us under what conditions our sadhana, fueled by these five ingredients—faith (*shraddha*), vigor (*virya*), retentive power (*smriti*), stillness of mind (*samadhi*), and intuitive wisdom (*prajna*)—bears fruit rapidly.

SUTRA 1:21

तीव्रसंवेगानामासन्नः ॥२१॥

tīvrasaṁvegānāmāsannaḥ ॥21॥

tīvra, steadfast or intense; *saṁvegānām,* to those with ardent desire; *āsannaḥ,* near

It [samadhi] is near for those whose aspiration is steadfast.

In this sutra, Patanjali tells us a bitter truth in a kind and tactful manner: samadhi is not for slowpokes. Samadhi is for those who are highly inspired. It is for vigilant, perceptive seekers—those who embrace the moment of inspiration and keep it in the forefront of their minds. Such aspirants understand the value of that inspiration and do everything possible to nourish it. They never fail to hear and heed the voice of their hearts. They are so absorbed in their sadhana that they are oblivious to the pains and pleasures of the world. The ideas of success and failure do not enter their minds, so they are free from anxiety and fear.

Vyasa divides aspirants into nine specific categories. Here, for the sake of simplicity, we will divide them into three broad categories: low, intermediate, and highest grade.

Those who, fearing obstacles, do not start their practice are the lowest-grade aspirants. They wait for miracles, hoping someone else will take away their misery. When they do become inspired, they demand simple solutions to their complex problems. They seek validation for their aspiration. They consult teachers, priests, and astrologers for an auspicious time to begin their quest and look to the stars for guidance. Their journey usually ends before it has really begun. Such seekers are far from attaining samadhi.

Intermediate-grade aspirants drop their practice when obstacles arise. They know the importance of making their minds clear and calm and becoming established in themselves, but they have not decided that this is their top priority. They do not make a clear distinction between means and goals. Because they do not clearly understand that material objects are only means, while inner tranquility—maturing into samadhi—is the goal, they drop their practice when faced with obstacles.

Obstacles cannot stop the highest-grade aspirants, however. They start their practice with clarity and enthusiasm and never allow their aspiration and motivation to wane. They are always aware of the meaning and purpose of life. They never forget that inner equanimity empowers the mind to face and conquer all calamities. Their understanding that no loss is greater than the loss of inner equanimity renders every obstacle impotent. Undaunted by obstacles, they invest all their resources in their practice. For them, the goal—samadhi—is near. How these highest-grade aspirants gain distinction within their own circle and quickly reach the most exalted state of self-mastery is the subject of the next sutra.

SUTRA 1:22

मृदुमध्याधिमात्रत्वात् ततोऽपि विशेषः ॥२२॥

mṛdumadhyādhimātratvāt tato'pi viśeṣaḥ ॥ 22 ॥

mṛdu, mild; *madhya,* intermediate; *adhimātratvāt,* supreme; *tataḥ,* from that; *api,* also; *viśeṣaḥ,* distinction

Depending on whether the seeker's steadfast aspiration is mild, intermediate, or supreme, there are further distinctions.

An aspirant of the highest grade rises to even greater eminence due to the intensity of the five *upayas* (the five means listed in sutra 1:20): a joyous state of mind resulting from unwavering faith (*shraddha*), inner elixir (*virya*), strong retentive power (*smriti*), a well-settled, unperturbed mind (*samadhi*), and the light of intuitive wisdom (*prajna*).

Even the highest-grade aspirants fall prey to carelessness. This is the most subtle and potent function of ignorance (*avidya*). For example, a monk renounces worldly life to commit himself wholeheartedly to his sadhana. He gives up his possessions and embraces the practice of non-possessiveness as a means of freeing himself of material and emotional baggage. His initiation signifies a departure from involvement in worldly affairs for a full engagement in spiritual matters. As time passes, however, a monk not endowed with a high degree of vigilance gradually becomes more involved in cultivating the outer appearance and paraphernalia of monkhood than in attending his spiritual quest. Eventually, monastic life becomes just another worldly pursuit and he is a monk in name only.

Maintaining and further intensifying the fervor that drew us to spiritual practice is the only way of ensuring we will continue our journey persistently and speedily. We intensify our fervor with regular self-examination and by assessing the quality of our thoughts, speech, actions, and the subtle forces that propel them.

The higher and more lofty the practice, the more carefully it must be tended. Highly advanced practice must be supported by intense fervor and must be tended with supreme care. Before undertaking an advanced practice, we must assess our capacity and preparedness. Once we decide to undertake it, we cannot afford to be lax. In this sutra, Patanjali tells us how to assess our current capacity and prepare ourselves to undertake increasingly advanced practices so that we can accomplish life's purpose without delay.

As stated in the last sutra, there are three kinds of aspirants: those with mild aspiration, those with intermediate aspiration, and those with supreme aspiration. These three degrees of aspiration depend on several factors, the most important of which is knowledge. The deeper our understanding of the practice, the more grateful we are that we have been guided to do it. Gratitude fills our heart with love and compels us to surrender trustfully to the higher reality, which created the conditions conducive to the practice and endowed us with the tools and means of doing it. The tradition calls trustful surrender *bhakti*. *Bhakti* means "to be joined in; to be yoked in." Trustful surrender, laden with gratitude, yokes us to our practice.

Trustful surrender cannot be fabricated. It is the spontaneous outgrowth of a mature understanding and the conviction grounded in that understanding. Working to gain knowledge is in our hand. *Bhakti* (trustful surrender) is a sign that we have truly gained knowledge. Thus, for all intents and purposes, our degree of aspiration depends on our level of knowledge. People with a mild understanding of their practice, therefore, will have only a mild aspiration, whereas those with an intermediate or supreme understanding will be much more highly inspired. That is why the same practice leads to three different levels of experiences. The following example will clarify this point.

In the Yoga tradition, there is a mantra, *om namah shivaya.* According to popular belief, it is the mantra of the Hindu god, Shiva, the destroyer. Shiva lives at the cremation ground. His hair is disheveled and his body smeared with funeral ash. His aspect is fierce and he surrounds himself with ghosts and goblins. He does not conform to standards of civility—he lives the way he likes and eats whatever he likes. His destructive wrath is one of his most notable attributes. Phallic worship pleases him the most. *Om namah shivaya* is a mantra for worshiping this god.

According to Hindu theology, Shiva is one of three top gods, in company with Brahma and Vishnu. Shiva is the master of one of the forces of Primordial Nature, *tamas,* the force of stability, darkness, and inertia. The universe comes into existence, remains in place, and, at the time of dissolution, is reabsorbed into Primordial Nature because he balances the forces of nature by controlling tamas. His knowledge and strength are unmatched. Nothing and no one can disobey his command. This valiant, omniscient cosmic being is the embodiment of unconditional love and compassion. He is always there for those who seek his help. He resides in our heart in the form of intelligence. The mantra for worshiping him is *om namah shivaya.*

According to tantric metaphysics, Shiva is Pure Consciousness. All powers, capacities, and capabilities are intrinsic to Shiva. Her power manifests in numberless names and forms, yet she remains above all. She is the source of both duality and non-duality and is untouched by confusion regarding duality and non-duality. Her pure will establishes law and order throughout the universe. Her light shines in the sun, moon, and stars, and her life force pulsates in each of us. Shiva is our essence and *om namah shivaya* is the mantra for experiencing it.

As we can see, the understanding of *shiva* in popular belief, in theology, and in metaphysics is quite different, as is the meaning of the mantra *om namah shivaya*. The popular meaning, "Salutation to Shiva," is based on the mantra's connection with Sanskrit. According to tantric metaphysics, however, the true meaning of the mantra lies in its pure inner vibration (*spanda*). *Om namah shivaya* is the mantric body of the purest state of consciousness; by merging our mind with this sound, we unite with Pure Consciousness. From this standpoint, *om namah shivaya* has nothing to do with physical or devotional prostration to an external deity. Rather, meditation on *om namah shivaya* is a process of embracing our own essence and becoming fully established in it.

These various levels of understanding of *shiva* and the mantra *om namah shivaya* fill our heart and mind with varying degrees of aspiration, inspiring us to do our practice with varying degrees of intensity and intention. Continually stretching the scope of our understanding will automatically make us aspire to gain a higher level of experience at a faster pace.

To stand out as an aspirant of the highest grade, therefore, we must have a profound understanding of our sadhana and its role in enabling us to accomplish life's purpose. This entails committing ourselves to an exhaustive study of the subject and dedicating ourselves totally to our sadhana. In other words, it is a full-time job. But living in the world while discharging our duties is also a full-time job—it never comes to an end. Furthermore, we are not all equipped to comprehend the subtleties of the practice necessary to accelerate our aspiration. Is there a less demanding and equally rewarding shortcut to accomplishing life's purpose? In response to this question, Patanjali offers the next sutra.

SUTRA 1:23

ईश्वरप्रणिधानाद्वा ।।२३।।

īśvarapraṇidhānādvā ॥ 23 ॥

īśvara, God; *praṇidhānāt,* from trustful surrender to; *vā,* or

From trustful surrender to Ishvara [God], samadhi also comes.

The subtle impressions created by our repeated actions are the source of the mind's roaming tendencies. The preceding sutras advise us to nullify and attain mastery over them by adopting the twofold method of abhyasa and vairagya. This method aims at actively creating desirable impressions and actively eliminating undesirable ones. In other words, Patanjali has advised us to undertake a course of sadhana to undo what we have done in the past and to rewrite our destiny in the light of the highest truth.

In this sutra, he says that when we surrender to God we will automatically be freed of our past deeds and the subtle impressions created by them. Although this may appear to be a marked departure from his teaching up to this point, it is not. Here Patanjali is introducing a new course of sadhana—surrender to God (*Ishvara pranidhana*)—as the surest way to attain samadhi.

In most cultures, the word *surrender* is associated with giving up—it conveys a sense of weakness, defeat, and hopelessness. But as we'll see in sutras 1:23–1:33, the path of surrender in Yoga is highly structured and complete in itself. For those who understand the essence of surrender, this path is easy and direct. But for those who are lazy and seeking an easy path, it is complicated and full of pitfalls.

Surrender to God is not an option but an inescapable reality. It rises on the horizon of our consciousness as the result of our sadhana, impelling us to embrace it joyfully. This is the path of *bhava pratyaya yogis*—yogis who in their past life were led to a higher level of realization by the grace of the Divine and are born with intuitive wisdom. Because they remember how grace has guided, protected, and nourished them, theirs is a life of surrender from the outset. They pray for divine grace to take its course once again and with greater force. They rely on God's grace, while doing their practice wholeheartedly, and they retain the purity of their knowledge with the help of vairagya.

The idea of surrender comes to the rest of us—the ordinary yogis (*upaya pratyaya yogis*)—only when we are faced with persistent obstacles or when our practice does not seem to be bearing fruit quickly. Just as many people turn to alternative medicine only after exhausting the options offered by conventional medicine, most of us consider surrendering to God only as a last resort, and even then only on a trial basis. Turning to surrender as a last resort prevents us from embracing it unreservedly. At the same time that we are hoping surrender will free us from our problems, we are regarding it with a skeptical eye. We are seeking a magical solution, and when it does not materialize quickly, we try something else.

Surrender to God is a central theme in all religions in spite of the fact that God is shrouded in mystery in most cultures and traditions. He cannot be seen or touched. He is all-pervading, yet is said to live in heaven or in a temple. He is the embodiment of forgiveness, yet is said to assign punishment for our smallest transgression. He is the father of all, yet is said to prefer certain castes, creeds, genders, and ethnic groups. According to the Yoga tradition, these concepts are simply different notions of God—products of the human mind, which is often disturbed, stupefied, distracted, and thoroughly confused.

Yoga tells us that God is as real as we ourselves. God is among us, is in us, is us, and yet is beyond us. It has no beginning, no middle, and no end. God is eternal, all-pervading, and beyond death, decay, and destruction. It is the total sum of all that is. It is everything—knower, known, and the means of knowing. It is endowed with limitless unrestricted power of will, power of knowledge, and power of action. God is Pure Being with the ability to become anything imaginable. It is one, with the ability to become many. It is transcendental, with the ability to become immanent. It is abstract, with the ability to become perceptible. It is beyond time, space, and the law of causality, with the ability to become part of the world existing within the domain of time and space. We attain samadhi by surrendering to this God.

What is surrender? How do we do it? We usually turn to God under one of four circumstances: desperation, curiosity, the desire for health and wealth, and out of correct understanding. The first three circumstances may make us God-oriented and God-fearing, but they do not lead us to embrace the reality of God or seek his unconditional love. We are simply seeking what we love the most—the fulfillment of our desires. Genuine love for God and surrender to God walks into our life only under the fourth circumstance—correct understanding.

When we have truly acquired knowledge, there is no need to make either an effort to love God or a plan to surrender. At the moment of inner awakening, we see the higher reality surrounding us and know it as our perennial source of guidance and nourishment. This luminous reality pervades every cell of our body and all the spaces between. It guides the expression of our genes and chromosomes so we don't grow toenails in our brains. It ensures that after conception, progesterone levels rise, preventing menses, so we are not flushed from our mother's womb. At birth, it ensures that our lungs begin to function. It trains our brain to comprehend the meaning of words. It infuses our mind with the power to solve problems. It gives us the courage and motivation to explore the vastness of life. It guides us to find our livelihood and to create a world of our dreams. And it does all this and much, much more without seeking anything in return. Its love and concern for us is unconditional. This realization fills our heart with deep gratitude. That gratitude finds its natural expression in love for God (*Ishvara*).

Faith in Ishvara means fully embracing our realization of his unconditional love. Living in the light of this faith is surrender. Making an effort to live in the light of this faith is the path of love and devotion (*bhakti*). Even though God is everywhere, bhakti enables us to experience God concretely. Cultivating constant awareness of God's presence and unconditional divine grace intensifies our conviction that we are not alone—that we are loved and nurtured. This conviction becomes a source of inner strength, enabling us to remain unperturbed in the midst of life's many storms. Even when powerful subtle impressions of the past begin to churn our mind, we remain fully aware of the guiding and protecting grace of the Divine. We witness the tendencies of our mind with trustful surrender, while remaining fully focused on one reality—the Divine within. Patanjali calls this *Ishvara pranidhana,* surrender to God.

According to Vyasa, the most powerful strand of realization leading us to spontaneously surrender to God is the realization that she is constantly meditating on us. She has joyfully taken us into her fold. Her concern for our well-being is infinitely more refined and focused than our concern for ourselves. By meditating on us, she has endowed our mind with the ability to meditate on her. The joy of her meditation on us makes our mind turn inward. Her intrinsic beauty, which she has transmitted to us, frees us from the charms and temptations of the world. Fullness is her essential nature, yet she seeks her ever-growing fullness in us. She is satisfied only upon seeing that we have acquired her grandeur. Our aspiration to be like her arises from her desire to see us in her image. This realization is the ground for true surrender. Surrender rising from this firm foundation pulls God toward us, and us toward God. Samadhi is the ground where the two meet.

From time out of mind, the notion of God has been shrouded in mystery. Is God one or many? Is God in heaven or everywhere? Is God with form or formless? Is God attainable or not attainable? Is our life on earth a reward or a punishment? Is God the creator or is nature the creator? Is God omniscient? Omnipotent? If so, why doesn't she free us from sorrow? Does God help only those who know her as almighty? Patanjali dedicates the next eight sutras to answering these questions and to explaining the concept of God in Yoga and the role of meditation on God in attaining freedom from our karmic bondage.

SUTRA 1:24

क्लेशकर्मविपाकाशयैरपरामृष्टः पुरुषविशेष ईश्वरः ॥२४॥

kleśakarmavipākāśayairaparāmṛṣṭaḥ puruṣaviśeṣa īśvaraḥ ॥ 24 ॥

kleśa, affliction; *karma,* action; *vipāka,* result; *āśayaiḥ,* repository; *aparāmṛṣṭaḥ,* untouched; *puruṣa-viśeṣaḥ,* special soul; *īśvaraḥ,* God

Ishvara is a unique being untouched by afflictions, karmas, the results of karmas, and the repository of karmas.

This sutra brings us to the heart of yogic metaphysics: the undeniable reality of God (*Ishvara*). Ishvara is pure intelligence, eternal, and beyond time and space. He is pure being. The world exists only because he brings it into existence. We come into being only after he empowers us to be. Ishvara makes the unmanifest manifest, causes dormant forces to pulsate, brings nonbeing into being, and the dead to life. This supremely Intelligent Being sees all that is, and in a single glance, creates a condition where infinite numbers of souls, dissolved in Primordial Nature and unaware of their existence, awaken and become self-aware. Primordial Nature (*Prakriti*) awakens in response to his infallible intention (*sankalpa*). At her awakening, everyone and everything contained in her awakens. Thus, Prakriti herself and all the potential—including time, space, and the law of cause and effect—

resting in her as non-being instantly come into being. This is the beginning of creation, the birth of our soul, and the genesis of our inexorable quest for fulfillment and freedom.

Awakening Prakriti, awakening us, and creating a world where we can find our fulfillment and freedom is an idea conceived by Ishvara. Its infallible intention (*sankalpa*) manifesting as the life force (*prana*) pulls the world forward. Its sankalpa causes us to breathe, think, and aspire to find life's purpose. In this context, gaining knowledge means knowing the dynamics of Ishvara's sankalpa. Trusting this sankalpa is surrender to God. The more we know the dynamics of Ishvara's sankalpa, the purer and more intense our surrender. The purer and more unshakeable our surrender, the closer we are to Pure Consciousness, the Divine within us. This is *bhakti yoga*, the path described in sutra 1:23. Here, in sutra 1:24, Patanjali describes the nature of Ishvara and its role in the manifestation of the universe, as well as its role in helping us find our life's purpose.

Previous masters, particularly the sage Kapila, have described the entire range of reality in two words: Purusha and Prakriti. Purusha is Consciousness and Prakriti is Primordial Nature, the total sum of all that exists and all that has potential to exist. For the sake of simplicity, Purusha is described as pure intelligence and Prakriti as the primordial cause of energy and matter. Everything in the world, including we ourselves, is a perfect blend of Purusha and Prakriti.

When addressing a general audience, philosophers of the Yoga tradition describe purusha and prakriti as two distinct entities. In that context, they appear to embody two totally different sets of qualities and attributes. Purusha is intelligent, prakriti is unintelligent; purusha is consciousness, prakriti is matter; purusha is pure witness, prakriti is fully involved in the process of creation. According to this description, only when unintelligent prakriti joins intelligent purusha is unmanifest primordial matter (*prakriti*) set in motion and the universe manifests.

Philosophers further dilute the profound metaphysics of Yoga by using the analogy of two people, one lame (*purusha*) and the other blind (*prakriti*). One cannot move and the other cannot see, but together they undertake a journey. They join forces because purusha is caught in the cycle of birth and death and the pain inherent in it. Purusha can see its problem but has no ability to escape it. Seeking help, it unites with prakriti. Using purusha's intelligence, prakriti manifests as intellect, ego, mind, senses, and the elements. A world of infinite forms in numberless shapes and sizes is created. This makes it possible for purusha to use worldly objects and experiences as a tool to extricate itself from the cycle of birth and death.

According to this metaphor, by bringing herself into manifestation, primordial nature (*prakriti*) does consciousness (*purusha*) a great favor—she releases him from the bondage of matter. This lame-and-blind metaphor makes purusha appear helpless and meek, yet it is with the assistance of this helpless, meek purusha that unintelligent prakriti unfolds her infinitely vast potential, resulting in the creation of the universe. This tangled explanation of how the universe comes into being becomes more confusing when philosophers of Yoga posit the theory of many purushas but only one prakriti.

This confusing explanation becomes even further convoluted when philosophers discuss the reason consciousness and matter join hands in the first place. By falling into the cycle of birth and death, consciousness becomes bound. Seeking freedom from bondage, it unites with primordial nature. This union results in the manifestation of the universe. What circular logic! The world is already in existence. Consciousness has already fallen into the worldly cycle. It is already trapped and helpless. Then somehow (mysteriously, as the philosophers say), it unites with prakriti so it can attain freedom from her. How many purushas does prakriti need to unfold her vast potential? Who is dependent on whom? How can the Absolute be dependent on anything? And most important, how can there be two absolutes? The *Yoga Sutra* answers these perennial questions—and the answer is Ishvara.

Ishvara is Purusha—a very special one. This Special Purusha is unique in that it has never been affected by the fivefold affliction: ignorance, distorted self-identity, attachment, aversion, and fear. Nor has this Special Purusha ever been subject to karmas, to the effects of karmas, nor to the karmic vehicles that lead consciousness into bondage. Ishvara is beyond time. Ishvara is omniscient. Ishvara is the absolute apex of knowledge (*jnana*), non-attachment (*vairagya*), virtue (*dharma*), and the limitless capacity to be and become (*aishvarya*). Consciousness in which these godly attributes are not fully manifest falls into the category of ordinary purusha.

Ordinary purushas are affected by the five afflictions, operate within the domain of time, and are subject to karmas and the effects of karmas, as well as to the karmic vehicles that have led to bondage. Ishvara is one; ordinary purushas are many. It is the union of Ishvara—the Special Purusha—with Prakriti that brings about the manifestation of the universe, not the union of ordinary purushas with prakriti. The relationship between this Special Purusha and Prakriti is nothing like the relationship between a lame person and a blind one. This metaphor applies only to ordinary purushas—to us. Purushas caught in the snare of bondage are lame. Prakriti entangled with these bound purushas is blind. And the union of these two is disastrous. We overcome this disaster through the grace of Ishvara. Ishvara's grace enables us to rise above our limitations. Then we are no longer lame or blind. We are pure Purusha—a perfect reflection of Ishvara herself.

Purusha is eternity of constancy (*kutastha nityata*) and Prakriti is eternity of ever-flowing change (*pravaha nityata*). Both are eternal and all-pervading. Both are absolute. Due to their eternal and pervasive nature they are contained in each other. They are always together. Their union is as eternal as their own eternity. In other words, there is no Prakriti without Purusha and no Purusha without Prakriti. For all intents and purposes, they are one and the same. The intrinsic capacity of Purusha is Prakriti; the intrinsic intelligence of Prakriti is Purusha.

Our long-cherished confusion fills our consciousness with the notion that duality and non-duality are incompatible. This confused notion forces us to study Purusha and Prakriti in isolation from each other. However, the Sri Vidya tradition I belong to dispels this confusion by explaining that Yoga posits the philosophy of dualism only from the vantage point of ordinary souls. From the vantage point of *brahma rishis*—those who have reached *asamprajnata samadhi* and achieved the highest level of realization—Yoga posits the philosophy of non-dualism.

This gives rise to a number of questions: If Purusha and Prakriti are two sides of the same coin, in what respect do they unite? In what respect does the universe begin to manifest? What does "begin" mean in this context? When the union of Purusha and Prakriti is as eternal as they themselves, why is the universe not always in existence? What does the creation and evolution of the universe mean?

The tradition of Yoga, as presented by Patanjali and expounded by Vyasa, holds that the universe is beginningless. The building blocks of the universe—the forces of *sattva, rajas,* and *tamas,* which constitute the very essence of Prakriti—are eternal. The changes occurring in them are eternal. Their interaction with

Purusha is eternal. The universe created by the interaction of these forces is eternal. The primordial cause of matter and energy—Prakriti—is so subtle that Patanjali calls it untraceable and irreferable (*alinga*). In an attempt to describe its indescribability, Vyasa calls it the existence of that which is devoid of existence (*nihsattasattam*) (YS 2:19).

"Creation and evolution of the universe" means simply that the dormancy of Prakriti is shaken off through the sheer intention of Prakriti's own intrinsic intelligence, Purusha. The evolution of the universe is a purposeful, finite manifestation of Prakriti's infinite properties, qualities, and attributes. In other words, "evolution" refers to the awakening of the infinite variety of subtle imprints (*bhavas*), which can be traced, seen, and felt by Prakriti's own intrinsic intelligence. With this awakening, Prakriti's vast field is filled with purpose and meaning.

Before this awakening, changes occurring in the vast field of the threefold forces of Prakriti (*sattva, rajas,* and *tamas*) are without sequence (*akrama*), without specific purpose. Thus, for all intents and purposes, there is no universe. The universe begins to exist only when Prakriti is impregnated by the purposeful embrace of the intention of Purusha. It is necessary to reiterate here that this intention of Purusha refers to the intention of the Special Purusha known as Ishvara, not to the intention of ordinary purushas, enveloped in the darkness of ignorance. This purposeful embrace—intention—causes changes to occur in a sequential fashion (*krama*).

In Yoga, the sequential flow of creation is known as *parinama krama,* the flow of cause and effect in a sequence comprehensible to our mind and senses. In order for sequence to be comprehensible, time and space must manifest. When Pure Intelligence (*Purusha*) divides time and space into numberless pieces and strings them together in a linear manner, time itself is born. This is when phenomena and the process of phenomena coming into being in time as well as in space become comprehensible to the mind. It is in this respect that the ever-existent, unborn universe is born. In other words, the untraceable, imperceptible, irreferable universe, which until this point was known only to the Seeing Power of the Pure Seer, the Special Purusha (*Ishvara*), now receives a traceable, perceptible, referable form.

To teach us further, the sages raise another set of questions: What is the exact nature of Purusha's intention in embracing Prakriti? Is there only one intention or many? The answer to these questions illumines both the evolutionary process of creation and our spiritual path.

As stated before, the universe is eternal. Individual beings—ordinary purushas—are also eternal. They are in the world and are part of the world. They are in bondage. Their bondage is due mainly to their ignorance (*avidya*) regarding their true identity. Groping in the darkness of ignorance, they become attached to what little they know of themselves (YS 2:24), and get caught up in preserving what they hold dear—their own false self-identity (*asmita*). Attachment (*raga*) to what gives them hope of preserving that false identity is their wealth. They hate (*dvesha*) anything or anyone posing a threat to this wealth. Excruciating pain caused by fear (*abhinivesha*) of losing their precious self-identity, attachment to this self-identity, hatred for those who threaten it, and ultimately, the prospect of losing it all to death is a cocoon they have spun around themselves. They live helplessly in the illusory safety of this cocoon and resort to death when they are exhausted by the strains of life.

With their death comes the death of both time and space; in relation to these ordinary purushas and their personal world, the sequential flow of time and space comes to an end. They are reabsorbed into untraceable, imperceptible, and irreferable Prakriti. However, from the vantage point of Ishvara, they remain as alive as ever. In the eyes of Ishvara, their surrender to death is an act of helplessness. Moved by his intrinsic compassion, he awakens them from their slumber through his sheer intention. He glances at his own intrinsic Primordial Nature (*Prakriti*), stirring her internal atmosphere, animating the numberless purushas and their personal worlds, all of which were absorbed into her vast field at death and which are still in need of fulfillment (*bhoga*) and freedom (*apavarga*). Ishvara's glance is imbued with the benevolent desire for these individual souls to attain their life's purpose—fulfillment and freedom. In one glance, the ever-free Purusha conveyed everything. And in her spontaneous response, Prakriti did everything.

The individual souls awaken from their timeless slumber to find not only a world made of earth, water, fire, air, and space, but also a world that responds to their thoughts, feelings, and sentiments. They are thrilled at the prospect of experiencing what they were not able to experience before they died. Their unfulfilled desires and powerful samskaras are stirred up. Those unfulfilled desires and samskaras influence their process of choosing the right time, the right place, and a suitable body in this so-called newly created world. Their unfulfilled desires determine the unique qualities and characteristics of their personality, as well as their overall physical characteristics, the range of their emotions, the capacities of their senses, and the availability of sense objects in the external world. In short, their unfulfilled desires shape their destiny. Thus, the major course of their experiences of pleasure and pain is determined, as is when and how the guiding and nurturing grace of God will walk into their life in the most significant manner.

The role of Ishvara in our life's journey is more intricate than we can imagine. He sheds the light of his intelligence on us when we are enveloped in the utter darkness cast upon us by death, bringing us back to become living beings. We become aware of our feelings. We begin to search for our lost identity. Our memories return. We start looking for those we loved and hated the most. Our cravings intensify. The drive for fulfillment and freedom gathers momentum. We again set out on the arduous journey we left incomplete—we are born. Ishvara is fully involved in this process in every respect. He is our companion before we are born. That is why another name for Ishvara is Ganesha, the lord of individual souls (*gana*).

Sages use the metaphor of two birds perched in the tree of life to describe the nature of the relationship between ourselves and Ishvara. One bird eats fruit from the tree while the other watches. We, the ordinary purushas, eat our karmic fruits while Ishvara watches. Seated at the core of our being she pervades every nook and cranny of our life. Every cell of our body and all our limbs and organs receive guidance and nourishment from this ever-free being. Ishvara guides us through the journey of life, which is normally made of pleasure and pain, success and failure, honor and insult. She accompanies us when we perform our actions, but remains untouched by our performance. Ishvara is the force of our pulsation, yet is untouched by the thoughts, feelings, and sentiments our inner pulsation stirs. She sets the direction for our emotions and enables us to revisit our unresolved issues while remaining untouched by them. Her actions are not tainted by ignorance, a false sense of self-identity, attachment, aversion, or fear. She is untouched by her actions, the fruits of her actions, and the karmic vehicles, which cause ordinary purushas to remain caught in the cycle of birth and death. She is untouched by those whose lives she touches so compassionately, yet is fully aware of our minutest needs and takes care of those needs with limitless care and attention. Her capacity to know the endless details of each of the numberless individual beings is due to her omniscience.

Among a long list of differences between God and us, this particular quality—omniscience—stands out. We are suffering mainly because we lack correct understanding of our true self. Our knowledge is limited, and we are attempting to unveil the mystery of life with this limited knowledge. Ishvara is the embodiment of infinite knowledge. The entire mystery of life is fully open to him. He knows the ins and outs of each karmic strand we have ever created. From the standpoint of Yoga sadhana, therefore, this particular attribute of God—omniscience—is the most important, because it relates directly to the fulfillment and freedom we are seeking. For this reason, Patanjali dedicates the next sutra to discussing the omniscience of God.

SUTRA 1:25

तत्र निरतिशयं सर्वज्ञबीजम् ॥२५॥

tatra niratiśayaṁ sarvajñabījam ॥ 25 ॥

tatra, therein; *niratiśayaṁ,* without limit; *sarvajña-bīja,* seed of omniscience

Therein [in Ishvara] lies the seed of unsurpassed omniscience.

In the preceding sutra, Patanjali describes the unique nature of God from a special vantage point. He states that, unlike us, Ishvara is completely untouched by the fivefold affliction, by karmas, and by the fruits of karmas, as well as by the karmic vehicles which transport us from one life to another.

Because we live and act under the influence of the fivefold affliction—ignorance, distorted self-identity, attachment, aversion, and fear—we undermine, dishonor, and disclaim our own potential. We suffer from inner poverty. We become weak and meek. We bring a crippling feeling of disempowerment on ourselves and consequently have little or no confidence in our ability to achieve life's purpose.

Ishvara is totally opposite. Her *shakti*—the power of containing and exhibiting her ability to do what she wishes to do, her ability not to do what she does not wish to do, and her ability to undo what so far has been done by anyone and anything—is utterly unobstructed. She is omnipotent, a subject elaborated on in sutra 1:24. This sutra describes Ishvara's intrinsic attribute from another vantage point—omniscience.

God's ability to know everything all the time is without parallel for he is not an individual. The sense of individuality draws a boundary around us in both time and space, separating us from the totality of existence and erecting borders between our various experiences. Each experience stands alone within a well-defined point of time and space. Thus, before we revisit our experiences we must use the power of our memory to create bridges among them. But because we have damaged our memory to a significant degree by clinging to the five afflictions, we have limited ability to store our experiences, and we store them only in the form of subtle karmic impressions.

Ishvara is not an individual. He is not trapped in the cage of time and space. His experiences are not separated by time and space, so he has no need to create bridges before revisiting these experiences. His various aspects have different names. The totality of knowledge—comprised of his direct experience of everything and everyone—stands continually before his consciousness. His memory is not damaged by the five afflictions. He is fully aware of each individual soul. He is the father of the most significant of all phenomena—the birth of creation itself. He knows the entire dynamics of birth—birth as a process, birth as an event, the cause that led each individual to be born, and the cause that carries the potential for an individual to be born again. That is why he is known as *Jatavedas,* the one who knows about all those ever born. It is to Jatavedas that the sages say, "We offer the essence of our being" (*sunavama somam*).

Due to our limited knowledge, we do not know the constituents of our life. We are not familiar with our karmas, samskaras, and vasanas. We do not know which of our karmic debts we must pay off by discharging our duties, which we can renounce, and which we must surrender. Jatavedas, the knower residing within us, knows precisely what brought us to this world and what we must do to find our life's purpose. This Omniscient Being is capable of destroying our doubt and fear by shedding the light of his intelligence on us. He is an embodiment of absolute wisdom; thus, the sages call him *Veda,* the knowledge.

Our knowledge is incomplete. It always seeks confirmation and is heavily influenced by the opinions of others. Groping our way by its dim light, we are filled with doubt. The light of Ishvara, on the other hand, is complete. It seeks no validation and is not influenced by opinion. Bathed in its brilliance, we are confident.

In the clarity and confidence conferred by the inner light we find ourselves utterly secure. We know we are sitting in the safety of Ishvara's castle of omniscience. This realization empowers us to conquer our long-cherished enemies—our karmas, samskaras, and all other mental tendencies. That is why Ishvara is called *Durga,* the valiant goddess who is both a shield and a sword. She is also a castle (*Durga*), who keeps us in and keeps our enemies out. Even though she is one, she is addressed by the sages in the plural; she is also beyond gender so the sages address her in neutral gender and plural number—*Durgani.* In relation to navigating the vast ocean of samsara, the worldly cycle, she is the boat, the boatman, and the final destination (*Naveva Sindhum*). God is the very essence of enthusiasm—the epitome of the indomitable will that makes us unstoppable in our quest. Thus, the sages call him *Agni,* the fire that illumines our path, burns our foes, and leads us to the castle of ultimate safety.

This omniscient being (*Sarvajna*); the knower of all those ever born (*Jatavedas*); the goddess of protection and conqueror of enemies (*Durgani*); our very personal boat, the rower of the boat, and the destination (*Naveva Sindhum*); and the ever-present fire of courage (*Agni*) is in us, is with us, and essentially *is* us. This realization fills our heart with gratitude, making us humble and strong. We realize how little we know of ourselves and of the immense reality surrounding us. In the light of this realization we begin to question our distorted sense of self-identity. Our belief in our self-incriminating and self-righteous ego drops away, replaced with a humbler and more enlightened ego, one with the willingness to listen. This realization-driven gratitude becomes the source of our strength. We are infused with a new understanding of ourselves.

We know we are not alone. Despite our long list of weaknesses and follies, we are accompanied by the Divinity who understands us perfectly. She knows our needs and she knows how to fulfill those needs. We no longer count our mistakes. We stop assessing our sincerity for we know the Knower within us is fully aware of all our strengths and weaknesses. Our motives cannot be hidden from that Omniscient Being—there is no point even in attempting it. Because we have realized the Omniscient Being knows us better than we know ourselves and her concern for our fulfillment and freedom is unconditional, our prayers and methods of meditation and worship become simpler. We no longer trivialize God with petty requests and demands. We stop begging and become a true seeker. We do everything in our power to maintain the awareness that the Omniscient Being is our guide and that every experience and circumstance—pleasant or unpleasant—is taking place under her watchful eye. We trustfully surrender to Ishvara and attend to our duties—both worldly and spiritual—without fear or anxiety.

In the next sutra, Patanjali describes the nature of Ishvara and his relationship with us from yet another vantage point—omnipresence. There, he tells us that Ishvara is not only an omniscient being but also the teacher who guides us in how to reach him, experience him, bathe in his omniscience, and accomplish life's purpose.

SUTRA 1:26

स एष पूर्वेषामपि गुरुः कालेनानवच्छेदात्
॥२६॥

sa eṣa pūrveṣāmapi guruḥ kālenānavacchedāt ॥ 26 ॥

saḥ, he; *eṣaḥ,* this one; *pūrveṣām,* of the previous ones; *api,* even; *guruḥ,* spiritual guide or preceptor; *kālena,* time; *anavacchedāt,* not limited by

He is the one who has been the preceptor of all previous teachers for He is not limited by time.

Our core is Consciousness. Consciousness is eternal but we are mortal. Consciousness is never born and never dies yet we are subject to birth and death. Consciousness is the Seer and the Power of Seeing, and yet in our conscious awareness we cannot comprehend it as anything other than an object of our experience. In daily life, the awareness of our self-existence is broken by sleep. When we sleep, we have no idea of who we are. We wake up with no knowledge of the process and phenomenon of sleep. How short-lived is the experience of our continuity!

Philosophers may boast of their doctrines regarding the eternity of consciousness and its continuous flow, but we all share a common experience: death brings our consciousness to a full stop. The idea that we are eternal—that we were there before we were born, that we will continue even after we die—is unconvincing, yet we force ourselves to believe this unconvincing truth.

We know we are mortal. We know we have little knowledge of our past and no ability to foresee the future. We know our knowledge of the dynamics of life is extremely limited, and we also know that expanding this knowledge is not among our priorities. And yet the desire to experience our eternity is inherent to our psyche. Lacking faith in ourselves, we hope to find someone who is immortal or, failing that, someone who has the knowledge of immortality.

The desire for a connection with someone who is holy and lack of faith in our own holiness are basic human characteristics that lead to personality worship. We search for a leader. If one is not readily available, we create one. We put the holy man on a pedestal. His words become authority and a cult begins. When our conscience questions his authority, we feel guilty because we believe our holy man—swami, lama, imam, priest, or guru—is enlightened, or is at least a conduit for enlightenment. The more religiously oriented our society, the less we trust our own conscience and the more inclined we are to rely on a holy man's pronouncements regarding eternity. According to Patanjali, this is a dangerous trap. Instead, he advises us to turn to the One who is eternal and immortal—Ishvara.

As explained in the commentary on sutra 1:24, when death renders us unconscious we lose our most valued possession—self-identity. From that perspective, we become a non-being. We have no means to even feel that we are dead. With death our sense of time also dies. Past, present, and future are absorbed into nothingness. Buried in the deep tomb of non-being, we are virtually non-existent. Then the imperishable Divine casts his glance on us and we emerge from the depths of darkness. We recognize our helplessness. We become aware that we have been absorbed into a state of non-being. We long for our most valued possession—our self-identity—but we have no tools to reclaim it.

Seeing our helplessness, Ishvara is moved. Out of compassion, he glances at all-pervading Primordial Nature, Prakriti, who instantly manifests everything we need to reclaim our sense of I-am-ness (*asmita*) and the private world we had before we died. The intelligence (*buddhi*) we once possessed awakens. The mind (*manas*), ego (*ahamkara*), and the senses (*indriya*) spring forth, but they need a locus. The urge for a locus spins the karmic wheel. Honoring the intention of the Primordial Seer (*Purusha*), his intrinsic Prakriti brings out from herself the world of endless diversity. The light of the Omniscient Being guides us to the right place and the right time to begin our life. We are born again. Nonbeing comes back into being. Death is transformed into birth. Once again we ride the current of time.

In his compassion, the Seeing Power of the Seer has assumed responsibility for much more than simply bringing us back to life. His guiding grace takes birth with each of us; thus, the sages call him *Sadyojata,* the one born instantly. For our sake, the ever-unborn is now born. In the wake of inner realization, the sages pray to him as *Bhavodbhava,* origin of the origin, father of the beginning. He is *Vamadeva,* the lord of everyone and everything ever created. He is the eldest (*Jyestha*) and the most respected (*Shrestha*). He is the breath of life (*Rudra*) and the very principle of time itself (*Kala*). He slices time into numberless divisions (*Kala-vikarana*). He is the principle of might (*Bala*). He slices his might into numberless parts (*Bala-vikarana*) and distributes them among us as strength and vitality. He churns our vitality (*Bala-pramathana*), so we can obtain the essence of his might. He rules over our little self (*Sarva-bhuta-damana*), yet is beyond our comprehension (*Manonmana*). He is peacefully active (*Aghora*), aggressively active (*Ghora*), and active to the point of fierceness and violence (*Ghora-ghoratara*). He is the essence of everything tangible, comprehensible, and defined by name, form, and number (*Sharva*). He is the master of the very principle of knowledge, the knowing power of the knower (*Ishana*). He is the lord of all living beings (*Ishvara*). He presides over all creation (*Brahma-adhipati*). He presides over the Creator herself (*Brahmano-adhipati*). The sages tell us to seek the guidance of this Creator of the Creator (*Brahma*). In this sutra, Patanjali tells us that this Special Being has been the master of all previous masters (*purvesham api guruh*), for he alone is unconfined by time.

Ishvara is our teacher. This fact is not dependent on our choosing. Due to her loving grace, we rose from the dead and came into being. This fact is not affected by our lack of belief in God or by our rejection of her. Her loving grace is unconditional. It came to us well before the birth of our mind and the power of speech.

As a dead person, we had no mind to think of her grace and no tongue to pray for it. As a living person, we can proclaim our rejection of Ishvara's grace, but the truth remains unaffected—we are alive only because her loving and guiding grace is keeping us alive. In compliance with her will, for example, oxygen is infused with the life-sustaining energy that fuels our cellular respiration. And it is in compliance with her will that oxygen no longer supports our life. We die. Nothing is more predictable than death, yet throughout our lives we go about our activities without much concern about dying because everywhere, within and without, we are surrounded and accompanied by the all-pervading divine being, Ishvara.

This Omnipresent Being is our guru and our guide. In him lies ultimate safety and security. By realizing the essence of this Omnipresent Being and embracing him consciously, we are freed from doubt and fear. This freedom gives us confidence in ourselves, respect for life, and gratitude toward the Divine Being who, for our sake, endures the pain of being born with us. This Divine Being is born again and again until we are completely free from our karmic bonds and the ignorance that sustains them. In one spontaneous intention (*sankalpa*) he has yoked himself to us. No force in the universe can obstruct his intention. The infallibility of his intention lies at the heart of our spiritual quest, and in its own mysterious way, this same infallibility guides us to our spiritual core. This guiding force is our guru.

The clearer our understanding of this guiding force, the more balanced we become in our understanding of external sources of guidance: physical gurus, guides, temples, churches, and holy texts. How we gain a clear understanding of this guiding force is the subject of the next sutra.

SUTRA 1:27

तस्य वाचकः प्रणवः ॥२७॥

tasya vācakaḥ praṇavaḥ ॥ 27 ॥

tasya, of that; *vācakaḥ*, denoter or indicator; *praṇavaḥ*, ever new, the sound *om*

***Pranava* [om] is the denoter of That [Ishvara].**

Everything—manifest or unmanifest, alive or dead—is an extension of Primordial Nature, Prakriti. Prakriti is always with Purusha, for both are eternal and all-pervading. As we saw in sutra 1:24, the union of Purusha and Prakriti, which results in manifestation, is an intentional union of the Special Purusha (*Ishvara*) and Prakriti. They are one in every respect and are expressive of a single reality. Purusha (Pure Consciousness) is not simply an observer nor is Prakriti (Primordial Nature) simply the material cause of the universe. Prakriti is in Ishvara. Ishvara is in Prakriti.

The question of whether the world evolves from Ishvara or from Prakriti remains only if we have forgotten the three preceding sutras. Purusha is the intelligence of Prakriti, and Prakriti is the creative power of Purusha. The problem lies with the limited capacity of our language to describe a reality beyond time, space, gender, and number. We are attempting to deconstruct and then reconstruct a reality that is inconceivable to the mind.

Our thoughts remain abstract until they become associated with a word. Words are associated with meaning. Meaning becomes concrete when its scope is narrowed to an object. An object is made concrete by differentiating it from other objects. This differentiation is made concrete by pointing out the dissimilar characteristics of various objects. Thus, in an attempt to describe the unitary reality, which issues forth a world of limitless diversities, our mind tries to deconstruct this reality, grind it into smaller parts, give each part a distinct meaning, and then attempt to explain the union of the two. By entering the realm of *asamprajnata samadhi*, a yogi rises above these mental constraints and sees the reality as it is, without deconstructing and reconstructing it.

Every entity is indicative of Ishvara, yet in this sutra, Patanjali states that *pranava,* a technical term for the sound *om,* is indicative of Ishvara. This raises three questions: Is *om* indicative of Ishvara while other sounds are not? Are the other four sensory objects—touch, sight, taste, and smell—and the world corresponding to them not indicative of Ishvara? Is *om* indicative of Ishvara but is not Ishvara? These questions come to the minds of those unfamiliar with the profound philosophy and metaphysics of the word and its meaning.

The philosophy and metaphysics of the word and its meaning constitute the central doctrine of Vyakarana Agama, Shaiva Agama, and the tradition of Sri Vidya. As the author of the *Mahabhashya*, the "Great Commentary" on the sutras of Panini, Patanjali is one of the foremost authorities on this subject. Vyasa, commenting on this sutra, states that the relationship between the word and the meaning conveyed by it is like that of light and the flame that emits the light. The word is the light; the meaning is the flame that emits the word. Just as the flame is the locus of the light, the meaning is the locus of the word. The word is contained in its meaning in the same way light is contained in the flame. The influence of avidya on our mind forces us to see the truth in reverse order, making us seek the meaning in the word and not the other way around.

At this stage in our evolution, this avidya-fed reality is quite real. The phenomenal world is substantial. The laws by which the phenomenal world operates are predictable. Every word indicates a meaning, every form expresses its function—these are predictable laws of our world. The world is an extension of Ishvara, and Ishvara is contained in the world. Our body is an extension of our soul, and our soul is contained in our body. Similarly, the word is an extension of the meaning, and the meaning is contained in the word. The world is indicative of Ishvara. The body is indicative of the soul. And the word is indicative of its inherent meaning. The relationship between the word and its meaning is forever fixed. With the evolution of language, words may evolve, undergo a change, and eventually become extinct, but the relationship between the words and the meaning they express never fades. Their relationship is set in the stone of eternity.

In *mantra shastra,* the science of mantra, phonemes are called *akshara,* indestructible, non-degradable expressions of eternity. Just as the essence of the flame is contained in each minute shade of light, eternity is contained in every nook and cranny of the phonemes. Words are made of phonemes. Thus words, like the phonemes of which they are made, are containers of eternity. Eons may pass. The cyclical creation and annihilation of the universe may repeat its course, but the relationship between the word and its meaning remains intact. When we reemerge from our timeless slumber of death, the meaning of words stored in the mind in the form of subtle karmic impressions spontaneously flashes upon hearing the sounds once associated with them. Every human being is innately endowed with this power of intuiting the relationship between the meaning and the word corresponding to it. That is how we learn a language as a child and how, in a conducive environment, we can learn several languages at once.

There is a unique relationship between Ishvara and the sound *om*. *Om* is an outward expression of an experience pertaining to the Omniscient Being. The experience of the Omniscient Being is contained in this expression. Each time *om* takes audible form, it expresses what it contains—the experience of God. Experiencing God means knowing and embracing the omniscience, omnipotence, and omnipresence of God—and the totality of this experience is contained in the word *om*.

Now let us revisit our questions: Is *om* indicative of Ishvara while other sounds are not? Are the other four sensory objects—touch, sight, taste, and smell—and the world corresponding to them not indicative of God? Is *om* indicative of God but is not God? These questions arise primarily from a long-cherished tradition of confusion.

There is confusion regarding the meaning of *pranava*. The idea that *pranava* stands for the sound *om* is only partially correct. Any mantra imbued with illuminative power is *pranava*. The literal meaning of *pranava* is "that which is precisely, astoundingly, or uniquely new." *Pranava* refers to the power that breathes a notable newness into us. According to mantra shastra, the infallible transformative power of God is *pranava*. Phonemes and those words, which by their intrinsic nature emit their transformative power, are *pranava*. In short, mantras of the highest caliber leading to enlightenment are *pranava*.

The idea that *pranava* is *om* and *om* is *pranava* is inaccurate. The sound *om* breathes the life of newness into us. Therefore, it is *pranava*, indicative of God. There are other mantras that also have power to breathe the life of newness into us. They too are *pranava*. In everyday language, many words have a similar general meaning. For example, "see," "look," "glance," "observe," "sight," "spot," "locate," and "glean" all share some elements of meaning. But each is also expressive of the unique meaning it contains. The same is true of mantras. God is infinite. Words belonging to everyday language are expressive of our finite experiences. Mantras, on the other hand, are embodiments of revelation.

Revealed knowledge and experience flow from the infinite and descend into the minds of sages absorbed in *asamprajnata samadhi*. Here, in higher samadhi, the mind has stretched all the way to infinity. Knower, known, and the power of knowing have become one. The experience that dawns in this state of samadhi is unique in the sense that its transformative power is extraordinary. It overshadows the influences of the past. It is its own kind of reality—ever-fresh and ever-new. Most important, this reality has no cause. It has emerged from a state beyond time, space, and the law of cause and effect; thus, it is beginningless. Because it has no beginning, it has no end. Its power is infallible. It continues breathing newness into the phenomenal world of which we are a part. Therefore, the sages refer to this self-revealed reality as *pranava*, "uniquely new." When it assumes a body made of pure sound, this reality is experienced as mantra. By meditating on a mantra, we eventually become absorbed in its inherent power. This elevates us to the same level of realization that the seers of the mantra had when the mantra was revealed to them. How we meditate on the mantric form of the Absolute Being is the subject of the next sutra.

SUTRA 1:28

तज्जपस्तदर्थभावनम् ॥२८॥

tajjapastadarthabhāvanam ॥ 28 ॥

tat, that; *japaḥ*, repetition; *tat*, that; *artha*, meaning; *bhāvanam*, reflection or contemplation

Repetition of That [Pranava] means to reflect on its meaning.

God is as real as we are and yet as abstract as our own soul. For many of us, surrendering to God makes sense only as a concept. A concept takes concrete form only when it falls within the range of our conscious awareness, thereby becoming comprehensible. Something is comprehensible when it is perceivable by one or more of our senses. The concept of God becomes concrete when it takes mantric form. It then becomes comprehensible because it can be perceived by our sense of hearing. However, comprehending the content of mantra—God—is somewhat tricky.

A child hears a word and comprehends its meaning because the word is spoken in context. The child is aware of the context and so can make an association between the word and the meaning it expresses. People around the child encourage and confirm his understanding by responding positively. But we hear a mantra and do not comprehend its meaning because we are not fully aware of the context in which the mantra was revealed to the Seer or of the process of transmission. We are aware only of the literal meaning of the word, and that only if the word is in a familiar language. We have a tendency to assign a word the simplest meaning possible. This tendency forces us to select the smallest element of the content denoted by the word, which robs the word of the richness it once contained. This is what has happened with the word "God," and with the different mantras expressive of the vast content denoting the omniscience, omnipotence, and omnipresence of God (*Ishvara*).

Remembering a mantra means remembering its meaning. The word for remembering a mantra is *japa*. More accurately, japa refers to the repetition of a mantra; each time we repeat a mantra, the mantric *samskaras* become deeper. There is no significant difference between japa (repetition of a mantra) and meditation on a mantra. Repeating the mantra while keeping track of the number of repetitions is japa; it is usually done with *mala* beads. Meditation is continuous remembrance of the mantra without keeping track of the number of repetitions. With or without a mala, remembering a mantra leads to one-pointedness of mind, which eventually evolves into freedom from the mind's roaming tendencies. The secret is to remember the mantra with constant awareness of its meaning.

The meaning of mantras, especially high-caliber mantras such as the Sri Vidya mantra, is as expansive as Ishvara itself. The meaning of these mantras unveils itself in segments as we methodically engage in self-study (*svadhyaya*) and in the study of scriptures containing the experiential knowledge of the sages. This form of study makes our knowledge of Ishvara shine. Our convictions come to life as they blend with the experiences of the sages, and our inquiry into the nature and reality of Ishvara becomes increasingly refined.

With each repetition, the mantra emits its unique meaning and we feel it deep within without deconstructing and reconstructing it. Our japa is accompanied by the awareness that for eternity Ishvara alone exists. A paraphrased passage from the "Hiranyagarbha Sukta" of the *Rig-Veda* describes this uninterrupted awareness:

> He alone brings us into existence. He is the Lord of all those caught in the cycle of birth and death. He is the One who holds heaven and earth together. To who else should I surrender? He is the giver of life and the giver of strength. All the forces of the universe abide by his laws. Life and death are his shadow. To who else should I surrender? As He opens his eyes, we awaken to life. As He closes his eyes, we drown in death. He is the Lord and Master of those with two feet and those with four feet. To who else should I surrender? It is through his power mountains rise into the sky and the earth and ocean coexist. His mighty arms manifest and spread as directions. To who else should I surrender?

The clarity and intensity of this realization, which came to the sages, brightens as we remember our mantra. The meaning turns into feeling, and the feeling becomes an integral part of our consciousness. What effect this feeling has on us, and ultimately, where it leads us in our spiritual quest is the subject of the next sutra.

SUTRA 1:29

ततः प्रत्यक्चेतनाधिगमोऽप्यन्तरायाभावश्च ॥२९॥

tataḥ pratyakcetanādhigamo'pyantarāyābhāvaśca ॥29॥

tataḥ, from that; *pratyak,* inner; *cetanā,* consciousness, awareness; *adhigamaḥ,* attainment; *api,* also; *antarāya,* impediment; *abhāvaḥ,* removal or absence; *ca,* and

From that comes the experience of Inner Being as well as the elimination of impediments.

J*apa* of high-caliber mantras fills our mind and heart with the essence the mantra embodies—Ishvara, the omniscient eternal being. Japa reinforces our feeling of the presence of Ishvara. This feeling eradicates all doubt about our safety and erases our fear of annihilation. We are not alone and we know it. Each repetition of the mantra reminds us that the Omniscient Being is always with us. Fear of losing our possessions, especially the dearest one—life itself—no longer grips our mind. Worry and grief vanish forever, a subject Patanjali elaborates on in sutras 1:36 and 3:34.

A mind free of doubt, fear, worry, and grief finds no reason to be distracted by worldly matters. The inner pull becomes irresistible. The forces of the mind, which once flowed outward attending one object after another, change their course and begin flowing inward. The joy of experiencing the presence of the Inner

Divinity is so intense that we become completely absorbed in it. The Seer, the Seen, and the process of seeing merge. At this stage, we need no reminder that we are Consciousness itself. Our sense of I-am-ness (*asmita*), which had been incessantly defending its own self-existence, loosens and begins to flow inward toward the very core of our being, Ishvara.

We maintain this effortless one-pointed flow of mind with japa. As the intensity of japa increases, we become less and less aware of ourselves doing japa. The meaning of the mantra and the essence it embodies occupies the forefront of our mind. Eventually, the mind dissolves into its essence, Pure Consciousness (*Purusha*).

As this sutra tells us, japa brings an end to all our impediments. Obstacles to our growth are rooted in ignorance (*avidya*). We are so strongly predisposed to our ideas of right and wrong, good and bad that we refuse to examine their validity. We insist that what we think is right is right. Our actions—physical, verbal, and mental—are propelled by this predisposition. When our actions bear unpleasant fruit, we blame the law of karma, destiny, and God. We never question the incorrect, unhealthy, and essentially distorted nature of our own predispositions. This is ignorance.

Actions rooted in ignorance carry the samskaras of ignorance. The effect of these impressions is so powerful that we refuse to see we have a problem and, further, that we are the cause of the problem. Denial becomes an integral part of us. We treat anyone or anything challenging our identity as an enemy. We become defensive. That is how a distorted, fearful, reactive personality evolves from ignorance. We spend all our mental and spiritual resources protecting it. Year after year, life after life, we continue serving ignorance and the distorted self-identity (*asmita*) springing from it. But even though obstacles to our spiritual growth are as strong and perennial as our ignorance and distorted self-identity, they can be eliminated with japa.

Japa of high-caliber mantras illumines our mind. Even though our mind, and the consciousness flowing through it, is heavily influenced by ignorance and distorted self-identity, proximity to Ishvara, engendered by japa, enables our mind to see reality as it is. Bathed in the light of Inner Divinity, the mind begins to see its own predispositions. In this same light, it finds the courage to face them and discover their deep-rooted cause. The experience induced by japa empowers us to examine the foundation of our self-identity and the actions we have been performing in an attempt to defend and nurture it. In other words, japa enables the diseased person within us to diagnose the causes of the disease and accept the cure flowing from deep within. Once this process begins, the numberless obstacles arising from the long chain of suffering diminish one by one. What these obstacles are and how they block our growth is the subject of the next sutra.

SUTRA 1:30

व्याधिस्त्यानसंशयप्रमादालस्याविरति-
भ्रान्तिदर्शनालब्धभूमिकत्वानवस्थितत्वानि
चित्तविक्षेपास्तेऽन्तरायाः ॥३०॥

vyādhistyānasaṁśayapramādālasyāviratibhrānti-
darśanālabdhabhūmikatvānavasthitatvāni
cittavikṣepāste'ntarāyāḥ ॥30॥

vyādhi, disease; *styāna,* mental inertia; *saṁśaya,* doubt; *pramāda,* carelessness; *ālasya,* sloth; *avirati,* inability to withdraw from sense cravings; *bhrānti-darśana,* confused understanding; *alabdha-bhūmikatva,* inability to reach the goal; *anavasthitatvāni,* inability to retain; *citta-vikṣepāḥ,* mental distractions; *te,* they; *antarāyāḥ,* obstacles

Disease, mental inertia, doubt, carelessness, sloth, inability to withdraw from sense cravings, clinging to misunderstanding, inability to reach the goal [samadhi], and inability to retain it throw our mind outward; they are obstacles.

Life is a long chain of pleasure and pain, success and failure, gain and loss. Transcending these pairs of opposites and reaching a state of inner equanimity is the essence of the spiritual quest. Along the way, a variety of obstacles emerge.

These obstacles are unimaginably numerous. For example, many of us neither know nor care to know that our life has a spiritual dimension. That is an obstacle. Some of us want to know our spiritual aspect but lack the will. That is an obstacle. Some of us search for our spiritual core but fail to set our priorities properly. That is an obstacle. We undertake practices leading to enlightenment but fail to drop habits that hamper our progress. That is an obstacle. We learn techniques for moving inward but begin doubting their validity as soon as we apply them. That is an obstacle. We find numberless reasons for not beginning the practice, or for starting and then stopping it, or for taking a detour and never returning to the path. These are all obstacles.

Patanjali divides all obstacles into nine broad categories: disease, mental inertia, doubt, carelessness, sloth, inability to withdraw from sense cravings, clinging to misunderstanding, inability to reach the goal of samadhi, and inability to retain samadhi. Although obstacles in these nine categories impede our growth in every sphere of life, Patanjali is focusing on them in the context of Yoga sadhana.

Disease is the foremost obstacle. In the final analysis, disease is caused by seemingly beginningless ignorance. We are ignorant about the innate wisdom of our body, so instead of discovering the cause and cure of a disease within the body, we search for it in the external world. We fail to realize there are more than ten times as many microbes—bacteria, archaea, and fungi—in a healthy human body as there are human cells. We insist alien agents—germs, bacteria, and viruses—are the cause of our sickness and seek to cure ourselves by eliminating them. But the truth is, outside forces can affect us adversely only when the host within us gives them an opportunity.

Disturbance in the natural balance of our inner ecology creates a hospitable environment for illness. According to Ayurveda,

Yoga's sister science, there are three bodily humors: *vata, pitta,* and *kapha,* the principles of catabolic, metabolic, and anabolic activities, respectively. Once their natural balance is disturbed, our entire system is thrown out of balance. One organ no longer cares for the well-being of other organs. Communication between the heart, the brain, the nervous system, and the endocrine system is impaired. The evolution of disease is an intricate, systematic process, but because we are cut off from our body's innate wisdom, we are barely aware of it. This lack of knowledge about ourselves forces us to rely instead on the tools and means available in the external world.

According to Yoga, the cure for disease lies in awakening the innate wisdom of the body and letting it heal us from inside. This deep healing occurs when we derive sustenance from deep within. Cultivating the ability to restore the harmonious balance of our bodily humors and thus maintain an internal atmosphere conducive to good health is an important aspect of Yoga sadhana.

The second obstacle is mental inertia. Some of us are more alert by nature than others, but all of us have the innate ability to overcome our mental sluggishness. Failure to acknowledge this innate ability and to then throw off the dense, dark blanket covering our mind is one of the biggest obstacles in our spiritual quest. Under the sway of inertia, we accept things the way they are and call this acceptance "destiny." We are stuck and our quest ends.

As disease and inertia tighten their grip, we begin to doubt ourselves and the very nature and process of the spiritual quest. Disease and mental sluggishness shake our conviction in our ability to help ourselves and to ensure a bright future. Doubt, which begins with lack of conviction and self-confidence, is a swiftly growing destructive force. It destroys the foundation of our inner peace. We become suspicious of everyone and everything, which generates an endless chain of negativity. This third obstacle is the stage where our inner turmoil becomes clearly visible. We are constantly on the lookout for anything that might harm us. Doubt fuels our mind's roaming tendencies—once in its snare, we find it difficult to focus our mind and turn it inward.

Exhausted by the onslaught of disease, mental inertia, and doubt, we succumb to carelessness, the fourth obstacle. To avoid facing reality, we indulge in activities that distract us from the pain arising from illness, inertia, and doubt. In other words, we bury our spirit in carelessness, tell ourselves we are carefree, and fail to notice that we are going nowhere.

Sloth is the child of carelessness. This fifth obstacle is fully developed and comes with its own justification. We make ourselves comfortable with our laziness by telling ourselves we aren't feeling well. We allow inertia to feed our laziness. Mental stupor gives sloth a pleasant flavor—a lazy person finds sloth enjoyable. Knowing how deep and strong the roots of sloth are, the sages call it a "grave sin." Sloth is incompatible with self-effort, the force that carries us along the spiritual path.

Now the sixth obstacle arises, the inability to withdraw our mind from sense cravings. Once we are firmly in the grip of carelessness and sloth, we employ our mind and senses indiscriminately. We fail to notice that our slow, foggy mind has fallen under the sway of the senses. We indulge without knowing why. The idea of refraining from indulgence makes no sense—we have neither the motive nor the ability to withdraw from the aimless, self-destructive activities of our senses. This unrestrained, uncontrolled, and virtually unconscious involvement of our senses with endless objects drains our vitality. We clearly see the damaging effects yet are unable to withdraw our mind from sense cravings.

Clinging to misunderstanding is the seventh obstacle and is a direct outgrowth of the indiscriminate, inexorable, self-destructive cravings of our senses. The actions we perform under the spell of sense cravings create powerful mental grooves. Because they were created by actions performed in an uncontrolled, unrestrained, unconscious manner, these samskaras emit a disorienting, aimless energy.

Under the influence of this disorienting energy arising from deep within, we become fully convinced that the sensory world and the experiences pertaining to it are the only reality. Not only do we no longer question the validity of the sensory world, we dismiss outright the possibility of a reality beyond it. At this stage, our senses are fully in charge of defining the truth: the world of the senses and sensory experiences is real and everything else is unreal. It no longer occurs to us that the senses are tools for knowing the truth, and further, that they are designed to know only that portion of the truth that pertains to the objective world. Complete dependence on the senses, which are the victims of their own cravings, poses a tremendous obstacle in our spiritual quest. To move forward, we must overcome this dependency and reverse the habit of replacing truth with our own mental fabrications.

The eighth obstacle is frustration caused by inability to reach our goal. Setting a worldly goal is much easier than setting a spiritual goal. Worldly affairs belong to the mental and sensory domain, so we have yardsticks for measuring our progress. But because spiritual matters lie only partially within the mental and sensory domain, we often set goals in the spiritual arena without understanding them clearly.

For most of us, descriptions of the spiritual quest are akin to fairy tales. We read books, hear about the experiences of mystics, observe others walking on the spiritual path, and get excited. Some of us decide God is our goal without having an understanding of God. Some of us seek love without a clear idea of what we mean by love. Others decide tasting divine ambrosia flowing from a thousand-petaled lotus blossoming in our brain center is our spiritual goal, even though we do not understand what this divine ambrosia is. Similarly, we crave enlightenment without having the slightest idea what it actually means. Such notions are not authentic spiritual goals and they become the ground for perpetual disappointment.

According to Patanjali, samadhi is the true spiritual goal. In the state of samadhi, our mind is as pure and luminous as unalloyed Consciousness itself. Once in samadhi, we see ourselves clearly—our mind, our habits, and the cause of the roaming tendencies of the mind. In the light of samadhi, we come to realize that the mind is the center of all mysteries. When the mind flows peacefully inward, we are connected to the inner reality. That is the goal we are striving for. Therefore, nothing is more important than training our mind to become still and turning it inward. How long it takes us to reach samadhi is not as important as attending our meditation practice. This realization enables us to overcome our frustration and instills us with courage and enthusiasm to do our practice.

The last obstacle, failure to retain samadhi, is even subtler. Through the practice of abhyasa, we cultivate a clear, calm, and tranquil mind, train it to flow inward, and reach samadhi. But due to deeply rooted habits, the mind runs back to its long-cherished sense objects. As soon as we realize the mind has slid from samadhi, we summon it back. Using the power of abhyasa and vairagya, we yoke it to samadhi. A little later, it slides back again. The desire to stay in samadhi, coupled with the inability to stay there for long, becomes the ground for frustration. This is the ninth obstacle.

The technical term for these nine obstacles is *chitta vikshepa*, which means "distractors of the mind." No matter how wise we are or how committed to our practice, if we are ill, drowning in inertia, or struggling with doubt, carelessness, and sloth, we have no way of preventing our mind from being victimized by its roaming tendencies. In the same way, sense cravings, a distorted understanding of reality, the inability to reach samadhi, and the inability to stay in samadhi make our mind spin. These potent obstacles have a strong negative effect on our body, breath, and mind. Vyasa calls them *yoga mala,* toxins in Yoga sadhana. If they are not removed, they lead to five conditions that are detrimental to yogic achievement. These five conditions, all of which arise from the nine obstacles, are the subject of the next sutra.

SUTRA 1:31

दुःखदौर्मनस्याङ्गमेजयत्वश्वासप्रश्वासा
विक्षेपसहभुवः॥३१॥

duḥkhadaurmanasyāṅgamejayatvaśvāsapraśvāsā
vikṣepasahabhuvaḥ ॥31॥

duḥkha, pain; *daurmanasya,* mental agitation; *aṅgam-ejayatva,* unsteadiness, trembling of limbs; *śvāsa,* inhalation; *praśvāsa,* exhalation; *vikṣepa-saha-bhuvaḥ,* conditions that accompany impediments

Pain, mental agitation, unsteadiness or trembling of limbs, [abnormal or disturbed] inhalation and exhalation all arise with the obstacles.

The nine obstacles described in the previous sutra rob the body of vitality, strength, stamina, and agility, and the mind of clarity and peace. The absence of these obstacles is the ground for joy. Their presence is the ground for pain, which leads to four other debilitating conditions: mental agitation, unsteadiness in the limbs, disturbed inhalation, and disturbed exhalation.

Vyasa describes the anatomy of pain in his commentary on this sutra. According to him, the nine obstacles bruise our body and mind. Our natural response is to attempt to stop these obstacles from hurting us, so a war begins between the obstacles and the defensive forces of our body and mind. The resulting strain is experienced as pain. In the attempt to defend themselves, our body and mind waste resources that could otherwise be invested to accomplish a higher purpose. We become short-tempered and agitated—quick to react and quick to take the offensive. Our positive attitude toward life vanishes and we latch on to negative thoughts.

Pain gives rise to mental agitation, which has a deeper source than we normally realize. Agitation arises from unfilled desires. We have the inherent desire to be happy. Driven by this desire, we do everything in our power to drive away pain. When obstacles such as illness, inertia, and doubt thwart our desire for happiness, we are swept into a whirlpool of anger, dejection, fear, and grief. Caught in this whirlpool, the mind attempts to ride the two opposing currents of despondency and hope. Eventually, it becomes exhausted and collapses into its long chain of negativities, led by anger and fear. Anger and fear lead to unsteadiness.

Unsteadiness is a sure sign we no longer have confidence in our ability to help ourselves. Lack of self-confidence spreads in concentric circles. Trust in our friends and relatives, and in our teachers, doctors, colleagues, and counselors declines. Our faith in ourselves and in everyone and everything else becomes shaky. This unsteadiness is extremely subtle. It nests in the very core of our being and blankets our understanding of the innate wisdom and healing power of our body and mind. It gradually matures into full-fledged doubt about our mental and physical capacities. Uncertainty clouds our consciousness. Our heart, brain, nervous system, circulatory system, and immune system are unnerved and no longer communicate clearly with each other.

At this stage, unsteadiness emerges at the physical level as vatic forces begin to dominate the kaphic and pittic forces. The stability of our limbs and organs is compromised. The efficiency of our bodily functions and communication among the various organs are obstructed. A person specializing in pulse diagnosis can see the trembling of the organs reflected in the nervous system. Aspirants with a significant degree of mental discipline can observe the subtle shakiness of their limbs and organs during relaxation practices. During deep relaxation, an experienced yogi can not only feel the fluttering of his heart and the uneven, jarring movement of blood in his veins and arteries, but also can detect the trembling of his stressed cells and tissues. The longer this unsteadiness continues, the more vital energy (*prana shakti*) is wasted. This waste of vitality is reflected in disturbances in our inhalation and exhalation.

As discussed in sutra 1:13, prana is a direct manifestation of Divine Will. It awakens us from our beginningless slumber of death and brings us back to life. We are alive because we breathe. The more harmonious the breath, the more peaceful and organized the mind. Unsteadiness in the limbs and organs caused by a vast range of mental negativity—particularly anger and fear—has a direct effect on the breath: Our inhalation and exhalation become erratic and noisy. We hold our breath. The pause between the inhalation and the exhalation lengthens, and the movement of the diaphragm becomes restricted. According to the yogis, fear and anger are the major causes of chest breathing. Chest breathing limits the intake of oxygen and the output of used-up gases. Our lung capacity declines, the level of vital nutrients in our blood drops, and the level of toxins in the body rises. Our physical vitality and strength decline, as does our mental clarity and ability to think linearly.

The negative effects of unhealthy breathing go far beyond the injurious effects noticeable to a layman. Disturbed inhalation and exhalation disrupts fluid pressure in the body, throwing the lymphatic and circulatory systems out of balance. Dysfunctional breathing not only dulls and disorients our brain, but also clouds the intelligence of the mitochondria, our cellular power plants. In other words, disturbed breathing puts a veil over the innate wisdom of our body and weakens our mental capacity.

Pain, mental agitation, shakiness of limbs and organs, and disturbances in our inhalation and exhalation solidify the connections among all nine impediments, magnifying their grip on body and mind. None of us are completely free from these obstacles—even the most advanced aspirants face at least one at some point. And each obstacle is, to some degree, accompanied by all these secondary conditions. Removing these obstacles and their accompanying conditions is as important as the methodical practice of abhyasa and vairagya. In sutra 1:29, Patanjali clearly states that obstacles are removed by the grace of Ishvara, which we attract through *japa*. To stress the importance of this point, in the next sutra Patanjali describes in greater detail how to embrace God's grace and attain freedom from obstacles blocking our quest.

SUTRA 1:32

तत्प्रतिषेधार्थमेकतत्त्वाभ्यासः ॥३२॥

tatpratiṣedhārthamekatattvābhyāsaḥ ॥32॥

tat, their; *pratiṣedhārtham*, the way to overcome; *eka-tattva*, one single reality; *abhyāsaḥ*, practice

Meditation on one single reality is the way to overcome these obstacles.

God's grace is unconditional. It has no beginning and no end. Grace is an integral part of the Seeing Power of the Seer and is as perfect as Ishvara herself. Grace is the intrinsic power of Ishvara. Time, space, and the law of causation have no power to stop its flow—its healing, transforming, and illuminating effect on us is unfailing. Grace precedes our birth, accompanies us when we are born, and has been with us every moment since. Accompanied as we are by omnipresent divine grace, it makes no sense that we suffer from illness, inertia, doubt, the other six obstacles and their five companions. And yet we are all suffering. Why?

We are victims of our karmic possessions. We are attached to our habits and find pleasure in clinging to them. Our idea of fulfillment is molded by our likes and dislikes. These, in turn, are shaped by our internal makeup—the subtle impressions of our thoughts, speech, and actions stored deep in our mind. In other words, we are defined by our samskaras and vasanas.

Samskaras and vasanas, the building blocks of our personality, color our mind. They shape our perception of ourselves and the purpose of life. They mold our ideas of bondage and freedom. Our samskaras dictate what we like or dislike, what we embrace or discard. Our beliefs have no independent status—they are simply products of our samskaras. And our samskaras stand between us and divine grace.

Because divine grace sheds the light of true understanding regarding our samskaras and their effect on us, we work hard to block its flow. Losing our most valued possessions—our samskaras—is so frightening that we prefer to reject divine grace. This rejection is too subtle for most of us to notice, but the tendency to seek fulfillment in achieving objects compatible with our samskaras is obvious. This tendency causes us to embrace familiar objects, regardless of how painful they are, rather than make an effort to renounce them.

Knowing that we love our samskaras more than we value God's grace, Patanjali again presents the infallible recipe for eliminating the conditions that block our quest for samadhi: abhyasa and vairagya (YS 1:12–1:16). As we have seen, abhyasa is an ardent effort to retain the peaceful flow of mind, free of roaming tendencies; vairagya is cultivating a clear mind, free of the coloring of vasanas. In sutras 1:12 through 1:14, Patanjali explains the general nature of the practice of abhyasa, making it clear that the first prerequisite is cultivating a clear, tranquil mind. In other words, abhyasa entails cultivating a state where the mind is peaceful and flowing toward the center of Consciousness. We become proficient in our practice when we do it with energy, enthusiasm, self-discipline, sense control, right understanding, and faith. Abhyasa becomes firm when done without interruption for an extended time, and with reverence.

But in these earlier sutras Patanjali does not describe the precise object of mental focus. Here, in sutra 1:32, which he has introduced in the context of removing obstacles to our attainment of samadhi, Patanjali prescribes a single reality—Ishvara—as the focal point. According to Vyasa, in this sutra, Patanjali is making a clear statement: the practice of abhyasa entails making an ardent effort to retain the mind's peaceful flow toward a single truth, Ishvara. Ishvara-oriented abhyasa is the ultimate remedy for removing all obstacles now and forever. He tells us that in order to nullify the nine obstacles and the five conditions they produce, we must direct our peacefully flowing mind toward Ishvara. That is what is meant here by abhyasa.

The purpose of this Ishvara-focused practice is to attenuate the obstacles, not to reach samadhi immediately. It is understood that we have surrounded ourselves with obstacles and are undertaking our practice with a distracted and stupefied mind. It is also understood that all our actions, including our practice, are powerfully affected by samskaras. Furthermore, our faith in the Inner Divinity is superficial and experimental, because the quality of our meditation on God is predictably poor. And yet we start our meditation with the hope of reaping a desirable fruit: the elimination of the nine obstacles and their five companions.

The success of Ishvara-focused meditation depends on our understanding. The more clearly we understand the nature of God and his unconditional intention to help and guide the souls who have fallen into the whirlpool of samsara, the easier and more straightforward our meditation becomes. God-focused meditation requires making contemplation on Ishvara, as described in sutras 1:23 through 1:29, part of our daily sadhana. Sutra 1:27 tells us, "*Pranava* [*om*] is the denoter of Ishvara." We must constantly remind ourselves that *om* is representative of the entire *mantra shakti,* and mantra shakti and Ishvara are one and the same. In other words, mantra embodies the essence of Ishvara.

Here, in sutra 1:32, Patanjali introduces mantra as an object for meditation. Mantra sadhana, according to Patanjali, is the shortcut that attenuates obstacles and eventually eliminates them altogether. It is one of the most dependable ways of freeing the mind from its roaming tendencies and strengthening our conviction in the Inner Divinity, which is our soul's eternal companion.

The first and most important prerequisite in mantra sadhana is to meditate on a revealed mantra. A bogus mantra leads nowhere. A revealed mantra is neither a set of randomly selected sounds and phonemes nor a poetic composition. A revealed mantra is a living entity, just as we are. The only difference is that our body is composed of physical elements, whereas the body of a mantra is composed of the most subtle of the subtle elements, the purest form of sound. We are conceived by biological parents, while a mantra is conceived—revealed—to a sage in the deepest state of samadhi. We confine our soul; mantra is "soul" itself. Our body, senses, and mind obstruct the light of the soul; the mantric manifestation of the Inner Divinity spontaneously and incessantly emits inner light.

The second prerequisite in mantra sadhana is to meditate on an awakened mantra. With the passage of time, even a revealed mantra may become dormant. Sages in the tradition tend a mantra like parents tend their babies. Through their meditation, they keep the mantra vibrant and potent. When a mantra is transmitted by a living tradition, it exerts its power on the mind and heart of the meditator. There are many, many mantras, but a qualified teacher specializing in *mantra shastra* knows which mantra is most appropriate for which aspirant. Spiritual traditions differ on the ground of their specialization in a particular mantra or set of mantras, and no single tradition can claim to be the custodian of them all.

The third prerequisite in mantra sadhana is to practice in the proper sequence (*krama*). It is a mistake to assume that the first mantra we get from a guru is a "guru mantra" or "personal mantra," and further, that this mantra is sufficient to destroy all our obstacles, burn our samskaras, lift us into samadhi, and connect us to Ishvara evermore. Neither a single guru nor a single mantra holds the solution to all our problems. If it does, we have found the primordial master, Ishvara, and have been initiated into the most sublime mantra, which embodies the complete essence of his being. In a normal course of mantra sadhana, however, a skilled, informed teacher leads a student step-by-step through a series of mantric practices. The exact sequence of mantras and their corresponding disciplines is the core of mantra science. As Patanjali tells us in sutra 3:15, a change in sequence leads to a drastic change in result.

The fourth prerequisite is to start the practice with whatever faith and self-discipline we can muster, and then do the practice regularly. To see a noticeable effect, we must engage in a relatively intense practice for a short time (*purashcharana*). This allows us to have a firsthand experience of the intended result. Nothing is more convincing than our own direct experience. Even a small experience gives us faith in our practice and in the Divinity whose grace we are seeking. Commenting on this sutra, Vyasa says that the value of a practice verified by direct experience can never be challenged. Meditation on a single reality—Ishvara—through mantra sadhana is the means of gaining this direct experience. As Krishna proclaims in the *Bhagavad Gita*, "Even a small experience protects us from the biggest fear."

The biggest fear is losing ourselves—death. Mantra meditation shows us beyond the shadow of a doubt that when the mind is absorbed in the mantra, we are more alive and peacefully vibrant than at all other times. This removes our doubt regarding whether or not there is a dimension of reality much deeper and more profound than our material existence. It fills us with confidence that we are not alone. When we are not tossed by the charms and temptations of the world, and the mind is not churned by its roaming tendencies, we are close to our eternal friend—Ishvara—who makes himself available to us at the sensory level in mantric form. This experience leads us to a previously unknown dimension of life. It becomes our personal experience—private wealth that cannot be taken away.

As we continue our practice of mantra meditation, this experience is repeated. It becomes more concentrated each time, strengthening our confidence in Ishvara's guiding and nurturing grace. Fear arising from the mundane level of reality loses its grip. We know who we are and what our relationship is both with the world and with our core being. We do not need an external source to confirm whether or not the soul exists; whether the mind is a continuous flow of separate cognitions or truly an indivisible entity; and whether our current life is a continuation of our past, or we just happened to pop out of nothingness.

It is deeply reassuring to realize that we have a vibrant mind that can be trained to serve the higher purpose of our soul. The mind is our best friend. It is the direct extension of Prakriti, who, in compliance with the benevolent will of Ishvara, bestowed it on us. Once the mantra and the mind join hands, accomplishing life's purpose is no longer a distant goal.

The biggest questions now become: How to protect our mind and the mantra? How to nurture their relationship? How to shield the mind from the hidden foes deep within that gnaw at the foundation of our spiritual aspirations? In response to these pressing questions, Patanjali introduces the next sutra.

SUTRA 1:33

मैत्रीकरुणामुदितोपेक्षाणां सुखदुःखपुण्यापुण्य-
विषयाणां भावनातश्चित्तप्रसादनम् ।।३३।।

maitrīkaruṇāmuditopekṣāṇāṃ sukhaduḥkhapuṇya-
puṇyaviṣayāṇāṁ bhāvanātaścittaprasādanam ॥33॥

maitrī, the essence of friendship; *karuṇā,* compassion; *muditā,* a joyful condition of mind; *upekṣāṇaṁ,* seeing without judging; *sukha,* happiness; *duḥkha,* pain, sorrow; *puṇya,* virtue; *apuṇya,* lack of virtue; *viṣayāṇāṁ,* in relation to; *bhāvanātaḥ,* by contemplating; *citta-prasādanam,* transparency of mind

Transparency of mind comes by embracing an attitude of friendliness, compassion, happiness, and non-judgment toward those who are happy, miserable, virtuous, and non-virtuous.

Animosity, cruelty, jealousy, and self-righteousness are the greatest mental contaminants. The antidotes are friendliness, compassion, happiness, and non-judgment. The importance of making these antidotes part of our daily practice, and thus keeping our mind clear and transparent, is the subject of this sutra.

Animosity originates from attachment. Attachment to our inner belongings—our habits, samskaras, and vasanas—is far stronger than attachment to any material object or achievement. The most precious of all our inner belongings is the desire to be bigger, richer, more powerful, more respected, and more influential than other people. We want the world to comply with our whims—we want to see it revolving around us. The more we see this desire being fulfilled, the happier we are. We measure our success in the light of this desire, and we cannot easily tolerate the prospect of someone being more successful than we are.

In yogic literature, this desire is called *kama.* Anger arises when a desire is not fulfilled. Anger disorients our mind. Our thinking becomes lopsided. We no longer see ourselves in the context of the larger world; rather, we see the world in the context of our own little self and its desire for dominance. We become confused. Confusion leads to loss of memory. Our linear thinking becomes impaired and our comprehension of cause and effect is dulled. Our power of discrimination is compromised. Lack of discrimination—even partially damaged discrimination—leads to despair. Yet our desire for success remains as fresh as ever. In desperation, we look outside ourselves for the cause of our failure. When people who are more successful come into view, our impaired power of discrimination and confused mind see them as the cause of our failure. This is painful, and the pain is intensified by our inability to do anything about it. As described in sutra 1:31, pain causes mental agitation (*daurmanasya*), which manifests in the form of animosity.

A mind contaminated by animosity perceives successful people as enemies. Now actively seeking fulfillment of our desire is no longer a priority—eliminating our enemy becomes the priority. We are on the offensive in our thoughts, speech, and actions. The peaceful condition of our mind is destroyed, replaced by inner turmoil. If we do not find a timely cure for this condition, our anger intensifies. Animosity throws our mind into such turmoil that it cannot think properly. An agitated mind is more interested in capturing the enemy than in meditating on a mantra—it has no inclination to reflect on Ishvara and her mantric manifestation. The mind's *sattvic* nature—its transparency, clarity, and illumination—is being consumed by anger and animosity. It becomes progressively darker, duller, and less competent to meditate and reflect on truth.

To help us free our mind to reclaim its transparent and illuminating power, Patanjali offers an antidote to the principle of animosity: cultivate an internal environment of friendship. This does not mean that we should run after successful people and ingratiate ourselves, but that we cultivate a positive attitude toward them—an attitude grounded in right understanding.

There are three levels of cultivating an internal atmosphere of friendship: nurturing a friendly attitude toward those who are successful and happy; transforming the element of animosity into friendship; and practicing the yogic technique of combining concentration, meditation, and samadhi (*samyama*) on the principle of friendship. In this sutra, Patanjali is introducing the practice of friendship at the first level. The two other levels are described in sutras 2:33 and 3:23.

Nurturing a friendly attitude toward those who are successful and happy cleanses the mind of the fundamental toxin of animosity. This practice also frees the mind from its dark, heavy properties, and makes it clear and transparent so it can attend its chosen focal point without distraction.

Cultivating a general attitude of friendship is a contemplative process. We remind ourselves that success depends on hard work and the act of divine providence. It is no accident that particular individuals are healthy, happy, peaceful, and prosperous. A long chain of good deeds led them to a positive result—we have no idea what positive karmas have intersected to lead specific individuals to a point where they seem to be successful. It is good if we can learn something from their success, but there is no need to examine their follies. For example, if we have joined an anti-corruption movement, there is no need to cultivate animosity toward politicians who have built their fortune through corrupt means. Our knowledge of their corruption must not be allowed to contaminate our mind with hatred, for by hating them we damage our own mind. Hatred, anger, and animosity fill our mind with negativity. We cannot create a positive result with a negative mind. We are the first and foremost recipients of our own negativity. And negativity takes our mind away from the single reality—Ishvara—on which we are trying to meditate.

As part of this contemplative practice, when we find ourselves intensely critical of a particular successful person, it is important to ask ourselves if this is because the part of us that craves power, prestige, and glamour is trying to demolish the competitor that we see in that successful person. Dismantling our justification for hating others and seeing our competitors in a positive light of friendship protects our mind from an inner enemy—the deeply rooted principle of animosity.

The second potent mental contaminant is cruelty. Cruelty originates from the desire to dominate those who are poor, miserable, and helpless. Cruelty and fear are part of our primitive nature. Cruelty makes us find violence thrilling, and fear channels our cruelty toward those who pose no threat to us. Exploiting the poor and helpless is the deeply rooted habit of the rich and powerful. Even when we are not particularly rich or powerful, the subhuman in us searches for those who are poorer and more helpless than we are and prompts us to exploit their helpless condition. Oppressive social practices are rooted in this ego-driven, self-centered desire. For example, this desire gave rise to the caste system in India.

Failure to fulfill our desire to dominate those weaker than we are breeds cruelty. Cruelty breeds violence. Violence-driven thoughts damage more than our concentration—they injure the loving, kind, and considerate part of our nature. If not checked, these thoughts not only kill the meditator in us, they also kill our spirit of humanity. That is an enormous loss. To prevent this loss, Patanjali advises that we practice compassion toward those who are suffering.

Practicing compassion is more subtle and potent than practicing friendship and it requires greater understanding and skill. For example, practicing compassion involves more than serving the poor and the sick, more than opposing war or campaigning against human trafficking. The practice of compassion begins with discovering and acknowledging the injured person in us.

The first step is to recognize where our own thoughts and feelings have been hurt. We must explore the scars in our own minds and hearts and heal our own emotional injuries—a process Patanjali describes in greater detail in sutra 1:36. The pain caused by emotional injuries has a powerful effect on our personality. It distorts our worldview and forces us to be hypervigilant. Suspicion becomes imbedded in our character. We are constantly on the offensive, quick to hurt others, slow to forgive, and insensitive to the injuries and pain of others. We are drawn to painful thoughts and memories.

Our inability to bear our painful thoughts and memories makes us angry with ourselves. As a coping strategy, we pour out our anger on those who are weak and helpless. This behavior is completely unconscious. We are unaware that the irritable and insensitive part of our personality has taken over. If left unchecked, this behavior becomes a breeding ground for violence and cruelty. That is why the practice of compassion begins with healing our own internal injuries. Self-destructive behavior and compassion do not go together. To practice compassion, we must first heal ourselves and rise above the turbulence caused by our own internal pain.

A mind free of painful tendencies is naturally drawn to a peaceful state. Happiness is the property of a peaceful mind. A peaceful, happy mind sees things clearly. It has the ability to discern good from bad, right from wrong, real from unreal. It has the ability to see and relate to others' pain while remaining unaffected. This is when the practice of compassion in its truest sense begins. Compassion is always accompanied by wisdom. It is not a random response to our own emotional turmoil, stirred up by seeing the suffering of others. Compassion has no room for pity or lamentation. We know our compassion is accompanied by wisdom when we neither grieve for those who are miserable nor are angry with those who caused their misery.

The loftiest and most effective way to practice compassion is to help, serve, and love others the way Ishvara helps, serves, and loves us. Ishvara's intention is pure. It is triggered by her essential compassion. She is not affected by the misery of the souls who have fallen in the cycle of birth and death nor is she touched by aversion to the conditions that led them into such misery. Ishvara always stands on the neutral ground of wisdom, yet her compassion is fully active. Thus, according to Patanjali, an active engagement in loving, caring, and serving those who are suffering, without judging anyone, is practicing compassion.

The third mental contaminant is jealousy. Jealousy, like cruelty, springs from desire. Here, jealousy is discussed in the context of our spiritual quest, and in this context, the source of jealousy is the desire for spiritual recognition. Therefore, Patanjali recommends that we cultivate an attitude of happiness in relation to those known for their spiritual virtues.

Finding joy in learning about someone's spiritual achievements is both subtle and tricky. Love for God, dispassion toward worldly objects, selfless service, and non-possessiveness are universally accepted indicators of spiritual virtue. We are told people blessed with these virtues are great souls. They are close to God. There is a sense of elation in being associated with them. We want to be like them. They are our guides and we should respect them. But in an attempt to respect them and benefit from their spiritual power and wisdom, we put them on a pedestal and build high hopes around them. And because we want to be recognized for our own spiritual virtues, it is only natural to be jealous of them and to feel happy when the recognition they have achieved is tarnished for some reason. This potent subtle contamination destroys the mind's ability to flow peacefully inward.

The world will always have both genuine and fake spiritual adepts and seekers, and both will gain recognition. Truth and the appearance of truth will be continually tested, challenged, condemned, and welcomed. Our job is to look into our own mind, examine its powerful tendencies, and work hard to make it crystal clear. We must remember it is self-examination, not examination of others, which lays the foundation for our spiritual quest. Cultivating a general attitude of respectful happiness toward virtuous souls, without ferreting out the details of their personal lives, is one of the surest ways to benefit from what is good in them while remaining unaffected by what may not be so good.

The fourth contaminant that clouds the mind is self-righteousness. The antidote is practicing an attitude of non-judgment toward those classified as "sinners." The concept of vice is more deeply ingrained in us than the concept of virtue. The concepts of sin and hell occupy more room in religious texts than the theories and practices that bring a positive change here and hereafter. Every religion has its own definition of sin, and even though these definitions are often childish, people take them seriously. Further, the scope of sin and sinful acts is so broad that few people escape being stamped as a sinner by someone. We tend to associate with those whose beliefs and values are similar to ours. The desire to be recognized as a "good" person within our own group causes us to discover and highlight "bad" attributes in others. The search for sin and sinners becomes our primary focus, and the quest to know the truth is forgotten. If this tendency is not checked, our inner world grows steadily darker, and we eventually lose our capacity to comprehend true spiritual values.

As a society we have become addicted to condemning others on the ground of piety-driven differences. It is obvious that this has caused an enormous amount of pain, but what is not so obvious is the powerful negative effect this attitude has on our personal growth. As part of nature's design, we are more adept at seeing things outside us than inside us. This makes it much easier to see a sinner outside us than to see the very element of sin within ourselves. We waste our time criticizing others. Our priority becomes correcting those we deem to be on the wrong path rather than discovering our own source of peace and happiness. As a result, we begin walking backward. Patanjali tells us that to overcome this problem we must stop judging those who, in the light of our personal beliefs, are sinful.

The term for cultivating a non-judging attitude is *upeksha.* Although it is frequently translated as "indifference," this is not what Patanjali means. *Upeksha* is a composite of *upa* (near, closely) and *iksha* (to see), and means "to see closely" or "to see in the proper context." For example, theft and violence are generally regarded as sinful. The more poverty and illiteracy in a community, the more theft and violence there is likely to be. This does not mean the poor and illiterate are sinful. Practicing upeksha in relation to poor, illiterate people caught in the painful cycle of theft and violence means understanding them in their context. This enables us to see them as downtrodden fellow beings and to develop love and genuine compassion for them.

The purpose of cultivating the four positive attitudes highlighted in this sutra is to instill higher virtues in our mind, which Vyasa calls *shukla dharma*. These virtues allow our mind to reclaim its natural, pristine, joyful state. A joyous mind has all the ingredients to become one-pointed and flow peacefully toward the center of Consciousness.

Knowing how mysterious the mind is, how powerful our habits are, and how difficult it is to change our attitudes, in the next sutra Patanjali offers another option for making the mind one-pointed and peacefully flowing toward a state of samadhi: a special practice of pranayama.

SUTRA 1:34

प्रच्छर्दनविधारणाभ्यां वा प्राणस्य ॥३४॥

pracchardanavidhāraṇābhyāṁ vā prāṇasya ॥34॥

pracchardana, forceful exhalation; *vidhāraṇa,* retention; *vā,* or; *prāṇasya,* of the breath

Transparency of mind also comes by practicing pranayama that involves forceful exhalation and breath retention.

Transparency is the foundation of a stable mind. A mind drowning in the darkness of the five *kleshas*—ignorance, distorted self-identity, attachment, aversion, and fear—is bound to be anxious and fearful. Such a mind loses touch with its natural inner joy. The attitudes of friendliness, compassion, happiness, and non-judgment described in the previous sutra illumine the mind and shield it from ignorance. But this illumination is not powerful enough to dispel the principle of darkness itself. The practice described here picks up where sutra 1:33 left off, taking us directly to the brilliance inherent in us—the brilliance of our essential life force (*prana shakti*).

The body is the repository of the limitless wealth of Primordial Nature. Although the body's innate wisdom gives us complete access to this wealth, to a large extent this wisdom is buried under thick layers of darkness and so has become dormant. The pranayama technique referred to in this sutra peels those layers away, awakening the body's innate wisdom and illuminating our mind. It drives away stupefaction, instills the mind with clarity and tranquility, and reinfuses it with the ability to flow peacefully toward the center of Consciousness. To understand the unique potential of this pranayama, we need to examine the design of our body, the powers inherent in our organs, the privileges these powers grant us, and the sustaining role of prana shakti.

The human body is nature's finest creation. It is superior to the bodies of other creatures in that it contains the most highly evolved brain and nervous system and is endowed with the most expressive intelligence. Our limbs and sense organs have developed in response to the irresistible desire of our intrinsic intelligence to express itself and experience its vast grandeur. This irresistible desire caused the body to evolve in a manner that allows us to feel and respond to an extremely wide range of emotions, a phenomenon unique to humans. For example, every human being has a sensitive endocrine system—even a slight change in emotion alters our body chemistry, enabling us to recognize our feelings and respond to them in a tangible way. At various intersections of energy within us, the body assigns cells and tissues to monitor and guide the currents and crosscurrents of our thoughts and feelings. In yogic literature, the most prominent of these intersecting energies and the cells emerging from them are called *chakras*.

In addition to a powerful drive to feel and express itself, our intrinsic intelligence also has a limitless appetite to explore the external world; thus, our highly refined limbs and sense organs evolved. With their help, we perceive and experience objects in the world around us. Were it not for our innate intelligence, neither the world outside us nor the world inside us would have come into existence. Every aspect of creation, including our mind, body, and senses, has evolved to satisfy the need of our intrinsic intelligence for fulfillment and freedom.

Prana shakti is the link between our inner intelligence and the tools—the mind and body—it uses to express itself. Prana is the direct manifestation of the Divine Will and its compassionate intention to awaken us from the timeless slumber of death. Prana is the life force itself, the very breath of Ishvara. It is the primordial principle of pulsation, the provider and enabler. It is the might of the Almighty breathing life into the aggregation of matter and energy that we know as the body and mind. Prana is infused with the intelligence of the Omniscient Being, an intelligence significantly superior to that of the individual soul, which has fallen into the cycle of samsara. Prana is the source of nourishment and inner guidance. By embracing its nurturance and guidance, we remove the veil of darkness hiding the innate wisdom of our body and the immense power of our mind.

This sutra refers to a unique practice for embracing our pranic force and using it to remove the veil of darkness. This practice is highly technical and Patanjali returns to it in sutras 2:49 through 2:53, then again in sutras 3:38 and 3:43. In the tradition of the ancient sages, this practice is taught step-by-step with several prerequisites and precautions. The primary prerequisite is the adoption of a sitting posture as defined in sutras 2:46 through 2:48. The primary precaution is to learn and practice this technique under the guidance of a competent teacher.

This is a highly specialized pranayama practice, characterized by forceful exhalation (*pracchardana*) and retention (*vidharana*)—hence the name *pracchardana vidharana pranayama*. It is important to observe the prerequisites and precautions, because even though this practice appears simple, it has a profound effect on the brain, the nervous and endocrine systems, and more precisely, on the pituitary gland and the function of the hypothalamus.

According to Vyasa, the core of this practice consists of the extremely specialized and forceful (*prayatna-vishesha*) exhalation and retention of breath. It is the final step in a series of pranayama practices, which begins with what is known in the hatha yoga tradition as *bhastrika pranayama.* In bhastrika, the exhalation and inhalation are brisk and forceful. This shows itself as a rapid contraction and expansion of the abdominal area, while the rib cage is suspended and remains relatively still. The breath is fast and short, somewhat similar to breathing that might lead to hyperventilation, although in bhastrika all movements are controlled and voluntary.

Following bhastrika, the next step leading to this special pranayama is the practice of *pratiloma pranayama,* also known as *surya bhedi.* This is the same as bhastrika, except that in pratiloma pranayama the practitioner exhales and inhales forcefully and rapidly through one nostril, then quickly switches to the other. One round of pratiloma pranayama may consist of a hundred to two hundred breaths, switching back and forth from one nostril to the other. To master this pranayama, it is important to conclude with a specific form of breath retention (*kumbhaka*), which must be learned and practiced under the guidance of a qualified teacher.

Finally comes the practice that this sutra refers to: pracchardana vidharana pranayama. Pracchardana involves breathing through both nostrils forcefully and rapidly. The uniqueness of this breathing pattern is that, during exhalation, the breath is directed to strike the region of the soft palate, which lies near the floor of the brain. This makes the soft palate vibrate, while diffusing the intensity of the outgoing breath. Similarly, with each inhalation, the breath enters the nostrils with great force, striking the soft palate before reaching the trachea. In short, the forceful and rapid exhalations and inhalations are both directed at the soft palate.

The vidharana portion of the practice is introduced in the advanced stage. This highly specialized form of concentration involves retaining the breath. To emphasize the unique nature of the concentration induced by this pranayama practice, both Patanjali and Vyasa avoid using the term *kumbhaka.* In this practice, retention is introduced between the inhalation and the exhalation.

To do pracchardana vidharana, exhale and inhale forcefully and rapidly as just described. Then, just prior to introducing retention, extend the exhalation and make it forceful, emptying the lungs to the fullest capacity. During this extended and forceful exhalation, the breath is still brushing the soft palate. Without creating a pause, take an extended and forceful inhalation, directing it at the soft palate. There should be no jerk or shakiness in the breath.

After this long, forceful, smooth, and extended inhalation, retain the breath without using the fingers to block the nostrils. Concentrate (*dharana*) in the specialized area (*vi*) in the region of the soft palate. During the long, extended, and smooth exhalation and inhalation, the mind is fully engaged in the area around the soft palate. This mental engagement is now further intensified because the mind is no longer involved in attending to the process of inhaling and exhaling, but is suspended in the mental space surrounding the soft palate. Concentrating while retaining the breath allows the mind to consciously recognize and imbibe the energy generated by the forceful exhalation and inhalation.

After holding the breath to your comfortable capacity, exhale gently and smoothly, take a few normal breaths, and then repeat the process. Do not practice the vidharana portion of this practice more than three times in one session.

The vibratory movement induced by pracchardana at the soft palate awakens and energizes the brain, in general, and the limbic system, the hypothalamus, and the pituitary gland, in particular. The limbic system, located on top of the brain stem and under the cortex, is directly involved in regulating powerful emotions, such as fear and anger. It also regulates sexual behavior. Thus, feelings of pleasure and the urge for survival are important facets of our limbic system. The limbic system is also responsible for storing and retrieving memories, and plays an important role in regulating a variety of hormones, our sense of exhilaration, and a broad range of activities vital for survival.

In the tantric scheme of the chakras, this part of the brain corresponds to the *talu chakra*, which is subsumed in the "command" center (*ajna chakra*). The ajna chakra is located in the center of the brain—inward from, and just above, the level of the space between the eyebrows. There is no practice as effective as pracchardana vidharana pranayama for awakening the inherent power of this important part of the brain.

Shortly after beginning this practice, the power lying dormant in the region of the ajna chakra is roused. This awakening emerges in the form of light experienced in the region of the ajna chakra. With this light comes a sense of joy so compelling that the scattered mind coalesces and rushes toward it. The causes of disturbance vanish and the mind becomes stable and tranquil. With prolonged practice, the mind becomes one-pointed and inwardly flowing, gradually reaching the state of samadhi. Remember, however, that the practice described in this commentary is not for beginners but presupposes that the student has mastered the fundamentals of breath training and pranayama.

Commentators and scholars have long debated whether or not the practice referred to in this sutra is an alternative to the practice set forth in sutra 1:33. According to the tradition of the Himalayan masters, such arguments are misplaced. Just as the trustful surrender to Ishvara described in sutra 1:23 is not an alternative to abhyasa and vairagya, the practice of this special pranayama is not an alternative to cultivating the attitudes of friendliness, compassion, happiness, and non-judgment described in sutra 1:33. These four attitudes help us protect our mind from the subtle contaminations of animosity, cruelty, jealousy, and self-righteousness, and cleanse them from our mind. But the practice of pranayama referred to in this sutra goes further—it peels away the layers of these contaminants, burns them in the brilliant light of the wisdom buried deep within us, and infuses our mind with vitality, clarity, and one-pointedness. In other words, this pranayama transforms and energizes our mind, and impels it to flow peacefully toward our core being.

As we will see in the second chapter of the *Yoga Sutra*, pranayama is the only practice with the capacity to remove the veil that hides the light. It is the only practice that helps the mind fulfill all the criteria for practicing concentration (*dharana*). But if we do not make an effort to cultivate the fourfold virtues described in sutra 1:33, we leave our mind unprotected. The pranayama practice described here provides further protection and enables the mind to discover and embrace the inner light. Practically speaking, just as abhyasa and vairagya (YS 1:12) form a complete practice, so do the fourfold virtues and the methodical practice of pracchardana vidharana pranayama. Together, they form the foundation for the techniques described in the following sutras, none of which will yield satisfactory fruit unless they are carried out by a mind which is to some degree already calm, clear, one-pointed, and trained to flow inward.

SUTRA 1:35

विषयवती वा प्रवृत्तिरुत्पन्ना मनसः
स्थितिनिबन्धिनी ।।३५।।

viṣayavatī vā pravṛttirutpannā manasaḥ
sthitinibandhinī ॥35॥

viṣayavatī, pertaining to a sense object; *vā,* or; *pravṛtti,* unique mental cognition; *utpannā,* arising from; *manasaḥ,* of the mind; *sthiti-nibandhinī,* that which compels the mind to remain one-pointed

A unique cognition pertaining to a sense object arising from within also anchors the mind to *sthiti,* the peaceful flow free from all thought constructs.

The body is a repository of nature's infinite wealth. Each of our cells, tissues, limbs, and organs is infused with limitless potential. Every cell is a locus of energy and intelligence. Further, specific tissues and the space containing them serve as a locus for unique powers. Only a small portion of these powers is available to us in manifest form—most remain dormant. For example, due to the unique energy and intelligence focused in our eyes, our capacity to see is unimaginably vast. But what we actually see is quite limited because only a small portion of that potential is manifest. Due to this limitation, we cannot see objects that are too big, too small, too far away, or too close. In addition, the eyes present an inverted image to the cortex. The cortex rights the image and helps us comprehend details the eyes do not register clearly and discretely.

We have the ability to awaken the potential dormant in our cortex and eyes, putting their extraordinary powers at our command. This is true of all the senses and the capacities lying dormant within them. However, we face three obstacles: we do not know the exact places in our body that serve as a locus for this unique energy and intelligence; we do not know how to awaken it; and once it is awakened, we do not know how to use it to anchor our mind and make it flow peacefully inward.

For thousands of years, yogis used their own bodies as laboratories. Through direct experience, they were able to identify the unique characteristics of energy and consciousness lying dormant in specific senses, limbs, and organs. For example, they discovered unique dormant potentials at the tip of the nose, at the tip of the tongue, in the soft palate, in the middle of the tongue, and at the root of the tongue. With practice, these potentials manifest in the form of extraordinary fragrance, taste, form, touch, and sound, respectively. The technique discovered by the yogis for awakening the dormant potentials at these locations is the subject of this sutra.

In his commentary, Vyasa clarifies how awakening these extraordinary powers anchors our mind, makes it flow peacefully, and accelerates our spiritual unfoldment. He begins by reminding us of the sources of truth. Scriptures are a valid source of knowledge, he tells us. A correct process of inference also leads to the truth, as does knowledge imparted by teachers ordained in the tradition (*acharyas*). But Vyasa adds that unless we gain a direct experience of truth—at least in part—we will never be fully convinced of its validity.

Spirituality is subtle. Because spirituality pertains to realities not perceptible to the senses, doubt is a substantial obstacle in spiritual practice. No matter how many scriptures we read or discourses we hear, without direct experience some degree of doubt regarding subtle spiritual matters invariably remains. But once we have direct experience of a reality beyond the ordinary domain of our senses, our belief in that particular aspect of reality—and in other aspects—unfolds naturally.

Direct experience removes doubt and breathes life into our faith in the scriptures. It confirms the truth gained both from inference and from the teachings of learned masters. Vyasa explains that this is why Patanjali prescribes purifying the mind by focusing on an object that manifests directly from inside. This gives us confidence in our ability to dive into the depths of our own body, mind, and senses and discover the extraordinary powers deposited there. It gives us the ability to discriminate between genuine spiritual experiences and the projections of our mind—between experiences that make us master of ourselves and those that make us slaves. And finally, direct experience enables us to become established in the state of vairagya known as *vashikara* (YS 1:15). Consequently, we recognize the difference between genuine revelation and fantasy, and thus are no longer prey to imagination—whether it results in visions of gods and goddesses, messages from angels, or delusions of ghosts. In short, a direct experience of the reality beyond the senses engenders faith, vigor, retentive power, stillness of mind, and intuition—the key ingredients we need to succeed in our practice.

As we have seen, Vyasa describes five different places in the body endowed with a unique energy. He also lists external objects, such as the moon, the sun, the planets, gems, or a flame, which can be internalized to awaken our inherent power (*shakti*). But as every aspect of our body and mind is infused with extraordinary power, the question becomes how to decide which to use as a doorway to discover our inherent potential.

In the tradition of the Himalayan masters, we awaken shakti by focusing our awareness in the region of the soft palate. This region is the locus of the energy and consciousness that gives rise to form. Among the various sense objects used for concentration, the mind is most strongly drawn to form because form constitutes a well-defined space. Form emerges when we visually isolate a portion of space and define its boundaries. This is a function of light, which gives definition to the space it illumines. Illuminated space in its various shades and densities is what we perceive as form. There is no ambiguity about how much space a form occupies, whereas the boundaries of a space containing smell, taste, touch, and sound are vague. That is why training the mind to remain focused on a form is easier than training it to remain focused on an object without form. As we concentrate on a form, the subtle properties contained in it and associated with it begin to manifest.

To get an idea of the subtle properties of the form that manifest when we awaken the inherent shakti that fills the region of our soft palate, it is helpful to consider some of the functions of this part of the brain. The soft palate lies near the base of the brain. Nearby structures include the brain stem, the limbic system, and various organs, including the thalamus, the hypothalamus, and the pituitary gland. Structures in the brain stem regulate functions necessary for survival, such as breathing and heartbeat. The hypothalamus and the pituitary gland are closely involved in the management of stress and the regulation of primitive urges, such as hunger, thirst, and sexual desire. The energies of emotional life are largely managed by the limbic system, which also functions in the storage of memories, especially long-term memories. All this happens outside our conscious awareness.

In yogic terminology, primitive urges, emotions, and long-term memories are known as samskaras and vasanas (YS 4:9). In everyday life, our experiences arise from the vast pool of our samskaras and vasanas, like mist rising from a lake. But because darkness and inertia render us unaware of our inner world, we grope our way through life, accepting the unconscious and involuntary functions of our body, mind, and senses as our destiny. Lifting this dark and stupefying veil allows the innate light in this region to shine unobstructed. The unobstructed flow of our inner luminosity is intrinsically accompanied by joy. This is a non-sensory joy. It is completely untainted by sorrow. Pure and unconditional, it is the joyful experience of our inner luminosity itself. This experience has three immediate effects: it anchors the mind in its peaceful flow (*sthitau nibadhananti*); it shatters doubt (*sanshayam vidhamanti*); and it serves as a gateway to the revelation that dawns in samadhi (*samadhi-prajnayam dvari-bhavanti*).

How do we lift the veil of darkness and allow the mind to become peacefully focused on the innate light in this region? The first part of this question was answered in the preceding sutra. At the peak of the practice described there, the veil of inner darkness is lifted and the light in the region of the *ajna chakra* is unveiled. The longer and more consistently we do the practice, the more stable our awareness of that light becomes.

As the practice matures, we become aware of awareness itself. We are aware not only of the light that fills the space in the region of our ajna chakra but also of the dynamic pulsation (*spanda*) of Consciousness that is its source. This experience leads to a subtle and extraordinary shift in our understanding. We realize that the space in the region of the ajna chakra is totally different from the space familiar to us in the external world. Furthermore, the inner light emerging there has no parallel in the external world. We are seeing neither space nor light through our physical eyes. We realize this space and light is not inside our forehead or in a particular part of our brain. Rather, it is an awareness of our inner luminosity filling our mental space. It is the non-physical, non-sensory experience of the luminosity of Pure Consciousness. In other words, it is self-revealed Consciousness—that is, Consciousness brought to awareness by its own natural presence and serving as a point of reference in the infinitely vast space of our mind. It enables us to anchor our awareness to a particular point—a particular locus in the space of our mind—rather than allowing it to be diffused throughout a nebulous mental space. It offers our mind no choice but to be one-pointed.

The practice of the unique pranayama (*pracchardana vidharana*) referred to in the previous sutra lifts the veil of darkness, allowing the luminosity of Pure Consciousness to emerge in the mental space that houses our ajna chakra. In this context, it is important to bear in mind that our physical body is superimposed on our mental body. Our limbs and organs are closely connected to the subtle design of our mind. The physical locations of the major organs and systems in our body help us locate precise points in the vast space of our mind. Yogis use the complex design of the physical body as a road map to navigate the intricate pathways of their mental body. It is in this context that they talk about meditating on different chakras or regions of the body.

Acquiring the ability to turn within and penetrate the inner recesses of awareness lying behind our physical organs requires systematic training and practice. This is where this sutra comes in. Vyasa lists five sensitive spots for concentration and tells us that by focusing on any of them we can attain victory over the mind's roaming tendencies. These five are at the tip of the nose, at the tip of the tongue, in the soft palate, in the middle of the tongue, and at the root of the tongue. As stated earlier, in the tradition of the Himalayan masters, we are trained to master our practice of concentration by focusing at the region of the soft palate. Meditation on this region leads us to the direct experience of form arising in the space of the mind. This form is not a product of our imagination nor is it symbolic of anything. It is the naturally manifesting experience of our inner luminosity illuminating a discretely defined space in the region of our soft palate, and more precisely, the mental space corresponding to the area around and above the soft palate. It is not form in any physical sense. It is form only in the sense that it is a segregated mental space lit by the luminosity of Pure Consciousness. This experience of form not only helps us train our mind to flow inward, it also helps us identify other meditative objects available in our mental space. Without this ability, we cannot comprehend what is meant by concentrating on the other four sensitive spots mentioned by Vyasa.

The space around and above the soft palate lit by inner luminosity contains the essence of our primordial memories. The most ancient among them are memories associated with the quest for fulfillment and freedom and our indomitable will to accomplish this quest. At the physical level, these memories are encoded in our brain, more precisely in the primitive brain. This part of the brain is buried beneath the cortex and above the brain stem. The longer we meditate on the luminous region of our soft palate, the clearer our quest for fulfillment and freedom becomes. The inner luminosity accelerates the process of refining our field of memory. Our retentive power is enhanced. Our willpower and determination increase. The memory pertaining to our ancient quest for fulfillment and freedom subtly transforms the functions of our primitive brain. Normally, this part of our brain governs and guides our primitive urges, such as hunger and other survival issues. But the subtle effects of inner luminosity make our primitive brain, at a deep level, understand that true survival entails accomplishing our quest for fulfillment and ultimate freedom. Such motivation becomes part of our personality. This is transformation from inside out.

In regard to meditating on the space lit by the inner light, however, many of us face a formidable obstacle: We do not allow the inner light to appear in its pure, undistorted form. Instead, we impose images of our own preferred gods, goddesses, deities, yantras, and mandalas—all with distinctive features—on that light. They have varying degrees of power and charisma. We are firm in our belief about their hierarchy. When one of these "sacred forms" occupies a central place in our mind, it blocks the inner light from manifesting in its purest form.

Those fortunate seekers not blinded by allegiance to a particular form may well struggle with other obstacles. For example, they may wonder just how the inner light is supposed to appear. Is it large or is it small? Is it white or is it blue? Is it precisely at the soft palate or is it somewhere between the eyebrows?

To overcome these and other obstacles created by our cultural habits and religious preferences, we need to constantly remind ourselves that the *Yoga Sutra* is talking about a formless form of inner light. Perceiving it is a matter of cultivating sensitivity and becoming aware of the experience itself. Meditation at the soft palate means first discovering our mental space and then experiencing the luminosity of Consciousness filling that space. Meditation on that experience helps us train our mind to become one-pointed and flow peacefully inward. This well-trained mind can later be directed to identify and meditate on other areas of the body and to benefit from the revelation unique to those regions.

As far as the actual practice of concentrating on the soft palate is concerned, the first requirement is to become fully grounded in the practice referred to in sutra 1:34. With the help of pracchardana vidharana pranayama, become fully familiar with the space in the region of the soft palate and gain a feeling of the energy generated there. Both during and after pracchardana vidharana pranayama, mentally observe how this newly generated energy seems to fill the entire space.

Next comes the practice referred to in this sutra. It consists of a special pranayama known as *kapala-bhedi*, which has two steps. Step one consists of inhalation (*puraka*) and exhalation (*rechaka*). Step two includes retention (*kumbhaka*).

In the first step, begin by uniting your mental awareness with your breath. Then breathe much as you do in *ujjayi pranayama*, except that in ujjayi your breath is quite audible, whereas in kapala-bhedi it is silent. Just as in ujjayi, restrain your glottis and force the air to move up toward the soft palate gently and slowly. Mentally continue beyond the soft palate as if, on an inhalation, you are drawing your breath upward through your brain all the way to your crown. When you have finished inhaling, exhale and descend while still restraining the glottis. After practicing for several weeks, go to step two.

In step two, use the same techniques you used in step one, but retain the breath between the inhalation and the exhalation. In other words, inhale slowing while restraining your glottis and mentally pull your breath all the way to your crown. When you have finished inhaling, retain your breath to your comfortable capacity. Then gently exhale and descend while continuing to restrain your glottis. It is important that you are comfortable during the retention, because the period of retention is the actual period of meditation on the luminosity that fills the mental space in the region from the soft palate all the way to the crown. Any discomfort involved in breath retention takes away the mind's ability to meditate on the inner luminosity.

On the surface, this particular variation of kapala-bhedi pranayama appears simpler and less vigorous than the practice of pracchardana vidharana pranayama, but in terms of experiencing the luminous nature of the space, kapala-bhedi is more penetrating and revealing. But remember, this practice is effective only after pracchardana vidharana has been practiced for a significant period of time.

The luminous nature of the space manifesting from this practice not only makes the mind flow peacefully, but also infuses it with the ability to enter our innermost space—our spiritual heart. The nature of our spiritual heart and the kind of fulfillment and freedom unique to it is the subject of the next sutra.

SUTRA 1:36

विशोका वा ज्योतिष्मती ॥३६॥

viśokā vā jyotiṣmatī ॥36॥

viśokā, free from sorrow; *vā,* and/or; *jyotiṣmatī,* infused with light

The state of consciousness free from sorrow and anguish and infused with inner light also anchors the mind to *sthiti,* the peaceful flow free from all thought constructs.

This appears to be one of the simplest sutras but it is actually the most cryptic and profound. To a casual reader, this sutra seems to tell us only that a mind free of worry and grief and infused with inner light automatically flows peacefully inward. But in the Sri Vidya tradition, this sutra is considered the core of the entire text. Here, Patanjali prescribes a course of sadhana—a comprehensive, well-defined practice—for the first time.

In the first thirty-three sutras, he created a context for introducing a system of practice by describing the general qualities and properties of practice. He explained how to assess whether or not a practice is of high quality, but he did not tell us exactly which practice to do. In this sutra, Patanjali identifies a precise practice—one with a clearly defined goal—but he does so in highly cryptic language. Only when Vyasa deciphers this sutra does the content begin to reveal itself.

Vyasa unravels this sutra by adding the phrases *hrdayapun-*

darike dharayato at the beginning and *pravrittirutpannamana-sah sthiti-nibandhini* at the end. This latter phrase is carried over from the previous sutra. Thus, the sutra now reads: *hrdaya-pun-darike dharayato vishoka va jyotishmati pravrittirutpanna mana-sah sthiti-nibandhini.* This can be translated: "By concentrating on the lotus of the heart, there arises a state of sorrowless joy [*vishoka*], which is infused with inner light [*jyotishmati*]; upon its emergence, such a state anchors the mind to a peaceful flow free from all thought constructs [*sthiti*]." Vyasa writes his commentary on this expanded version, but it is almost as cryptic as Patanjali's original sutra. It can be fully understood only when interpreted by a living tradition.

Vyasa explains what he means by concentrating on the lotus of the heart. He offers an important clue by telling us briefly of the limitless possibilities that come into view when we concentrate on the lotus of the heart. And he also provides a sense of how concentrating on the lotus of the heart looks and feels. But a clear understanding of the practice requires that we decipher Vyasa's commentary accurately. The reason masters like Patanjali and Vyasa are so secretive about their most profound and advanced teachings will become clear as we learn about the highly sought, extraordinary fruits of this practice.

Vyasa tells us that meditation on the lotus of the heart leads us to two unique states: vishoka and jyotishmati. Vishoka is a state in which there is no trace of sorrow and anguish (*shoka*). In this state, we are free from doubt, fear, anger, grief, guilt, regret, and shame. We are absolutely certain of who we are and of our relationship both with the higher reality within us and with the external world. The mind is so clear that we see our deeply rooted samskaras without being perturbed by them. We can distinguish unalloyed Consciousness from the consciousness fully entangled with our deeply rooted subtle karmic impressions. We know the truth about ourselves: we are the creator of our personal world. We also know we have the ability to transform and redesign that world. This realization frees us from the fear of losing ourselves by becoming entangled in our personal world. We live in the world while remaining above it.

The state of vishoka brings the realization that life is not confined to the material world nor to the loss and gain, failure and success, insult and honor integral to it. We see that our life stretches to a realm where fear, old age, death, hunger, and thirst do not exist—a realm where we are not dependent on anything for our sustenance. We know we exist beyond the confines of our body, senses, and mind (*videha*). Perennial joy itself is our locus—it goes wherever we go. In other words, our inherent joy has manifested fully. Riding that wave of joy, the mind moves freely within the space of Consciousness. Our emotional injuries have been healed so completely that no trace of sorrow remains. This inner healing nullifies our understanding of the world as full of sorrow, and therefore also nullifies our desire to attain freedom from the world. There is no need to disconnect ourselves from life for we are at peace. Inner healing and joyfulness are the defining characteristics of vishoka, the state of sorrowless joy.

The second state identified in this sutra, jyotishmati, is a condition of inner luminosity. In this state, our sense of I-am-ness (*asmita*) is fully illuminated by the light of Pure Consciousness. We, the little self, begin to see the Special Purusha, whereupon our notion of ourselves as an isolated individual consciousness dissolves (YS 4:25). We are filled with the realization that all the subtle impressions of the mind and the roaming tendencies arising from them are fully known to the all-pervading Seer (YS 4:18). This realization leads to trustful surrender to our eternal companion.

We are naturally inclined to embrace our true essence and turn away from the objective world (YS 4:26). This unique state, which is characterized by inner healing, sorrowless joy (*vishoka*), and inner luminosity (*jyotishmati*), dawns on the horizon of our consciousness when we meditate on the lotus of the heart.

But what does Vyasa mean by "the lotus of the heart"? The lotus is the most pervasive esoteric symbol in Eastern spirituality. Hinduism, Jainism, Buddhism, Sikhism, and Tantrism all employ the symbol of the lotus to express their deepest doctrines and esoteric experiences. In Hinduism, the deities of creation, protection, and dissolution are linked to this icon. Brahma, the creator, is said to emerge from a lotus that blossoms from the navel of Lord Vishnu, the protector of the universe. It is the creative power (*shakti*) of the lotus that infuses Brahma with creativity. In that sense, Brahma is fused with the image of the lotus, which, in one version of the story, is said to be the essence of the universe. The lotus is Brahma's origin and his permanent abode—he is eternally connected to its primordial and ever-blossoming realm.

Vishnu, the all-pervading provider and protector of the universe, is also characterized by his relationship with the lotus. He is the lotus-eyed one. During the cosmic dissolution, when the universe is reabsorbed into Primordial Nature, Vishnu resorts to his yogic sleep, awakening only when the lotus of the navel opens. As the lotus blossoms, Vishnu opens his eyes, and the seed of worldly existence begins to germinate.

In many traditions, a lotus blossom is used as the seat or base for images of the Divine. As the conqueror of death (*Mrityunjaya*), Shiva sits on a lotus growing in an ocean of ambrosia. Lakshmi, the wife of Vishnu, is often depicted standing or sitting on a lotus, representing the blossoming of wealth and potency. Similarly, Sarasvati, Tara, Buddha, Padmasambhava, the Chinese goddess Quan Yin, and the Japanese goddess Dainichi Nyorai are all associated with the lotus. And in the tantric system of philosophy and metaphysics, the centers of energy and consciousness in the human body are all described as lotuses, centers of blossoming energy.

As we navigate through the rest of Patanjali's text, particularly sutras 2:19, 2:20, 3:34, 3:49, 3:54, 4:18, 4:22, and 4:25, it becomes clear that "the lotus of the heart" refers to the state of consciousness in which the individual soul and God (*Ishvara*) are united in a common being. Sutra 3:34 states, "By meditating on the heart, one gains complete knowledge of one's mind." Commenting on that sutra, Vyasa writes, "In this city of Brahman [the human body] there is a space. In that space is the lotus shrine. In the lotus shrine, there is unique wisdom (*vijnana*). By practicing meditation (*samyama*) on that unique wisdom, one gains complete understanding of one's mind." This unique intuitive wisdom is known as *pratibha jnana*. According to sutra 3:33, it is the precursor to the power of discernment and to the highest samadhi. This intuitive wisdom is the deliverer (*taraka*), for it grants us freedom from the binding forces of the objective world, including the binding forces of our mind. This freedom-granting intuitive wisdom subsumes the experiences of the entire objective world and is not bound by the linearity of cognition. In other words, this knowledge is unconfined by notions of past, present, and future, or by any other form of sequence (YS 3:54).

This sorrowless and luminous state, says Vyasa, is the very essence of our own mind (*buddhi sattva*). It is the highest level of inner purity. Here Purusha (the Seer) and Prakriti (the Primordial Cause of the Universe) are face-to-face. In this field of intelligence, the Seer and the Seen are completely in each other's view. According to Vyasa's commentary on sutra 2:19, this state refers to both collective intelligence (*mahat*) and the field of individual intelligence (*buddhi*). It is the locus for our mind, senses, and body, and for all the karmas—the subtle impressions lying within us—including those lying dormant (*sanchita*), those awakened and manifesting in the form of destiny (*prarabhdha*), and those yet to be encoded (*kriyamana*). This state is so subtle and thus so incomprehensible that Vyasa calls it "the existence of non-existence" (*nihsatta-sattam*). Here, Consciousness and mind are so close and so reflective of each other that they appear neither similar nor dissimilar (YS 2:20). Lit by the light of Pure Consciousness, the mind loses its long-cherished illusion of I-am-ness. Its lust for preserving a sense of personal identity vanishes. Its fear of merging into higher reality is destroyed. The mind is grateful that this inner light (*jyotishmati*) has swept away any sense of spiritual darkness. It is a state of purest joy (*vishoka*) for it has gone beyond the conditioning of the body, senses, and mind (*videha*).

Two key questions remain: What is the lotus of the heart? How do we meditate on it? In sutra 4:22, Vyasa tells us, "It is all-pervading, eternal intelligence. It is neither in the netherworld nor in a mountain cave nor in the darkness of the deepest ocean. It is contained in the depths of Brahman. It is eternal and the very cognition of intelligence itself (*buddhi vritti*)."

The lotus of the heart refers to a unique space—the space in the city of Brahman (YS 3:34). It is the space of Consciousness (*chid-akasha*) as well as the epicenter of Consciousness. It is the seat of Ishvara, the Special Purusha, and the seat of the individual soul, the ordinary individual purusha. The lotus of the heart is our own very essence—our true abode. While residing here in the lotus of the heart, we seek our fulfillment (*bhoga*) and ultimate freedom (*apavarga*). Our primordial guru, Ishvara, is seated next to us. Out of sheer compassion and unconditional love, she dispenses protection and guidance as we strive for fulfillment and freedom. In other words, this lotus embodies the intelligence of both Ishvara and ourselves—the Enlightened Being and the one seeking enlightenment; the One Who Is Ever-Full and the one seeking fulfillment; the One Who Is Ever-Free and the one seeking freedom.

At the center of this lotus lies its essence, primordial desire (*kama*). Our primordial desire is to experience lasting fulfillment and attain ultimate freedom. Ishvara's primordial desire is to help us find that fulfillment and freedom. Our timeless intention is to be fulfilled and free. Ishvara's timeless intention is to help us find what we have been seeking for eternity. This primordial desire, this infallible intention, is the nectar of the lotus of the heart. It is intrinsically imbued with the power to manifest its limitless potential. From deep within the lotus, this primordial desire (*kama*) exerts its self-propelled influence, causing the petals to open, whereupon both Ishvara and the individual soul are drawn to drink its nectar. Inebriated by the nectar's sweetness, they sing and dance in complete accord (*Saundaryalahari* 38).

This is a state of supernal bliss. In this state, we no longer resist the love, protection, and guidance of Ishvara. Our *asmita*—our petty I-am-ness—is filled with gratitude that it has been embraced by the pure and perfect Consciousness. We are overcome by joy at seeing our circumscribed individuality melting away and dissolving into the higher reality. This joy transports us directly to a state of samadhi known as *ananda anugata samadhi,* the samadhi induced or preceded by joy. The result is *videha,* a state of realization in which we are no longer confined by the limitations of our body, senses, and mind. We are free from the fear of losing our individuality, and we delight in the prospect of expanding to a higher reality.

Inner illumination (*jyotishmati*) is closely related to sorrowless, joyful vishoka. In the discerning light of Consciousness we know who we are and what the building blocks of our individuality are. This clear understanding of ourselves transports us to a state of samadhi known as *asmita anugata samadhi*, the samadhi induced or preceded by a pure and fully expanded I-am-ness (*asmita*). The result is *prakritilaya*, the realization that we are resting in Prakriti. We know we are not losing our individuality, but are gaining access to the vast kingdom of Primordial Nature and expanding into it. Thus, we are free of all vestiges of sorrow and anguish. This realization demolishes our confusion about who we are, why we have come to this world, our relationship with higher reality, and what happens to us when we die. This perfect clarity is described as inner luminosity (*jyotishmati*).

The state of sorrowless joy and the state of inner luminosity are two facets of the same experience—the experience arising from meditation on the lotus of the heart. It is difficult to predict which will emerge first. We are all unique. Some of us are primarily driven by faith and devotion (*bhakti*), while others use logic and reason to verify our faith before we embrace it. Many of us are convinced of the effectiveness of our meditative techniques; for us, faith and devotion are secondary. In the case of meditators primarily driven by faith and devotion, the experience of vishoka comes into view first and jyotishmati follows. In the case of meditators primarily driven by logic and reason, jyotishmati dawns first. In most people, however, faith, devotion, logic, reason, and respect for technique are well balanced. Therefore, in most cases the experiences of vishoka and jyotishmati emerge almost simultaneously.

Regardless of which experience dawns first, the end result is the same—absolute clarity. We know our mind well. We are aware of its binding and releasing properties. We are no longer burdened by subtle impressions of the past for we have the power and wisdom to preside over them. We are aware of our karmic impressions but they no longer influence us. Doubt and fear vanish. We have confidence in the healing and guiding embrace of Inner Divinity. We trust and respect our own discerning power. Our desire to prove ourselves vanishes. We are free. We enjoy this freedom while in meditation and while going about our daily lives. We are established in vishoka and jyotishmati. The result? Our mind is with us and we are with our mind. Our inner guide is with us and we are with our inner guide.

This is the most crucial stage in our spiritual development. Once we reach this level of realization there is no possibility of ever falling backward. Even if we attain this experience only while drawing our last breaths, it remains with us forever. Death has no power to nullify it. The experience of vishoka and jyotishmati infuses our mind with unwavering retentive power. We return to this world with our wisdom and power intact. We remember that our inner guide, protector, and provider is within us. Because this indelible memory protects us from doubt and fear, our life is joyful and luminous from the outset. As soon as our body and mind are fully mature, we resume our spiritual quest exactly where we left it. In other words, after attaining vishoka and jyotishmati, we are able to live in the world and yet remain above it. We are free.

In sutra 1:19, both Patanjali and Vyasa tell us that one who has attained this level of experience will be born as an extraordinary yogi (*bhava pratyaya yogi*). To underscore the radical nature of the freedom brought by vishoka and jyotishmati, Vyasa does not list the yogis of extraordinary caliber (*videha* and *prakritilaya*) in his scheme of the planes of existence (*loka*) (YS 3:26). According to him, yogis of this caliber are established in their own unique world, the world made of freedom. They may live in the world but they are not part of it. They are born free, live free, and die free. After they attain the state of vishoka and jyotishmati, the purpose of their birth and death is simply to complete their remaining journey while established in their sorrowless, luminous Consciousness. At every stage in their life—both here and hereafter—they are joyful and lucid.

This raises a question of enormous importance for our practice: How do we meditate on the lotus of the heart? Here it will be helpful to remember that we were able to decipher the meaning of sutra 1:35 only by carrying over a portion of sutra 1:34. Similarly, in order to delineate the precise steps of the practice of meditation on the lotus of the heart, we have to carry over the practice described in sutra 1:35.

The unique system of meditation I have described in the commentary on sutra 1:35 enables us to experience a luminous field of energy throughout the subtle space within and around our forehead. As we continue to practice, this luminosity intensifies and expands. Eventually, both the space occupied by our body and the space immediately surrounding it is infused with luminosity. Experientially, it is as if this luminous field of consciousness has replaced our body. It becomes the locus for our self-awareness—we exist in it. As implied in sutra 1:14, if we continue our practice for a prolonged period, without interruption, and with reverence, this self-luminous field becomes stable and well defined.

Just as we feel the presence of our self-existence in our physical body, as we meditate with this awareness we feel the presence of our self-existence in this luminous space. This luminous space is the locus of our awareness. We are in it, and this awareness is in us. While residing in this awareness, we feel that we are breathing. When we inhale, we feel our awareness traveling upward, and when we exhale, we feel our awareness traveling downward. In general, we are aware of our entire locus—the entire luminous field—but we are particularly aware of the pathway within this field that our awareness is using to move up and down. We are breathing in the space corresponding to the region between the tip of the nose and the eyebrow center. Each time we breathe, we feel a sense of self-awareness traveling up and down. At the peak of our meditation, we are aware of only this feeling of self-awareness moving up and down. This is where the meditation described in sutra 1:35 culminates. The meditation described in this sutra picks up from here.

As part of the meditation on the lotus of the heart, we stretch this feeling, allowing ourselves to become aware of the breath moving between our heart and the eyebrow center. We are generally aware of the entire locus of radiant light—the luminous space itself—but we are particularly aware of the space covered by the movement of our breath. We are breathing in the space corresponding to the space between our heart center and the eyebrow center. As we immerse ourselves in meditation, all that remains is the sense of self-existence—an awareness of pure being—moving up and down. And this awareness is in the luminous space that has replaced our physical body as the locus of our self-existence.

The difference between this and the meditation described in sutras 1:34 and 1:35 is subtle but potent. The methods described in those two sutras are stages of a single meditative practice. In sutra 1:34, the emphasis is on meditating on the light filling the space corresponding to the center of our forehead, the *ajna chakra*. As we meditate there, the light intensifies and becomes well defined. The luminous energy engendered by this meditation pulls our consciousness toward the higher reaches of our head and beyond, awakening and energizing areas of the brain associated with conscious awareness; the meditation described in sutra 1:35 further enhances and intensifies that experience. As part of the meditation described there, we meditate on the luminous space corresponding to the region of the forehead. If done properly, this meditation pulls our energy upward. This upward pull is felt most noticeably in our eyes. Meditative vibrations fill the space in the region of our brain. These vibrations are extremely peaceful and yet very active. If we exceed our capacity, we feel lightheaded.

Meditation on the chakras above the ajna chakra is highly technical. According to the Sri Vidya tradition, it is dangerous to force our awareness to move from the region of the ajna chakra to the crown or to force ourselves to meditate at the crown without proper preparation and without fulfilling the prerequisites. Masters belonging to the *samaya* school of Sri Vidya meditate on the crown chakra, but theirs is the path of perfection, pursued in complete isolation from worldly existence. Sutra 1:36 advises us to meditate on the lotus of the heart; this particular form of meditation is the specialty of the *mishra* school of Sri Vidya.

While learning to meditate on the lotus of the heart, it is important to understand that we are concentrating neither on the image of a lotus nor on the heart muscle. Rather, we are meditating on the luminous space in the region of our spiritual heart. Furthermore, this luminosity is not the product of our imagination. As our practice of meditation on the luminous space in the area of the ajna chakra matures, the inner luminosity intensifies and expands. Although this expanded field of luminosity has no border, there is a sense of it occupying a discrete body of space—our mental space. Even though this field is not physical—it is purely a field of awareness—it surrounds our body; at the level of feeling, it subsumes our body. Our sense of self-existence is transported from our physical body to this field of awareness. It is in this field of awareness we have to locate our spiritual heart.

Just as our physical heart is located in the center of the body, our spiritual heart is located in the center of the luminous body of our Pure Being. The center of our inner luminosity is our core. This is where the awareness of our self-existence is felt most strongly. It is the resting ground of our Consciousness, the most prized space within us, because our sense of self-identification, along with all its karmic possessions, is concentrated here. Our numberless samskaras and vasanas are buried here. This is the home of our primal desire—the desire to preserve our self-identity—and the home of our sense of belongingness. Life after life, this space is where we have been holding on to our loved ones and struggling to get rid of what we hate and those we hate.

Our spiritual heart is also the abode of the Lord of Life, Ishvara. No matter how thick the veil of ignorance and how oblivious we are of our attachment, aversion, and fear of losing what we value the most, the Lord of Life is fully aware of us and the world in which we have buried ourselves (YS 4:18). The lotus of the heart is our personal world; we are at its center. The Lord of Life is next to us. Sankhya Yoga calls the spiritual heart *linga sharira*, the body made of endless samskaras and vasanas. At the time of death, our spiritual heart leaves the physical body; it then descends into a new body as we awaken from the slumber of death.

How do we locate the lotus of the heart? As stated before, the practice of meditation described in sutra 1:35 intensifies and expands the field of self-awareness. Even though this field of awareness does not have shape, size, or color comparable to anything in the objective world, it does have a quality identifiable by the mind. It is lucid, transparent, and infused with the sense of self-existence. This luminous field of self-awareness appears to have lower and upper limits, and a unique dimension. We can see it and feel it with our inner eyes. If we are sitting cross-legged on the floor, the luminous space, which has subsumed and replaced our body consciousness, is almost as big as the space from the floor to the crown of the head. The area of the perineum is the lowest limit, and the crown is the highest limit. At its center is the luminous space corresponding to the region of our physical heart. This is the lotus of the heart.

The ajna chakra, the luminous space corresponding to the region of our forehead, is the gateway to the lotus of the heart. This is how the human body has been designed, which is why, before delving into the lotus of the heart, the sages in our tradition emphasize meditation at the ajna chakra. A consistent and prolonged practice of meditation at the ajna chakra results in the manifestation of inner luminosity filling the space in the region of the forehead. With the help of an unwavering, one-pointed mind, devotion, and the strength gained through Yoga sadhana, we can intensify this luminous field.

By using a yogic technique unique to the samaya school of Sri Vidya, we can lift our pranic force and make it penetrate this luminous field. In scriptures, such as the *Saundaryalahari,* this technique is known as *bindu bhedana.* It is used to lift our consciousness to the upper limit of this luminous field. Yogis are advised to do bindu bhedana in the last phase of their life, and more precisely, at the time of final departure from this world (BG 8:10). This technique, which is expounded by Lakshmidhara in *Saundaryalahari* 14, 32, 41, 92, and 99, is not the subject of this sutra.

The process of meditating on the lotus of the heart under discussion here involves allowing our consciousness to descend from the ajna chakra to the center of the luminous field, the spiritual heart. To help us comprehend the phenomenon of consciousness descending from the ajna chakra to the heart, the tradition advises applying a technique that leads us in the opposite direction. By virtue of the contrast, it helps us understand where our heart is located and how it feels to reach there.

This technique is as follows: First become established in the luminous field of the ajna chakra. With practice, let this field intensify and expand. Let this expanded luminosity replace your bodily consciousness. Now mentally observe its lower and upper limits. Come to the space corresponding to the area of the ajna chakra and stay there for three breaths. Then let the feeling of self-awareness move from the ajna chakra to the crown by combining your awareness with the movement of your breath. When you inhale, feel as though your inhalation begins from the ajna chakra; as you continue inhaling, feel the flow of your awareness moving up until it reaches the crown. Then, without creating a pause, exhale as you descend from your crown to the ajna chakra. During the exhalation, feel the descent of your self-awareness. Repeat this process three times.

While doing this practice, you will notice an upward pull in your eyes as you inhale and mentally move your awareness toward the crown. Even though you are not using your eyes to see anything at the crown, the combined forces of self-awareness and breath subtly pull your eyes upward, and at a deep level, you feel it. By the time you reach the crown, there is noticeable tension in your eyes. As you descend, the level of tension drops. This allows you to sense a correlation between a part of the physical body and its corresponding part in the luminous field.

Note that this practice of lifting your awareness and moving it from the ajna chakra to the crown is only an experiment. The purpose is to gain a direct experience of the effort involved in reaching the crown center, the neuro-energetic exertion it creates, and the quality of one-pointedness it induces. Keep this experience in your memory and retrieve it to compare with the experience you gain from the following practice, which brings you to the lotus of the heart.

Begin this practice after you are already established at your ajna chakra. The field of luminosity and self-awareness has expanded and has enveloped your entire field of self-awareness. You are already aware of the upper and lower limit of the luminous field and of its center. Now take a deep breath. Begin exhaling from the ajna chakra to the center of this luminous field. As you exhale, feel your self-awareness descending from the ajna chakra to your spiritual heart. The movement of breath and self-awareness are fully coordinated. Upon completing your exhalation, begin inhaling. Your inhalation begins from your heart center and, accompanied by your self-awareness, goes all the way to the ajna chakra. Repeat this three times.

You will notice the journey between the ajna chakra and the lotus of the heart is accompanied by a totally different kind of feeling than what you experienced when moving between the ajna chakra and the crown. The upward movement of awareness from the ajna chakra to the crown causes a sensation of upward movement and a noticeable tension in your eyes. But during the downward movement of awareness to your spiritual heart, the tension in your eyes melts away. The slight upward movement in your eyes when you are inhaling from your heart center to the ajna chakra is gentle and does not create tension in your eyes. While exhaling from the ajna chakra to the heart, you feel a slight downward pull in your eyes and a profound sense of relaxation in the entire region of the ajna chakra. As you continue breathing between the heart and the ajna chakra, a natural rhythm of movement arises that restricts the pranic flow and the awareness accompanying it to the area between the lotus of the heart and the base of the ajna chakra.

Within a week or two of uninterrupted practice, your innate wisdom and inner guide will transport you to a state of understanding where you will no longer feel a need to travel from the heart center to the ajna chakra. You are now naturally inclined to stay at the heart center. All you want is to mentally observe the feeling of your self-existence at the lotus of the heart. The pull of your self-presence is so strong that your interest in coordinating your awareness with the movement of your breath fades. You are oblivious of the physiological dimension of breathing, which continues of its own accord. You do not need to make any effort to focus your mind on the lotus of the heart, for in the presence of this inner luminosity, the mind is naturally one-pointed. There is no ground for disturbance, stupefaction, or distraction. The lotus emits a unique joy, and the mind, fully engaged in experiencing it, loses all interest in entertaining its roaming tendencies.

As the center of our inner luminosity, the lotus of the heart is our true abode. This is our core, where we reside along with all our samskaras. This is where we are caught in a seemingly unending war of duality—good and bad, success and failure, life and death. For an ordinary soul, this is an impenetrable, inescapable reality the mind has been creating since the dawn of time. But this is also the home of our conscience, our power of discernment. It is also the center of intuitive wisdom. As soon as we enter this luminous field, we begin to realize that our mind is as pure and luminous as Consciousness itself. The mind is transparent and perfectly reflective of the reality within. It is capable of knowing itself and the samskaras it has stored. The mind is also capable of observing its own functions and the influence the samskaras exert on our thoughts, speech, and actions.

We see that we have been searching for lasting happiness in a complex world run by the fivefold affliction: ignorance, distorted sense of self-identity, attachment, aversion, and fear. We have been seeking freedom while clinging to our likes and dislikes. We have been trying to find fulfillment while complying with our cravings. This newly discovered inner luminosity at the lotus of the heart enables us to see reality in a different light. We realize we have been running away from ourselves. We have been trying to hold someone or something—God, karma, destiny, friends, family—responsible for our failure, sorrow, and misfortune. We have been keeping ourselves busy to avoid seeing within. This understanding dissolves our misperception of ourselves, of others, and of the world around us.

This understanding does not dawn during our meditation on the lotus of the heart, however. While we are meditating, the intrinsic luminosity of our spiritual heart infuses our mind with unaccustomed joy—joy untainted by sensory or mental conditions. It is pure and sorrowless joy. Vishoka is deeply nurturing. It instills the mind with strength to face and accept reality. Every time we meditate, we become clearer and stronger. The experience of sorrowless joy arising from meditation infuses our mind with the understanding that the world within us is much more predictable and reliable than the external world. Our inner reality is ever present and unaffected by the changing conditions of the external world—there is an extraordinary feeling of protection and safety. We are clear about who we are and have no interest in knowing what we are not. This state is self-luminous, and sorrowless joy is intrinsic to it. Meditation on the lotus of the heart leads to this state. During meditation we are in it, and it is in us.

Meditation on vishoka and jyotishmati transforms our mind. Our perception of life becomes clearer and our discerning power sharper. The mind begins to understand itself (*buddhi samvit*) and to comprehend its own essence (*buddhi sattva*). Enlightenment dawns in installments. We become aware of an ever-present truth: we are not alone. We realize the Lord of Life has always been with us and is always there for us. Her own unique law—pure unconditional love—binds her to us as our eternal friend, guru, guide, protector, and provider. She has never—and will never—abandon us. This supremely reassuring and nurturing realization drives away our primordial feeling of loneliness. We feel complete. When we return to our day-to-day world after meditation, the gift of this realization comes with us. Regardless of how outward-oriented our awareness and how hectic our life, this realization continues to nurture our mind and brighten our consciousness.

The most noticeable change brought by this meditation on the lotus of the heart is that we are able to face ourselves. The numberless labels we have been carrying are replaced with one: child of Divinity. Our essential nature is pure and divine. All other identities are acquired and transitory and we have no fear of losing them. We are grateful that the Inner Divinity never judges us. He bestows his love and guidance without counting our merits and demerits. This knowledge-driven gratitude gives us the courage to surrender to the Lord of Life. To many, the Supreme Being is merely a concept and a source of doubt, fear, and conflict. But for us, the Supreme Being is more alive and more present than we ourselves. He is imperishable (*akshara*), yet he accompanies us, the perishable beings (*kshara*). He is with us in both birth and death. He is omniscient and knows our habit of running away from him, yet always keeps us in his embrace. This realization fills us with unconditional love and devotion. We become loving, kind, and trusting. Our suspicious nature is replaced with simplicity and innocence—our purity is restored.

With sustained practice our meditation matures. It takes less time to enter the state of jyotishmati and vishoka. The longer we stay in this self-luminous, joyful state, the more refined and subtle our experience becomes. As we will see in sutra 1:43, this refinement purifies our memory field. The memory pertaining to our quest for fulfillment and ultimate freedom, and our memory pertaining to the love, guidance, and protection flowing from Ishvara, become clear and firm. We no longer need to remind ourselves of our perennial quest or of our relationship with the Supreme Being—it is now an integral part of our understanding. As we progress in our meditation, this understanding is transformed into feeling. Both during meditation and at other times, this feeling fills our consciousness. Even when we are not aware of it, this feeling is aware of us. We have entered *nirvichara,* the state of samadhi that arises when the mind is absorbed in an object that transcends the thought process (YS 1:44).

When this absorption matures, we enter the realm of *prajna,* the field of intuition (YS 1:47). In the bright light of intuition, we distinctly see both the trivial nature of our limited self-identity and the Special Being (*Purusha Vishesha*). We understand what we are and what we are not. The desire to know anything further vanishes (YS 4:25). We are free and we see the Seer within. The purity of our mind at this stage is equal to the purity of Pure Consciousness (YS 3:55). The mind now sees and conquers its long-cherished samskaras; it rises above its self-created karmic vortex. It dwells joyfully in the lotus of the heart (YS 3:34). There is no cognition of the mind seeing Purusha, the Inner Being. Instead, Purusha sees the mind within itself (Vyasa on sutra 3:35). Both Vyasa and Patanjali call this realization *taraka,* the knowledge that empowers us to transcend the cycle of samsara (YS 3:54). This state of realization is the furthest frontier of lower samadhi.

From this point on, we make no effort to push ourselves further. If we do make an effort, the samskara created becomes an obstacle to higher samadhi. Effort no longer has a role; our consciousness is lifted by the grace of the Divine. This is a transitional state from the furthest frontier of lower samadhi to perfect *nirbija samadhi.* This transitional state is known as *dharma megha samadhi.* Here the agitating and dulling forces of *rajas* and *tamas* no longer dominate the mind, which is infused with the inner luminosity of Consciousness. It is clear, peaceful, and flows effortlessly inward (Vyasa on sutra 1:47).

At this stage, practice is simply "being there." It is practice only in the sense that we make an effortless effort to stay in this joyful state. The longer we stay there, the brighter, more stable, and more spontaneous our intuition becomes. In our day-to-day life we operate in the light of this intuition. We perform our actions without identifying ourselves with them or their results. Our thoughts, speech, and actions are no longer motivated by ignorance, I-am-ness, attachment, aversion, or fear. Our actions no longer yield karmic fruit (YS 4:26–4:30). Every action—physical, verbal, and mental—carries the benevolence of the Inner Divinity. The quality of our actions is conducive to our meditation, and meditation enhances the quality of our actions. All our actions are good and auspicious. That is why this transitional state is called *dharma megha samadhi,* samadhi of the cloud of virtues.

Dharma megha merges into nirbija samadhi. Because this highest state is beyond mental cognition, it is called *asamprajnata*, samadhi beyond mental cognition. After reaching this state of realization, we are no longer part of the worldly cycle. We do not die an ordinary death, but are absorbed in the luminosity of the Divine Being, who resides in the lotus of our heart. We live neither in hell nor in heaven, but in the realm of freedom (Vyasa on sutra 3:26). Inspired by Divine Will, when the lotus blossoms again, we return. We are born with our memory and knowledge intact. We are not born to find life's purpose—fulfillment and freedom—for we have already found it; rather, we reincarnate in response to Divine Will. While living the life of a mortal, deep within we remain aware of our immortal, self-luminous nature.

We live in the world and perform our actions only as an extension of Divine Will. Our actions, including our spiritual practices, no longer bind us to the world governed by time, space, and the law of cause and effect. We are free from both worldly and spiritual karmic consequences (YS 4:29–4:33).

In the next three sutras, Patanjali describes three distinct practices, which, according to our tradition, are heavily dependent on the practice described here in sutra 1:36.

SUTRA 1:37

वीतरागविषयं वा चित्तम् ॥३७॥

vītarāgaviṣayaṁ vā cittam ॥37॥

vīta-rāga-viṣayaṁ, one whose perception is not colored by desire and ego; *vā,* and/or; *cittam,* mind

Or the ability to retain the peaceful flow of mind comes by focusing on someone who is free from all desire.

The practice of concentration and meditation described in this sutra is based on the premise that the mind shares the qualities of the objects of its thought. The mind is like a crystal. When placed next to a red object, it looks red; when it is placed next to a black object, it looks black. Thus, one of the best ways to make our mind stable is to focus it on someone with a stable mind. By definition, a person free from desire has a stable mind. Meditation on such a person infuses the mind with stability.

Desirelessness is a subtle quality, however. It is impossible for an observer to assess who is truly free from all desires and who is not. Only after we are established in higher states of samadhi and have attained intuitive wisdom (*prajna*) do we have a relatively reliable sense of who is actually free of all desires. But if we have already attained a high state of samadhi and the intuitive wisdom that accompanies it, there is no reason to use a person as an object of meditation.

The practice described in this sutra makes sense only to aspirants steeped in a culture with unquestioning reverence for its spiritual figures. Almost all spiritual traditions rooted in India revere a long line of saints and sages. These masters are selfless and free from all desires. They are endowed with extraordinary powers. They are immortal—guiding seekers and bestowing blessings even after their death. Patanjali and Vyasa are examples of masters of this caliber.

The problem is that most of us have difficulty distinguishing true faith from blind faith. We are accustomed to trusting religious leaders and gurus. Further, we have been told that scrutinizing someone reputed to be holy is a violation of spiritual values, and many of us believe it. This belief causes us to follow spiritual leaders blindly. But blind faith does not make our meditation on them the ground for acquiring a peaceful mind.

It is true, as Patanjali and Vyasa tell us, that meditating on the masters who are completely free from all desires and attachment results in freedom from desires and attachment. But because we do not know how to distinguish a genuine sage from someone who merely appears to be a sage, it is better to cultivate a dispassionate mind and use that mind to meditate on the Inner Divinity, the master of all previous masters.

SUTRA 1:38

स्वप्ननिद्राज्ञानालम्बनं वा ॥३८॥

svapnanidrājñānālambanaṁ vā ॥38॥

svapna, dream; *nidrā,* sleep; *jñāna,* knowledge; *ālambanaṁ,* object of focus; *vā,* and/or

Or by meditating on the knowledge gained from dreams and sleep, one acquires stability of mind.

During the waking state, the mind perceives the objective world through the five cognitive senses: hearing, tasting, touching, smelling, and seeing. When we are awake, our mind has access to logic and reason. Even remembering past experiences or conjuring up an idea involves logic. We are fully aware of what we are remembering and imagining. Everything we do when we are awake pertains to the objective world, and every experience carries the limitations inherent in its object. Objects are always associated with our likes and dislikes; they are good or bad, pleasant or unpleasant, desirable or undesirable. Every object and the experience pertaining to it is in constant flux. Furthermore, no worldly object or experience is purely *sattvic,* peaceful, and illuminating. Therefore, sensory objects are not ideal objects of meditation.

Knowledge gained in dreams or in deep sleep can be used as an object of meditation provided it is revealed knowledge and rooted in intuitive wisdom. There are two kinds of dreams:

ordinary and prophetic. The subtle impressions stored in our mind are the principle source of our ordinary dreams. These dreams, which are products of repressed desires, fantasies, and the chaotic behavior of our brain and nervous system, have no meditative value. During dreamless sleep, our mind and brain are at rest, engendering the comprehension of knowing and remembering nothing. When we wake up, we remember our lack of comprehension. This has no meditative merit.

Dreaming and sleeping states that serve as a source of knowledge and which can be used as an object of meditation are in a different category. There are specific mantric practices for purifying our dreaming and sleeping states and for allowing deeply buried spiritual experiences to come forward. Mantras we receive in dreams, and visions we receive during intense spiritual practices (*purashcharana*), can be used as objects of meditation. Such objects make our mind stable and inwardly flowing. Specific practices, such as *svapna varahi* and *nrisimha,* are used to receive guidance in dreams and to assess whether our practice is leading us in the right direction. It is only with the help of these unique practices that we can distinguish a prophetic dream from an ordinary dream.

SUTRA 1:39

यथाभिमतध्यानाद्वा ॥३९॥

yathābhimatadhyānādvā ॥ 39 ॥

yathā, accordingly; *abhimata,* well-considered choice; *dhyānāt,* by meditation; *vā,* and/or

Or by meditating on a well-considered object of one's choice, one attains steadiness of mind.

This sutra can be taken as evidence that Patanjali was an irresponsible person who recorded the information he gathered without assessing its validity. A simplistic translation of this sutra is: "By meditating on an object of one's preference, an aspirant achieves stability of mind." It can be interpreted to mean that if we choose any object we like, by focusing on it we can reach a state where our mind can flow peacefully inward (*sthiti*). Nothing can be further from the truth.

In cultivating a clear, tranquil, inwardly flowing mind, the object of concentration plays a more important role than the technique-oriented process of concentration. As we will see in sutra 1:41, as meditation deepens, our awareness pertaining to the object of meditation, the process of meditation, and ourselves as the meditator merges. If the object of meditation is not intrinsically imbued with peaceful and illuminating properties, meditation on that object will not induce peace and enlightenment. An object of meditation must be selected wisely.

Vyasa comments, "One should meditate only on that which has been accepted or agreed upon (*abhimatam*)." In our tradition, we add the word *shastra* or *acharya* to *abhimatam*. According to our tradition, we can select an object of meditation that originated in the scriptures (*shastra*) or has been taught and practiced by the teachers in a living tradition (*acharya*). Scriptures establish the standards. Learned teachers and adepts refine those standards. When they gain experiential knowledge through deep study and prolonged practice, they share it with other adepts. They do this not because they are seeking validation but because they want to make sure it is appropriate to document that method of meditation for posterity. That is how new techniques and objects of meditation came to be added to the scriptures, and this is what is meant by "the object of meditation that is agreed upon or accepted by the teachers in a living tradition."

Many objects are appealing but not necessarily uplifting. It is important to select an object of meditation whose spiritual virtues have withstood the test of time. The lotus of the heart, the Sri Chakra, the Star of David, the cross, an unwavering flame, personified forms such as Christ, Krishna, Buddha, Ganesha, Dainichi Nyorai, and mantras are examples of objects that have been accepted by a long lineage of teachers and their students. This sutra is referring to those objects—centuries of experience have shown that meditating on them infuses the mind with purity, stability, and peace.

SUTRA 1:40

परमाणु परममहत्त्वान्तोऽस्य वशीकारः ॥४०॥

paramāṇu paramamahattvānto'sya vaśīkāraḥ ॥40॥

paramāṇu, the smallest particle imaginable; *parama-mahattva,* the biggest entity or the highest expansiveness; *anthaḥ,* the end; *asya,* of this one; *vaśīkāraḥ,* mastery; a fully-controlled state of mind

A yogi's mastery stretches from the smallest particle to the biggest object.

Here Patanjali gives the precise result of the practices described in sutras 1:33 through 1:39. Through practice, he tells us, we reach a stage where we have complete mastery over our mind. With this mastery comes the mastery of all that is inside and outside us. Every object, from the tiniest to the most immense, is within the range of our comprehension. We can focus our mind on any object, regardless of size, and penetrate the mysteries of subatomic particles as well as gigantic stars. We can also focus on subtle and ordinarily incomprehensible objects, such as the movement of our pranic force, brain waves, and the flow of our own thoughts and feelings. We can walk through solid rock and through the veil of our own ego and intellect. We can go back and forth between extremes without being affected by them. Earth and heaven are both within our reach. We know the mysteries of life here and hereafter. We have mastered the forces of life and death and we are no longer subject to them.

The self-mastery engendered by Yoga sadhana is technically known as *vashikara,* an accomplishment described in some detail in sutra 1:15. Vashikara is a state of non-attachment in which we are no longer affected either by the world's charms and temptations or by heavenly temptations. We are free from desires and completely content. Even the subtle causes of the roaming tendencies of our mind have been rendered inert. In other words, the practice of meditation frees us from the binding forces of our mind.

Yogis established in vashikara are known as *videha* and *prakritilaya.* Once we reach this level of realization, we have the privilege of being born as an extraordinary yogi, a concept described in sutra 1:19. We are born with an exceptional degree of spiritual wisdom and the innate desire to discover the inner dimensions of life. Prakriti arranges our destiny so we resume our quest from the point where we left it. Why the practice of meditation is capable of elevating us to such a high degree of self-mastery is the subject of the next sutra.

SUTRA 1:41

क्षीणवृत्तेरभिजातस्येव मणेर्ग्रहीतृग्रहणग्राह्येषु
तत्स्थतदञ्जनता समापत्तिः ॥४१॥

kṣīṇavṛtterabhijātasyeva maṇergrahītṛgrahaṇagrāhyeṣu
tatsthatadañjanatā samāpattiḥ ‖ 41 ‖

kṣīṇavṛtteḥ, a mind free from roaming tendencies; *abhijātasya,* of a transparent gem; *iva,* like; *maṇeḥ,* of a jewel; *grahītṛ-grahaṇa-grāhyeṣu,* in relation to the perceiver, the process of perceiving, and the object of perception; *tatstha-tadañjanatā,* assuming the characteristic of what lies next to it; *samāpattiḥ,* complete absorption

A mind free from its roaming tendencies is like a crystal. It takes the form of whatever object is in its proximity, whether the object is the perceiver, the process of perceiving, or the object of perception. This is *samapatti,* complete absorption.

The practice of meditation as described in the preceding sutras enables us to cultivate a clear, tranquil mind unencumbered by roaming tendencies. Subtle impressions of the past no longer grip the mind. It is free from likes and dislikes and no longer colored by its prejudices, preoccupations, desires, and cravings. The mind has become as clear and transparent as a high-quality crystal. When an object of meditation is placed next to it, the mind assumes that form. When the awareness "I am the meditator" is in close proximity, the mind blends into that awareness. When awareness pertaining to the process of meditation is predominant, the mind is absorbed into that process.

We usually begin meditating by presenting the mind with an object. The effort we make to ensure that the object stays in the forefront of our mind evolves into the process of meditation. The longer we maintain this effort—without interruption and with reverence—the deeper the meditation. The deeper the meditation, the freer the mind is from distracting thoughts. The mind is free to attend the object one-pointedly. As meditation deepens further, the mind is aware only of the object. Although the mind is absorbed in that object, there may still be a trace of two other streams of awareness: ourselves as the meditator and the process of meditating. The traces of both streams vanish as meditation deepens. Both the awareness of ourselves as the meditator and the process of meditation dissolve into pure awareness of the object of meditation. And when even this awareness and the mind merge, the mind takes the form of the meditative object. Patanjali calls this complete absorption (*samapatti*).

When the object of meditation is gross and the mind is absorbed in it, the mind takes the form of that gross object. When the object of meditation is subtle, the mind becomes subtle. When absorption is induced by meditating on a person who is liberated (*mukta purusha*), the mind takes the form of a liberated person. Similarly, when meditating on a mantra, the personified form of a deity, or the state of *vishoka* and *jyotishmati* induces absorption, the mind takes those forms. In short, the mind becomes settled in whatever is placed next to it (*tatstha*) and is transformed into it (*tadanjanata*).

This sutra tells us quite clearly that meditation on different objects leads to different experiences. If the purpose of meditation is to purify the mind and awaken its sorrowless, joyful properties, we should select an object that is intrinsically *sattvic*, purifying, liberating, and joyful. The mind is an instrument (*karana*). Because it is deep within us, it is called inner instrument (*antahkarana*). By itself, the mind is neutral—it behaves differently in the company of different objects. The mind chases one object after another, with the purpose of leaning on an object. It invariably complies with the law "similar attracts similar" and so is particularly attracted to objects compatible with its deeply rooted samskaras. Meditation is the means of breaking the mind of its negative and self-destructive habits. It begins with consciously and wisely choosing an object and skillfully placing it next to the mind. Determined effort is required to ensure that the mind does not run away from this chosen object. The effort we put into focusing the mind on the object is meditation.

The practice of meditation restores the mind's pristine nature. A pristine mind makes us master of ourselves. The secret of mastering the mind lies in meditating on a spiritually illuminating object. How different objects of meditation lead to different kinds of absorption, how one stage of absorption matures into the next, and how object-centered meditation ultimately leads us to the highest state of samadhi is the subject of the remaining sutras in this chapter.

SUTRA 1:42

तत्र शब्दार्थज्ञानविकल्पैः संकीर्णा सवितर्का समापत्तिः ॥४२॥

tatra śabdārthajñānavikalpaiḥ saṁkīrṇā savitarkā samāpattiḥ ॥ 42 ॥

tatra, there; *śabda-artha-jñāna-vikalpaiḥ,* distinct perception of the word, its meaning, and cognition of both word and meaning; *saṁkīrṇā,* mingled; *savitarkā,* accompanied by a tangible object; *samāpattiḥ,* complete absorption

Meditation that has an object mingled with the distinct awareness of a word, the meaning of the word, and the awareness of focusing on the word and its meaning leads to a form of absorption known as *savitarka.*

To understand this and the remaining nine sutras in this chapter, it will be helpful to revisit sutras 1:17, 1:18, and 1:19 in which Patanjali delineates the full range of samadhi. In those sutras, he divides samadhi into two main categories: *samprajnata* and *asamprajnata.* For the sake of simplicity, these were translated as "lower samadhi" and "higher samadhi." In lower samadhi, there is an object of focus and we are fully aware of that object. We are also aware of ourselves and of the process of focusing on the object. In the final stage of samprajnata samadhi, only meditative and spiritually illuminating samskaras remain in the mind. As soon as these meditative samskaras are eliminated, higher samadhi dawns. In asamprajnata samadhi, there is no object. Consciousness, the Seeing Power of the Seer, is reflecting in a crystal-clear mind. The reflection of the Seeing Power is not a meditative modification; it is not a thought construct or a function of the mind. The mind is not seeing the Seer as an object. Rather, the mind is so well lit it has become one with the light of Pure Consciousness.

In sutra 1:17, Patanjali divides lower samadhi into four categories: *vitarka anugata samadhi, vichara anugata samadhi, ananda anugata samadhi,* and *asmita anugata samadhi.* As we have seen, this division is based on the quality of the object used in meditation. Vitarka anugata samadhi emerges when we meditate on a gross object; vichara anugata samadhi when we meditate on a subtle object; ananda anugata samadhi when we meditate on joy manifesting from within; and asmita anugata samadhi when we meditate on the feeling of I-am-ness. In other words, the four divisions of lower samadhi described in sutra 1:17 are based on the four categories of meditative objects.

In sutras 1:42 through 1:46, Patanjali explains the entire range of lower samadhi by dividing it into two main parts—*vitarka* and *vichara*—and then subdividing both parts. Vitarka is subdivided into *savitarka* and *nirvitarka*; vichara is subdivided into *savichara* and *nirvichara.* In addition to delineating the divisions of lower samadhi based on different categories of objects, here Patanjali is also delineating the subtle process of meditation, which automatically transforms one category of object into another. He is showing the natural progression of meditation and the transformation of the meditative object, demonstrating how, through our prolonged practice of meditation, that object undergoes a natural metamorphosis. As our meditation deepens, the form of the initial object becomes subtler. This subtler form presents itself to the mind and we spontaneously begin to meditate on it. As the process of refinement continues, new and increasingly subtler objects of meditation continually replace the previous objects until we reach the upper frontier of lower samadhi.

In sutras 1:42 through 1:47, Patanjali replaces the word *samadhi* with *samapatti*. *Samapatti* means "complete absorption; two blending in one." Samapatti is the process by which the mind becomes completely absorbed in an object. It leads to the experience of samadhi—different states of samadhi emerge at different stages in this process. There is a precise correlation between the degree of mental absorption (*samapatti*) and the category of samadhi induced by it. Mental absorption always precedes the experience of samadhi. In other words, samapatti is a process and samadhi is the state of experience arising from it.

Here, in sutra 1:42, Patanjali describes the most basic stage of mental absorption, *vitarka samapatti*. This stage is characterized by meditation on a gross object (*vitarka*). As meditation deepens, the grosser dimensions of the object drop away, leaving the subtler dimensions to occupy the mind. On the ground of this natural process, Patanjali further divides vitarka samapatti into two subcategories: *savitarka* and *nirvitarka*. To understand the distinction, we need to know what is meant by gross and subtle dimensions of the meditative object. We also need to know how the grosser dimension of the object drops away and its subtler dimension comes forward.

Vyasa uses a cow as an example of a gross meditative object. A cow is tangible. It has shape, size, and other qualities that distinguish it from other animals. When we hear "cow," qualities associated with the animal—horn, udder, hoof, milk, etc.—flash in our mind. All these qualities are denoted by the word "cow" and are the meaning of the word. When we use a cow as an object of our meditation, we are meditating on three things: the word "cow," the meaning of "cow," and the awareness of focusing on the word and its meaning. Our meditation is thus split into three streams: We are meditating on the sound "cow" (*shabda*); we are meditating on the meaning of "cow" (*artha*), which contains all the qualities and properties of the cow; and because we are cognizant of our self-existence, we are also meditating on this cognition (*jnana*). We are not focusing on any of these three streams fully, but are going back and forth among them. Either we are more predominately aware of the word "cow," more predominately aware of its meaning, or more predominately aware of the cognition of ourselves as the meditator.

"Cow" as a word accompanied by a meaning and its cognition is a gross object. The absorption induced by meditating on this object is shallow and incomplete. It is split—part of our mind is absorbed in the word, another in the meaning, and yet another in cognition itself. We are meditating, yet the mind is not completely quiet—it is busy attending one object after another. Its process of focusing is mingled (*sankirna*) with selecting one option (*vikalpa*) and pushing others away. Clearly, at this stage our meditation is accompanied by (*sa*) three different thought constructs (*vitarka*). The mental absorption (*samapatti*) arising from this stage of meditation is called *savitarka samapatti*, and the samadhi arising from it is called *savitarka samadhi*.

Meditation on a cow is only an example to explain the process of mental absorption. As meditators, we must each find an appropriate meditative object. To experience the deeper dimensions of our mind and consciousness, we must achieve an ever-deepening level of mental absorption and experience how, at different levels of absorption, the grosser dimension of the meditative object naturally drops away, allowing the next level of absorption to emerge. What is involved in bringing refinement to our current level of mental absorption, thereby allowing the grosser dimension of the meditative object to drop away and the next stage to take its place, is the subject of the next sutra.

SUTRA 1:43

स्मृतिपरिशुद्धौ स्वरूपशून्येवार्थमात्रनिर्भासा निर्वितर्का ॥४३॥

smṛtipariśuddhau svarūpaśūnyevārthamātranirbhāsā nirvitarkā ॥ 43 ॥

smṛti-pariśuddhau, upon refinement of memory; *svarūpa-śūnyā,* devoid of one's own form; *iva,* as if; *artha-mātra-nirbhāsā,* where meaning alone is illumined; *nir-vitarkā,* cognition affording no room for options

Upon the refinement of memory, there arises mental absorption named *nirvitarka samapatti,* in which the object of meditation seems devoid of its own form and is expressive only of its meaning.

Here Patanjali explains that as we refine our memory, the grosser dimension of the meditative object fades and the subtler dimension comes forward. In this subtler dimension, only the meaning of the gross object remains. The meaning is the essence. When we meditate on the meaning, a subtler and more profound mental absorption arises called *nirvitarka samapatti.* In this stage of absorption, the object of meditation seems to have lost its form—only the meaning remains. In other words, the mind is aware only of the meaning and is oblivious of the form. Refinement of memory is the key to reaching this level of absorption. This raises two questions: Refinement of which memory? And what is the process of refining it?

In this context, refinement of memory means the refinement of the entire memory field. As Patanjali and Vyasa elaborate later in sutra 4:9, there is no difference between memories and samskaras. Memories are deposited in our mind and carried over from one lifetime to another. Birth, death, time, and space are powerless to obstruct their flow. Yet as long as the mind lacks stability and clarity, it is unable to see the memories it contains with any degree of precision. We barely remember our recent past, let alone the experiences pertaining to previous lifetimes.

An unsteady, scattered mind fails to attend to an object for a significant period of time. A dull and opaque mind fails to perceive an object clearly. Thus, a disturbed, stupefied, and distracted mind has no ability to comprehend the essence of an object unless that object is brought to it repeatedly. That is why we must study and review our lessons over and over before we can comprehend the content clearly and store it in our memory. In contrast, with a clear and focused mind we can comprehend instantly and retain the memory forever. This is also true of the object of meditation and our comprehension of its essence—the meaning.

As I explained in the commentary on sutra 1:27, there is a lasting relationship between a word and its meaning. By the time someone utters a word and we hear it and comprehend its meaning, the sound and its meaning have been absorbed in space. Weeks, months, or even years later, when we remember the word, its meaning—the content—comes forward. How clearly we remember it depends on the strength of our retentive power. We may remember the word without its meaning, or we may remember the word with a vague feeling of what it meant, or we may vaguely recollect the feeling but not the word itself.

The relationship between the word and its meaning is more profound than we normally realize. The word and its meaning are inseparable. Together, they form a unique reality; the Greek philosophers called this reality *Logos*. In mantra shastra, *logos* corresponds to the concept of *pashyanti*, a highly refined dimension of the power of speech (*vak shakti*), where word and meaning coexist indistinguishably. *Logos/pashyanti* is integral to the consciousness belonging to the self-luminous field of intuition, a subject discussed in greater detail in the commentary on sutras 1:47, 1:48, and 1:49. Here, in the context of a commentary focused on refining our meditation, I am offering only the simplest and briefest presentation of this subject.

A discussion of the word and its meaning lies at the core of mantra shastra and has been central to Shaktism, Shaivism, and Vyakarana-Agama. According to these schools, words, sentences, paragraphs, books, and their meanings are stored in the infinite field of intuition (*prajna* or *pratibha*). From the field of intuition, meaning descends into our mind. When we hear a word, the meaning flashes from inside. Similarly, when we read a cluster of sentences, paragraphs, or an entire book, the meaning continues flashing. When we read those sentences and paragraphs again later, or when we remember them, the corresponding meaning flashes spontaneously from the field of intuition. How clearly we comprehend it depends on how clear, calm, stable, one-pointed, and inwardly flowing our mind is. The secret of sharp intelligence and retentive power rests solely with the transparency and one-pointedness of our mind. Thus, practically speaking, "refinement of memory" means cultivating a calm, transparent, one-pointed mind.

The most effective way to refine our memory is to meditate on an object that is intrinsically *sattvic* and illuminating. Our own breath is among the most sattvic, benevolent, and illuminating objects. Breath is the direct manifestation of the life force, the intention of Divine Will pulsating in us. The breathing practice described in sutra 1:34, which serves as a foundation for the unique technique of meditation described in sutras 1:35 and 1:36, leads the mind to the state of sorrowless joy (*vishoka*) and inner luminosity (*jyotishmati*). By using sorrowless joy and luminosity as objects of meditation, a profound purification of the entire field of memory begins automatically. Not only a particular memory, but the very principle of memory itself becomes clear and stable. The firmer we are in the practice and experience of vishoka and jyotishmati, the brighter and firmer our power of intuition. The firmer our intuition, the more refined and stable our retentive power. The more refined and stable our retentive power, the more easily and rapidly the grosser dimension of meditative objects fade, allowing the subtler dimension to come forward. The subtle dimension consists of only the meaning of the word. The word as well as the awareness of self-cognition recedes into the background.

At this stage in our mental absorption, the word and the awareness of self-cognition have not vanished. The subtle feeling of their existence remains, but due to our high degree of absorption in the meaning, it appears as if they no longer exist. This level of absorption is known as *nirvitarka samapatti,* the state of absorption devoid of the threefold differentiation of a word, its meaning, and the awareness of self-cognition. In this state of absorption, we are cognizant neither of the word nor of our self-existence. Our mind is deeply absorbed in the meaning—the essence—of the object.

This level of absorption is more refined and profound than when the mind is absorbed in the threefold division of the object. And yet what seems to be complete mental absorption is simply the mind being occupied by a slightly subtler dimension of a gross object. It is a significant milestone in our inner journey, but the journey by no means ends here. How we bring further refinement to our practice and reach the next level of absorption is the subject of the next sutra.

SUTRA 1:44

एतयैव सविचारा निर्विचारा च सूक्ष्मविषया व्याख्याता ।।४४।।

etayaiva savicārā nirvicārā ca sūkṣmaviṣayā vyākhyātā ॥ 44 ॥

etayā, accordingly; *eva,* only; *sa-vicārā,* accompanied by thought or feeling; *nir-vicārā,* that which is beyond thinking; *ca,* and; *sūkṣma-viṣayā,* that which has a subtle object as its focus; *vyākhyātā,* explained

Accordingly, the *savichara* and *nirvichara* levels of mental absorption, which have extremely subtle objects as their focus, are explained.

Meditation on a subtle object leads to the level of mental absorption known as *savichara samapatti.* Here the meditative object has no correspondence to a physical object. The image held in the mind does not represent an object composed of the five gross elements—earth, water, fire, air, or space—as in *savitarka samapatti,* but belongs to the subtle realm pertaining to smell, taste, sight, touch, and sound, which are the essence of earth, water, fire, air, and space, respectively. In Yoga philosophy, the essence corresponding to these gross objects is called "that alone" (*tanmatra*). In savitarka samapatti, we focus on an idea corresponding to the gross elements, and through sustained practice, the mind becomes absorbed in it. In savichara samapatti, we focus on the idea corresponding to the essence of its physical counterpart.

No matter how subtle the object of meditation, there is cognition. We are cognizant of the thought (*vichara*) we have chosen as the object of meditation. Each time the mind is carried away by a distracting thought, we bring it back. We make a conscious effort to stay focused on the meditative thought. The mind and the thought are flowing together; hence, this stage of meditation is *savichara,* meditation accompanied by (*sa*) thought (*vichara*).

The mind comprehends a thought when it is expressed by a word. In savichara samapatti, this subtle meditative object—thought or feeling—is denoted by a word. We are simultaneously aware of three things: the word indicating the thought; the meaning of the word, which is the thought itself; and ourselves as cognizant of the word and its meaning. These three streams of awareness are intermingled, yet distinct. Mental absorption in this threefold stream is savichara samapatti.

As we continue meditating, our memory becomes refined and the next level of mental absorption arises. This is known as *nirvichara samapatti,* the mental absorption devoid of the threefold division of cognition: the word indicating the thought, the meaning of the word, and ourselves as cognizant of both.

An example will help clarify the distinction between these two levels of mental absorption. In sutra 1:35, Vyasa tells us that by concentrating on different parts of the body, such as the tip of the nose, the tip of the tongue, and the soft palate, different extraordinary sense experiences manifest. In the commentary on that sutra, I explained the preference in the Himalayan tradition for concentrating on the soft palate, which engenders the manifestation of "light" in the *ajna chakra*. This is a non-sensory awareness of the luminosity of Consciousness itself. When we meditate on the light in the ajna chakra, we are fully aware of the word "light"; we are aware of the content, which is the awareness of luminosity itself; and we are aware that we are meditating on these two. The level of mental absorption arising from this meditation is savichara samapatti, for we are fully aware of the thought pertaining to the awareness of light.

As we continue meditating on the awareness of light, our memory pertaining to the word "light" and light itself becomes so purified that they flow together spontaneously—no effort is involved. At this stage of mental absorption, the light seems to have lost its form. Only the awareness of it, which is its own essence, remains and the mind is absorbed in it. This stage of mental absorption is nirvichara samapatti, for in this stage we are aware only of the feeling (*vichara*) pertaining to light, devoid of (*nir*) its own form.

These different levels of mental absorption (*samapatti*) leading to different levels of samadhi help us map the entire process of meditation. As Patanjali explains in sutras 3:1 through 3:6, the terms concentration (*dharana*), meditation (*dhyana*), and samadhi refer to three different stages of the peaceful, inward flow of the mind. They are neither disjointed nor three different processes, but a continuum (*samyama*). The idea of mental absorption (*samapatti*) described here in sutra 1:44 and in the two preceding sutras helps us understand exactly what we must do to meditate successfully and eventually experience the pinnacle of meditation—samadhi.

As far as the actual practice goes, meditation always begins with an object. With practice, we reach a state of mental absorption in that object. As we continue to meditate, we experience an increasingly fine level of mental absorption. Our memory becomes refined and we begin to comprehend, as well as meditate on, subtler objects. As the process continues, the time comes when we are no longer conscious of the object of meditation, the process of meditation, or even of ourselves as the meditator. The three have merged. At this juncture, a higher state of meditation, technically known as samadhi, begins to emerge. Here there is no object. The Seeing Power of the Seer experiences its sheer existence. This is the realization of Pure Being by Pure Being. Initially, this state of experience may last only a few minutes or even a few seconds. But with persistent practice the duration lengthens, and one day we become fully established in it.

From the standpoint of practice, the stages of mental absorption precede their corresponding stages of samadhi, but from the standpoint of the experience itself, they are identical. However, the concept of mental absorption (*samapatti*) conveys a powerful message: Do not be content with meditation/samadhi on a gross object; do not be content with meditation/samadhi even on a subtle object; discover and become absorbed in the subtlest of all objects, for only such absorption can open the door to the highest samadhi—*asamprajnata samadhi.* This subtlest of objects is the subject of the next sutra.

SUTRA 1:45

सूक्ष्मविषयत्वं चालिङ्गपर्यवसानम् ॥४५॥

sūkṣmaviṣayatvaṁ cāliṅgaparyavasānam ॥ 45 ॥

sūkṣma-viṣaya-tvaṁ, meditation on the most subtle object; *ca*, and; *aliṅga-paryavasānam*, that which dissolves into irreferable prakriti

That which ultimately dissolves into irreferable Prakriti is the subtlest of all objects.

The subtlest of all objects is the mind itself. The mind comes into its own view when all other objects—gross and subtle—have dissolved. When all thought constructs have ceased and the mind has reached a state of complete stillness (*niruddha*), it has only itself as an object of awareness. In this state, the mind experiences its pure essence (*buddhi sattva*). As described in sutra 1:36, this state refers to complete understanding of one's own mind (*buddhi samvit*). The mind is free of all roaming tendencies. It is crystal clear and lit by the unalloyed light of Pure Consciousness. It is luminous (*jyotishmati*). In the presence of Pure Consciousness, it is inebriated with sorrowless joy (*vishoka*).

I am using the word "mind" here for the sake of simplicity, although this is not mind in the ordinary sense but the most *sattvic* and enlightened state of mind known as *buddhi*. Buddhi is the first evolute of Primordial Nature (*Prakriti*) and the subtlest object of meditation imaginable. Object-driven meditation comes to an end when the mind is absorbed in buddhi. Beyond this point lies the domain of unmanifest Primordial Nature, where there is no differentiation of object and subject. This domain is unfathomable; unmanifest Primordial Nature is not an object of comprehension and cannot be an object of meditation. It is the resting ground of all powers, potentials, and possibilities.

Vishoka and jyotishmati rise on the horizon of our consciousness when we meditate on the lotus of the heart, as described in sutra 1:36. Mental absorption in this unique joy is known as *vishoka samapatti,* and absorption in inner luminosity as *jyotishmati samapatti.* Vishoka samapatti results in *ananda anugata samadhi* and jyotishmati samapatti in *asmita anugata samadhi.* These states are the furthest frontiers of lower samadhi. Those who have attained these states of samadhi are known as *videha yogis* and *prakritilaya yogis*, respectively. Yogis of this caliber incarnate with their knowledge and power fully intact. They resume their spiritual journey exactly where they left it (YS 1:19).

When we reach this level of mental absorption and gain such a high level of experience, what happens to our karmic impressions, including the impressions created by the meditation itself? That is the subject of the next sutra.

SUTRA 1:46

ता एव सबीजः समाधिः ।।४६।।

tā eva sabījaḥ samādhiḥ ॥ 46 ॥

tāḥ, those; *eva,* indeed; *sa-bīja,* with seed; *samādhiḥ,* completely still, pristine state of mind

Those are indeed samadhi with seed.

The four stages of samadhi arising from the four levels of mental absorption described in sutras 1:42 through 1:45 belong to the category of lower samadhi. In sutras 1:17 and 1:18, Patanjali calls lower samadhi *samprajnata samadhi.* Here he calls it *sabija samadhi.* This change in terminology is significant. In the earlier sutras, Patanjali is explaining lower samadhi from the standpoint of the experience, but here he is explaining it from the standpoint of the transformation the experience brings.

The highest state of samadhi is characterized by the experience of the Seer being established in its own nature. In this state, the Seer is cognizant of its own Power of Seeing. In other words, in the highest state of samadhi we are established in Pure Consciousness. We realize we are Consciousness itself. No trace of the mind's binding forces remain. On reaching this state of realization, we are free from the bondage of karma, the fruits of karma, and all karmic vehicles. Our karmic seeds, which propel the worldly cycle (*samsara chakra*), are rendered null and void. By contrast, in lower samadhi, our karmic seeds (*bija*) still exist; hence, the name *sabija samadhi.*

Lower samadhi is characterized by a high degree of inner stability, the result of acquiring a clear and tranquil mind. The clarity and tranquility of the mind is due to its absorption in the meditative object. This mental absorption refines our memory, making the mind sharp and intuitive. In the final stages of lower samadhi, we are able to experience sorrowless joy (*vishoka*) and inner luminosity (*jyotishmati*).

By using vishoka and jyotishmati as objects of our meditation, we become fully established in the essence of our own buddhi, the field of discerning wisdom (*buddhi sattva*). In the light of this discerning wisdom, we see our mind as it is. We see our karmas, samskaras, and vasanas, yet are not perturbed by what we see. We accept ourselves—our mind, samskaras, and karmic consequences. We are at peace. We know karmic seeds still exist, but we trust we will eventually attain freedom from them. This trust is not an intellectual conclusion, but is grounded in direct experience. This experience-based trust pulls us forward until, with further practice, we reach the next level of realization, which eventually matures into the highest state of samadhi, *nirbija samadhi,* samadhi without karmic seeds. The nature of this next level of realization and the transformation it brings is the subject of the next sutra.

SUTRA 1:47

निर्विचारवैशारद्येऽध्यात्मप्रसादः ॥४७॥

nirvicāravaiśāradye'dhyātmaprasādaḥ ॥ 47 ॥

nir-vicāra, that which is beyond thought and feeling; *vaiśāradye,* upon purification; *adhyātma,* spiritual; *prasādaḥ,* illumination or enlightenment

Spiritual transparency and joy come from the continued purification of *nirvichara samapatti.*

As described in the commentary on sutra 1:44, the furthest frontier of lower samadhi emerges from the stage of mental absorption known as *nirvichara samapatti.* It is the result of meditation on the subtlest of all objects, the essence of our own inner intelligence (*buddhi sattva*). Meditation on the lotus of the heart, as described in sutra 1:36, lifts the veil covering our inner intelligence. As a result, a state of sorrowless joy (*vishoka*) and inner illumination (*jyotishmati*) arises.

As our meditation on vishoka and jyotishmati deepens, our intuitive field expands. We begin to see ourselves clearly. The charms and temptations of the world and our samskaras lose their grip on our mind. The mind is spontaneously flowing inward, which results in the experience of a unique joy. Through continuous practice, this joy intensifies, making the mind sharper and more intuitive. Our comprehension expands, transforming our understanding of time, space, and the law of cause and effect. Past, present, and future merge. The notions of far and near vanish. Seated above the realm of time, space, cause, and effect, we see the objective world non-sequentially. The mind is so well illumined by the unalloyed light of Pure Consciousness that we see the world of sensory experience as it is. We comprehend the samskaras stored in our mind as a single, indivisible experience. Our actions and their consequences blend into a single cognition. Patanjali calls this non-linear, indivisible experience "intuitive wisdom" (*prajna* or *pratibha*), the source of knowledge pertaining to everything (YS 3:33).

The intuitive wisdom rising from this refined form of meditation sheds a fresh light on life. From this perspective, we realize life has a purpose and we must find this purpose now. We must not waste our life counting our follies or burden it with hubris concerning our accomplishments. We no longer mourn the past or worry about the future. We are no longer haunted by doubt, fear, anxiety, or insecurity. We live in the present, fully connected to the essence of our being, and we cherish that connection. Loneliness has vanished. We have found our best friend—a mind free of all roaming tendencies. We are at peace, content with the joy arising from within and unencumbered by the propensity to lean on sense objects. We are fulfilled and free.

Guided by the light of prajna, we continue moving toward the higher rungs of samadhi. Even when we are not in meditation, that light guides us. We perform our actions without losing sight of life's purpose. We work hard without identifying with our work or its intended result. We are free while engaged in the world and free when our work in the world is over. The experience of fulfillment when we are in meditation continues when we are engaged in the world. In the light of prajna, we are aware of the reality within and without. This awareness empowers us to live in the world yet remain above it. This is the life of a *jivanmukta,* one who is free here and now.

In the next sutra, Patanjali explains the distinctive attribute of prajna and methods for making it more refined and stable.

SUTRA 1:48

ऋतम्भरा तत्र प्रज्ञा ॥४८॥

ṛtambharā tatra prajñā ॥ 48 ॥

ṛtam-bharā, laden with truth; *tatra,* that; *prajñā,* intuitive wisdom

There that self-luminous field of Consciousness is laden with truth.

Truth is the core of *prajna.* Truth and truth alone radiates from the infinite field of intuition. The discerning power of prajna has no parallel. In the light of intuitive wisdom, we see things as they are. Our understanding of ourselves—our mind, subtle impressions, thought constructs, sensory experiences, actions and their consequences—is so clear there is no need for verification. We are certain.

In this sutra, Patanjali describes the fundamental characteristic of prajna. Later in the text—most significantly in sutras 1:49, 1:50, 2:27, 3:5, 3:25, 3:33, 3:36, 3:49, 3:51, 3:54, 4:23, 4:25, and 4:29—he elaborates on this concept from different perspectives and in different contexts. We will explore this as we come to each of these sutras, but here we will take a closer look at sutra 2:27 to better understand why Patanjali emphasizes prajna in the course of his discussion on samadhi.

As we have seen, long before we reach samadhi we are free of the mind's roaming tendencies. The mind is clear, one-pointed, and peaceful. By the time we reach the outer frontier of lower samadhi, we are established in a state of sorrowless joy (*vishoka*) and our mind is bathed in inner luminosity (*jyotishmati*). The unalloyed light of Pure Consciousness enlightens the world within us. This illumination is prajna.

In sutra 2:27, Patanjali explains that prajna grants sevenfold freedom. This is a distinctive characteristic of prajna. In the light of prajna, we realize the true nature of sorrow, the cause of sorrow, the state beyond sorrow, and how to reach that state. This fourfold realization frees us from the consequences of our karmic deeds (*karya vimukti*).

The remaining three levels of realization free us from the fundamental forces of the mind itself (*chitta vimukti*). This threefold realization consists of knowing our own mind. Guided by the light of intuitive wisdom, we first come to know the luminous essence of our mind (*buddhi sattva*), and at this, all the mind's acquired properties—the subtle impressions of our karmas—drop away. Second, in the light of intuition, we are confident these karmic impressions have no power to return. Finally, we realize Pure Consciousness, our core being, is untouched even by the building blocks of our mind—*sattva, rajas,* and *tamas.* At this seventh stage of intuitive illumination, we are devoid of even the subtlest of impurities (*amalah*). Pure Consciousness alone occupies the field of our experience—we have become that experience (*kevali*).

All of us are endowed with prajna, but samskaras and the mind's roaming habits block it. Meditation, which evolves into different levels of samadhi, washes away these impurities. The mind becomes progressively clearer and more perceptive. The field of memory, where samskaras are stored, becomes increasingly refined. We begin to see our inner creation and its influence on the world outside us. With practice we gain mastery over this inner creation. The highest level of mastery—the apex of intuitive wisdom—dawns when we are able to renounce our inner creation joyfully.

According to Vyasa, we brighten our intuition and attain the highest goal of Yoga by embracing the knowledge imparted in the scriptures, by committing ourselves to self-analysis and self-observation, and above all, by the ardent practice of meditation. But even though scriptures may embody the experiences that dawn in the field of intuition, prajna is not dependent on scriptural knowledge. Scriptures guide us in the right direction. They enable us to learn from the experiences of those who have trodden the spiritual path, but it is the practice of meditation that puts us on the path and pulls us forward. Similarly, self-analysis and self-observation help us identify our strengths and weaknesses, but ultimately it is the practice of meditation that strengthens us further and helps us transcend our weaknesses. There is no substitute for practice, just as there is no substitute for prajna.

Intuitive wisdom alone is the gateway to lasting fulfillment and ultimate freedom. That is the subject of the next sutra.

SUTRA 1:49

श्रुतानुमानप्रज्ञाभ्यामन्यविषया विशेषार्थत्वात्
॥४९॥

śrutānumānaprajñābhyāmanyaviṣayā viśeṣārthatvāt
॥ 49 ॥

śrutra-anumāna-prajñābhyām, intuitive wisdom from the knowledge gained from scriptures or the oral tradition and from logic and inference; *anya-viṣayā,* that which is totally different; *viśeṣārthatvāt,* due to having *viśeṣa,* "the unique," as its meaning

Because intuitive wisdom contains the meaning (or essence) of "the Unique," it has a different scope than the knowledge gained from scriptures and from inference.

This sutra tells us there are two kinds of knowledge: the knowledge that dawns in samadhi (*samadhi prajna*) and the knowledge we acquire when not in samadhi. They are quite different. As described in previous sutras, the knowledge we receive in samadhi is intuitive wisdom (*prajna*). In the light of prajna, reality is known in its fullness, with no distinction between subject and object. Prajna is suprasensory, whereas the knowledge we acquire when we are not in samadhi is incomplete, objective, and belongs to the realm of sensory experience. The major difference between these two forms of knowledge is that prajna is unique, and non-meditative knowledge is not. Prajna is unique in the sense that it is clear, precise, conclusive, and most significantly, illuminates all the particulars of the object. Non-meditative knowledge, on the other hand, includes only general information regarding the object and lacks clarity, precision, and conclusiveness.

Knowledge pertaining to the objective world is always general and subject to interpretation. We acquire it through our senses, which have their own limitations. The strength of the senses varies from species to species and from person to person. A rattlesnake can sense a temperature shift of one-thousandth of a degree, for example, but we cannot. Our perception of the world is molded by the qualities, characteristics, and properties of our senses. Within their limited scope, the senses present their experiences to the mind, which then interprets them. This interpretation is heavily influenced by our likes, dislikes, prejudices, and preoccupations. Furthermore, the senses and mind can perceive objects only if there is no obstruction. For example, we cannot see objects on the other side of a concrete wall. Also, we see only the surface of an object, not what lies beneath. Comprehension of size and shape is dependent on the health of the senses and the perceiving power of the mind. That is why objective knowledge compiled by the senses and mind is general, vague, and inconclusive. Intuitive wisdom is focused, precise, and conclusive.

The knowledge contained in the scriptures is also general, vague, and inconclusive. For example, "God lives in heaven" is a piece of indistinct, inconclusive, general information. This statement is found in reputable scriptures and makes sense linguistically, but it adds nothing to our comprehension of God, what is meant by "God lives," or what exactly heaven is. Furthermore, such statements are contradicted by equally reputable scriptures, and sometimes even by statements in the same scripture. We are instructed to believe in our scriptures and in the truth documented in them. To validate our beliefs, we gather more references and more proof, evidence in itself that our belief is unfounded and laced with doubt. Scriptural knowledge is general and inconclusive. It has little influence on our enlightenment and does not help the mind stop roaming and free itself from its samskaras. Intuitive wisdom, by contrast, is precise, conclusive, self-luminous, and purifying.

Inference, which is based on reason and logic, has its own limitations. If the ground for the inference is valid and the process of reasoning correct, then inference can help us reach an accurate conclusion, but one still devoid of specifics. Because we have seen a concomitant relationship between smoke and fire, for example, when we see smoke we infer the existence of fire. Our repeated experience is the ground for this inference. But inference does not tell us the fire's exact location—it only points us in the direction of the smoke. Further, seeing only the smoke will not tell us for certain whether what is burning is brush, a pile of wood, or a house. We cannot know whether the smoke is from an accident or from a sacred ceremony. In other words, inferential knowledge of fire neither contains nor conveys specifics, whereas intuitive wisdom includes all the specifics of fire.

Because they are subject to the conditioning of time, space, and the law of cause and effect, sensory perceptions, scriptural information, and inference fail to contain or convey the specifics of an object. We cannot perceive an object that is too far away, too close, too big, or too small. We cannot perceive the entire Himalayan range in one glance because it is too big. We cannot see an atom because it is too small. We cannot see a tree in a seed because we are able to see either cause (the seed) or effect (the tree), not both at once.

Objective knowledge gained through perception, inference, and scriptural sources flows linearly, as does the power of comprehension contained in our senses and mind. In other words, our comprehension is characterized by the phenomenon of linearity. We perceive the objective world one aspect at a time. Objective comprehension is invariably associated with time, space, and number. Each objective experience is stored in our mind along with its associated time, space, and number. When any of these three factors fade or vanish, we fail to recollect the experience. Confusion of time, space, and number blurs our recollection. That is why the knowledge gained from perception, inference, and scriptural sources is general, vague, and inconclusive, as is our recollection of it.

Prajna is utterly different for it is non-linear (*akrama*) and beyond the phenomena of time, space, and the law of cause and effect. In the light of intuitive wisdom, we have an integrated vision of the entire object. We see all its aspects and components. For example, in the light of intuitive wisdom we know how many individuals there are in a large crowd without counting them. We know all the cells of our body without separating one from another. This particular quality of prajna sets it apart from all other forms of knowledge. This is the distinctive meaning (*vishesha artha*) of prajna, a subject Patanjali elaborates on in sutra 3:25.

Prajna is also unique (*vishesha*) because it has the unique Purusha—Consciousness—at its core (YS 4:25). Prajna is the light of Consciousness itself. It is the Power of Consciousness (*Chiti Shakti*). The Power of Consciousness and Pure Consciousness are one and the same. To be established in the Power of Consciousness is to be established in Pure Consciousness (YS 4:34). It is both the ultimate source and the means of illumination and purification.

In the outer frontier of mental absorption, the mind is completely illumined and purified by this light. In this state, we are fully cognizant of our mind (*buddhi samvit*), yet the mind is not an object of our cognition. We, as the perceiver, are not separate from our mind. Due to the high degree of absorption, the light reflecting from the mind is as pure, illuminating, and revealing as the light of Pure Consciousness itself. The mind has reached the highest degree of purity (*buddhi sattva*). At this level of purity and illumination, the mind does not retain a distinguishable identity (YS 4:25). Its self-identity (*asmita*) has taken the form of Pure Consciousness (*Purusha*) (YS 3:55).

Experientially, the essence of the mind (*buddhi sattva*) is established in Pure Consciousness. This perfectly purified and enlightened mind is no longer associated with its samskaras, which once fueled the mind's roaming tendencies, for they have vanished. We are free from the mind's binding forces. This level of enlightenment helps us rise above the entire domain of mind; thus, Patanjali calls it *taraka*, "that which enables us to swim to the other shore; that which makes us free; the deliverer" (YS 3:54). Everything pertaining to our inner and outer worlds is an object of this wisdom (*sarva-vishayam*), yet this wisdom is not itself the object of anything (*sarvatha-avishayam*). Everything and everyone is within the fold of its comprehension, yet it is itself beyond comprehension. Experience gained intuitively is non-linear.

From the spiritual standpoint, however, the uniqueness of prajna lies in the fact that it transports us from the furthest frontier of lower samadhi to the highest samadhi. How prajna leads us to higher samadhi is the subject of the next sutra.

SUTRA 1:50

तज्जः संस्कारोऽन्यसंस्कारप्रतिबन्धी ॥५०॥

tajjaḥ saṁskāro'nyasaṁskārapratibandhī ॥ 50 ॥

tat-jaḥ, born of that; *saṁskāraḥ,* subtle karmic impression; *anya-saṁskāra-pratibandhī,* that which blocks or cancels other samskaras

Samskaras born of intuitive wisdom cancel all other samskaras.

When we become firmly established in intuitive wisdom (*prajna*), the quality of our meditation changes. We find great joy in it. The memory pertaining to the experience of joy yokes us to meditation. Our meditation is no longer goal-driven but an integral part of life, like breathing. Meditation for its own sake engenders a distinctive samskara—one with the innate power to neutralize all other samskaras. To understand why, it is helpful to examine the unique quality of this level of meditation.

At this stage, the mind is illumined by the unalloyed light of Pure Consciousness (*jyotishmati*) and is established in the state of sorrowless joy (*vishoka*). It is clear, perceptive, and at peace. We are experiencing our Pure Being, and the mind coalesces around this experience. This experience is non-sequential. The mind is like a waveless ocean—the experience arising from it and subsiding in it comes into view seamlessly. In this state, the mind is peacefully and inwardly active. The scriptures describe it as the action of an inactive mind. The samskaras created by these meditative actions are totally different from those engendered by actions undertaken in the normal course of life.

Meditative samskaras are illumined by the luminosity of prajna (*jyotishmati*) and accompanied by vishoka. They are imbued with clarity, purity, and peace. The experience of Pure Being lies at their core. They contain no trace of time, space, sequence, or the law of cause and effect. They are not stained by ignorance, distorted self-identity, attachment, aversion, or fear. Further, these meditative samskaras are laced with the power to counter contrary samskaras. As our meditation deepens, prajna brightens. The brighter our intuitive wisdom, the deeper we are led into meditation. This self-sustaining cycle creates a new and unique world of samskaras (*navo navah samskarashaya*). Eventually, this newly created realm becomes our true abode. Living in the security and comfort of this unique realm we perform our actions and discharge our duties. The more established we are in this realm, the more successfully and wisely we are able to live in the world, which is predominantly run by fear, greed, and false expectations.

Wisdom-driven meditative samskaras bring a qualitative change in our worldview and philosophy of life. We perform our actions with no thought of reward or punishment, propelled by the intrinsic virtue of our heart. In thought, speech, and action, we are constantly aware of the higher reality that constitutes our core being. Our actions are not motivated by our personal desires, for there are none. While in meditation, we enjoy experiencing our Pure Being, and when not in meditation, we maintain a constant awareness of it.

The meditative samskaras engendered by this awareness dissolve when they have consumed all other samskaras. We are then led to the highest state of samadhi, known as *nirbija samadhi.* That is the subject of the next sutra.

SUTRA 1:51

तस्यापि निरोधे सर्वनिरोधान्निर्बीजः समाधिः ॥५१॥

tasyāpi nirodhe sarvanirodhānnirbījaḥ samādhiḥ ॥ 51 ॥

tasya-api, of even that; *nirodhe,* upon restraint, control; *sarva-nirodhāt,* due to the cancellation of everything; *nirbījaḥ,* without seed; *samādhiḥ,* completely still, pristine state of mind

Upon cancellation of even that, everything else is cancelled. This is *nirbija samadhi.*

As we have seen in the preceding sutra, the light of intuitive wisdom lifts the veil of ignorance. Our identification with worldly objects and accomplishments disappears. We do not grieve over the past or worry about the future, but live fearlessly and confidently in the present. The mind is luminous and joyful. We meditate seated in the midst of joy and luminosity. The mind spontaneously radiates joyful and luminous energy, which destroys all dark and painful tendencies. We see that the world is beautiful and life is a gift. We are filled with a sense of gratitude for what we have and enthusiasm to achieve what we need for true fulfillment and ultimate freedom.

This transformation creates an internal environment that has no room for obstacles to our spiritual quest. Eventually our dark and painful tendencies (*klishta vritti*) are destroyed, along with their subtle causes. The mind regains its pristine nature.

Metaphorically, it stands still next to Pure Consciousness (*Purusha*). In this state, the mind is naturally motivated to flow inward toward the center of Consciousness; it flows outward only when propelled by Divine Will. When it interacts with the objective world, it is untouched by what it touches. Actions performed by this kind of mind do not engender samskaras. What is more, the mind is now free from even meditative samskaras.

Samskaras are like seeds germinating in the mind. They cause the mind to think, imagine, desire, and crave. Spiritually oriented samskaras neutralize our worldly samskaras and thereby induce a significant degree of freedom. From a higher perspective, however, they are a source of a subtle but potent form of spiritual bondage. Freedom from the spiritually oriented samskaras engendered by meditation itself comes from vairagya—cultivating a mind free from the coloring of potent samskaras (*vasanas*). As Vyasa explains in his commentary on sutra 1:40, the practice of process-driven meditation (*dhyana-abhyasa*) can purify the mind and lead it all the way to the outer frontier of lower samadhi. Thereafter, the journey is dependent on the highest level of vairagya (*para vairagya*) (YS 1:16). This level of vairagya prepares the ground for the grace of the Supreme Being (*Ishvara*) to lift our consciousness to a realm unreachable through self-effort. Self-effort by definition means we are cognizant of our action (in this case, meditation). Meditation accompanied by self-effort creates samskaras, and samskaras bind us to lower samadhi. When we trustfully surrender to the guiding light of prajna, which is the light of higher Divinity itself, we are spontaneously transported to seedless (*nirbija*) samadhi. This is the highest goal of Yoga.

The difference between seedless samadhi and prajna is extremely subtle. The field of prajna lies between the furthest frontier of lower samadhi and seedless samadhi. This field is not static but vibrant, continually assuming an ever-more-radiant form (*nava-navonmeshashalini*). As our meditation deepens, our memory becomes more refined, pure, and transparent. This purity and transparency reveal the inner joy buried deep within us. As we have seen, joy (*vishoka*) and inner luminosity (*jyotishmati*) go hand in hand. With practice, vishoka and jyotishmati expand all the way to the realm beyond time, space, and the law of cause and effect. Scriptures call this expanded field of vishoka and jyotishmati the field of intuition. At the dawn of this lofty level of prajna, the veil of samskaras no longer hides the *sattvic* qualities of the mind. The samskaras that once agitated it from inside are gone, and the mind is as transparent as a flawless crystal.

In this state of wisdom, both the dark and heavy qualities (*tamas*) and the qualities that agitate the mind (*rajas*) are nullified. The entire mind is dominated by illuminating qualities (*sattva*). In this state of buddhi sattva, the mind is so pure and well illumined that it sees itself as well as the light illuminating it. At this stage, a twofold realization dawns: the mind has been falsely identifying itself with its samskaras, and it has been denying its primordial association with Purusha. This realization empowers the mind to simultaneously disassociate itself from its samskaras and close the gap between itself and Pure Consciousness. The mind is infused with the highest degree of the power of discernment (*prakhya shilam*). It is laden with true knowledge.

The absolute disassociation from all samskaras enables the mind to see Pure Consciousness without distortion. In the truest sense, however, this is not a direct realization. Rather it consists of the cognition of the light of Pure Consciousness reflecting on the mind—the mind is cognizant of itself as an agent of cognition. And yet, the mind is so pure and transparent that it experiences itself as if it is the light of Pure Consciousness.

In this experience, the mind and Pure Consciousness are so well blended that there is no awareness of a differentiation between them. The mind appears to be Pure Consciousness and Pure Consciousness appears to be the mind (*chetana-achetana-svarupa-apannam*). Even though the mind is an object of cognition, it no longer appears to be an object (*vishayatmakam api avishayatmakam iva*). In this state of prajna, the wall between duality and non-duality and between subject and object has disappeared. But the mind has not yet dissolved into its primordial causal domain—Prakriti. It still exists as a cognizant entity. The experience of joy arising from this realization is still mediated by the mind—it is still the mind's personal, private experience. As soon as we rise above this level of experience, we land in the domain of seedless (*nirbija*) samadhi.

Nirbija samadhi is neither a part nor a function of mental cognition. It is a realization of Consciousness by Consciousness itself. Nirbija samadhi is not an experience of a process but the experience of Pure Being. It is the Seeing Power of Consciousness experiencing itself as the Seer. Just before reaching nirbija samadhi, the mind was able to experience Consciousness reflecting in it. It was able to see Purusha as neither completely similar to itself nor completely dissimilar from itself (Vyasa on sutra 2:20). Vyasa calls this experience *jnana vritti,* mental cognition with knowledge of Purusha as an object. It is a supremely refined mental cognition, but it is still cognition. We enter nirbija samadhi only when we go beyond this level of cognition.

Understanding how to go beyond this supremely refined state of prajna and enter nirbija samadhi requires an experiential analysis of this field. We have to discover how mental absorption in the supremely refined cognition (*jnana vritti samapatti*) evolves into absorption in Pure Consciousness (*purusha samapatti*).

Elaborating on the concept of prajna, Patanjali and Vyasa introduce two terms: *madhumati bhumi* and *dharma megha samadhi.* From the standpoint of Yoga sadhana, these terms are highly significant. Both describe the experiential nature of the intuitive field that lies between the outer frontier of lower samadhi and nirbija samadhi.

Madhumati means "consisting of (*mati*) honey (*madhu*)" and *bhumi* means "ground or state." Thus, *madhumati bhumi* is the state of samadhi filled with a unique sweetness. The theory and practice describing how to reach this state is known as *madhu vidya,* the science of honey. According to the Sri Vidya tradition of the sages, sutra 1:36 embodies this science, which is elaborated on in a wealth of Tantric, Vedic, and Puranic texts. The masters in our tradition consider madhu vidya the essence of the *Yoga Sutra,* in general, and of "Samadhi Pada," in particular. The *Yoga Sutra* of Patanjali, the *Kalpa Sutra* of Parashurama, and the *Saundaryalahari* of Shankaracharya are considered the primary texts on this subject.

Until we taste the sweetness of sorrowless joy and receive guidance and protection from our innate luminosity, the mind chases one object after another. The practices described in sutras 1:33 through 1:36 enable us to taste our intrinsic vishoka. The longer we stay with this experience, the more refined our meditation becomes. Eventually, the vast field of prajna rises on the horizon of our consciousness. At the peak of this experience, we become absorbed in its intrinsic sweetness, *madhumati bhumi* (YS 3:51). In his commentary, Vyasa describes the range of this experience in four stages: *prathama-kalpika, madhubhumika, prajna-jyoti,* and *atikranta-bhavaniya.*

In the first stage of madhumati bhumi, we glimpse our inner luminosity, which is invariably accompanied by sorrowless joy. As it attempts to follow the stream of vishoka and jyotishmati, the mind begins to flow peacefully inward. The desire to taste this newborn joy and bask in inner luminosity is so strong that the mind no longer has any interest in paying attention to its disturbing and distracting thoughts and other habitual tendencies, and so this peaceful inward journey is effortless.

With practice, the mingled stream of jyotishmati and vishoka intensifies, enabling us to experience the next level of sweetness. At this second stage, luminous awareness expands and joy deepens. The mind becomes infused with the true nature of the objects in view. We comprehend our strengths and weaknesses. We know the subtle causes of the roaming tendencies of our mind and are happy we know them. We know the power of jyotishmati and are confident that under its guidance and protection we will eventually eliminate the samskaras that cause our mind to be disturbed, dense, dull, and distracted.

As we continue our practice, we reach the third stage. Here the experience of joy and inner luminosity is so intense that we can identify it vividly in the space surrounding our forehead. We can also transport this vivid experience to any part of our body. We can feel its presence in the deeper niches of our physical and energetic body—a feeling previously beyond the domain of our conscious awareness. Accompanied by vishoka and jyotishmati, we can move from our frontal lobe to the region of the hypothalamus and the limbic system, for example, and attain greater mastery over the parasympathetic nervous system. We can transport the experience of joy and luminosity from the ajna chakra to our heart center and discover the loving, kind, selfless, forgiving, and compassionate aspect of ourselves. This level of vishoka and jyotishmati enables us to conquer and crush all our inner enemies (*bhutendriyajayi*). Here, in this third stage of madhumati bhumi, we find ourselves fully protected from our past, present, and future karmas. We are confident that we have all the tools and means to find true fulfillment and ultimate freedom.

In the fourth and final stage, the mind is utterly absorbed in the sorrowless joy and inner light of the intuitive field. It is no longer seeing Pure Consciousness through a flawless lens; rather, Consciousness has pulled the mind into its fold. Experience as a process has come to an end. The Seeing Power of Consciousness alone is in the view of Consciousness. As scriptures belonging to the tantric tradition put it, the mind is transformed into Pure Consciousness. At this stage, nirbija samadhi dawns spontaneously.

Another term Patanjali and Vyasa use for the field of prajna is *dharma megha samadhi,* samadhi made of the cloud of virtues. As is clear from the previous discussion, in the transitional state between lower and higher samadhi, the mind is no longer smeared by subtle karmic impressions but is like a flawless crystal. It functions under the guidance, nurturance, and protection of Inner Divinity. At this stage in our spiritual evolution, Divine Will alone motivates our thought, speech, and action. We are grounded in, and surrounded by, inner peace. Meditation has become as effortless as breathing.

When we are not meditating, our thoughts, speech, and actions are still propelled by Divine Will, for it has taken charge of our destiny. Fear of failure and doubt about success have vanished. We perform our actions in compliance with Divine Will, not under compulsion from outside forces. Action and inaction bear equal weight, for we know they are shaped and implemented by Divine Will. We no longer identify ourselves as a doer. We know intuitively what we must acquire and what we must renounce, and act in the light of that insight. Neither our involvement in the world nor our renunciation of it creates the slightest karmic impression. All our worldly and spiritual endeavors are directed toward serving Divinity and the creation conceived by her.

Both our worldly activities and our spiritual practices create spiritually illuminating samskaras, which by their intrinsic virtue arrest and eventually eliminate all negative karmic impressions. These illuminating samskaras are described as the cloud of virtues (*dharma megha*). The joy and luminosity raining from it manifests in an experience known as *dharma megha samadhi*. In this state, only sattvic samskaras remain—the mind is flawlessly transparent.

The advent of dharma megha samadhi brings freedom from the fivefold affliction—ignorance, distorted self-identity, attachment, aversion, and fear of death—as well as from karmas and the impressions created by them (YS 4:30). With the dissolution of the samskaras, the mind operating under their sway also dissolves, replaced by a mind filled with the cloud of virtues. This newborn mind is not veiled in any way—its power of comprehension is unlimited. It is as expansive as Pure Consciousness (*Purusha*) itself. Its power of cognition is larger than any objects of its cognition (YS 4:31). This newborn mind no longer contacts the objects of its cognition, for they are already within its fold—it knows the objective world without making an effort to know it. Vyasa uses an analogy to describe the power and function of this extraordinary mind: "A blind man pierced the pearl, he without fingers threaded it, the neckless wore it, and the tongueless praised it."

The use of *dharma megha* to designate this transitional state is highly significant. This state is called *dharma megha* for, in layman's terms, it is filled with the cloud (*megha*) of virtue (*dharma*). This term conveys the idea that only the samskaras of our good karmas now remain. But *dharma megha* has another more compelling dimension. In this state, Prakriti unveils her limitless potentials (*dharma*) and her intrinsic divinity (*aishvarya*), and with this comes the realization that we are not—and have never been—alone. In this state, the thinnest of all the veils of ignorance is lifted. We begin to partake of the infinite knowledge (*jnana*) and vairagya of the Absolute Divine Being. Prakriti unveils her limitless secrets, including the complex structure of the human body and the intricacies of the mind. It was in this state, for example, that yogis learned the subtle anatomy of the human body without dissecting cadavers and discovered the subtle properties of herbs without analyzing their chemical components. They intuited subtle planes of existence far beyond the universe of matter and energy. Simply put, in dharma megha samadhi, the limitation imposed by darkness (*tamas*) is removed, allowing the light of knowledge (*jnana sattva*) to shine all the way to infinity. In this state, even the slightest movement of the force behind the process of manifestation (*rajas*) is enough to bring forward the vast wealth of nature incomprehensible to our senses and ordinary mind. This is how the sages received mantric revelation—they "saw" the extraordinary power of sounds and words.

We find our life's purpose in dharma megha samadhi. We are fulfilled. We are filled with deep gratitude for we have come to realize that the door to Mother Nature's infinite treasury has always been open. She gave us a pristine and perfectly illuminating mind to recognize this immense treasure. Now we no longer see our mind and its functions as a source of bondage, but recognize them as the greatest gift. And we no longer see the world as a source of bondage, either. The concept of attaining liberation from the cycle of birth and death becomes meaningless. At the peak of the experience of dharma megha samadhi, we spontaneously slip into seedless samadhi, for even the subtlest cause—the desire to live as an isolated being—has dissolved. At this stage, we perceive Prakriti as intelligent, vibrant, beautiful, and perennially engaged in providing everything we need for our true fulfillment (*bhoga*) and ultimate freedom (*apavarga*). She is the Divine Mother, Chiti

Shakti, the Power of Pure Consciousness (YS 4:34). In nirbija samadhi, we are immersed in the experience of being held in her immutable essential being (*svarupa-pratishtha*).

Monasticism has been a dominant force in many religions for millennia. It is particularly esteemed by those with roots in the East, the homeland of Yoga and the *Yoga Sutra*. In these religions, piety has become associated with refraining from pleasure derived from the senses, and the spiritual quest with renouncing worldly possessions. Worldly life is regarded as a source of sorrow. The soul is said to have an urgent need to extricate itself from this world, never to be born again. This religious conditioning has led some commentators and scholars writing on the *Yoga Sutra* to adopt the view that nirbija samadhi is the highest objective of Yoga because this state of samadhi pushes us out of this world once and for all. According to the sages of our tradition, however, this view is incorrect and highly misleading. In the state of seedless samadhi, we are as luminous, free, and fulfilled as the Divinity in which we are fully immersed.

In nirbija samadhi, we attain complete freedom from the binding forces of our ordinary mind. With the dissolution of our samskaras, when our ordinary mind is also dissolved, we acquire a pristine, extraordinary mind, unsmeared by even the slightest trace of I-am-ness. It is not a mind in the ordinary sense, but the creative light of Purusha—Pure Consciousness. This creative light becomes our locus. After reaching this state, there is no possibility of helplessly falling back into the worldly cycle. We become "unfalling" (*achyuta*), a term used for such high-caliber masters as Krishna and Parashurama. They have no desire to return to this world, but they have no aversion to it, either. The will of the Divine manifests in their pristine, extraordinary mind as desire (*kama*) and they see the world through the eyes of this desire.

Because this level of desire is self-luminous and ever-revealing (*deva*), it is known as Kamadeva. It is the Seeing Power of the Seer, our pure, pristine core being, our guru and guide. For this reason, Kamadeva is Vidyeshvara, the Lord of the wisdom of Sri Vidya, which is the core of sadhana in our tradition.

In sutra 3:26, Vyasa describes the extraordinary existence of these pure beings. He says that, having attained the highest yogic accomplishment, some continue to enjoy lower levels of samadhi. Their true abode is an extraordinary level of consciousness (*loka*). For example, *satya-loka* and *tushita-loka* are the abodes of Krishna and Buddha, respectively. These lofty planes of awareness are untouched by even the subtlest trace of want or need. Masters like Krishna and Buddha descend from these planes without losing sight of their pure essence, walk among us in the flesh, then return to their true abode. These masters are immortal; they live neither inside nor outside, neither below nor above, but rather at the center of the universe (*trailokya-madhye*) (Vyasa on sutra 3:26). Attaining this level of immortality and experiencing everlasting fulfillment and freedom is the ultimate goal of Yoga—a goal we are all equipped to achieve.

The Practice of the Yoga Sutra: Sadhana Pada

The Secret of the Yoga Sutra: Samadhi Pada is the first volume in a series of commentaries on the *Yoga Sutra*. Here, in *Samadhi Pada*, Patanjali and Vyasa have shown clearly that each of us is an island of excellence, that the goal of life is lasting fulfillment and ultimate freedom, and further, that we are all equipped to achieve this lofty goal. They have also shared time-tested techniques for experiencing the wonder that we are.

In the next volume, *The Practice of the Yoga Sutra: Sadhana Pada*, these two masters teach us how to apply these time-tested techniques in our daily life. The modern world is dominated by forces that are not particularly loving, kind, nurturing, or spiritually uplifting. We find ourselves living in a world run by fear and greed. We are not as physically, mentally, or spiritually vibrant as we wish to be, yet we long to experience our unbounded joy and freedom. Deep within, we know we have the power to achieve anything we wish, provided we commit ourselves to a sustained and methodical practice. *The Practice of the Yoga Sutra: Sadhana Pada* delineates the steps of a fruitful practice, telling us how to conquer our self-defeating tendencies and embrace the joy and freedom that is our birthright.

APPENDIXES

APPENDIX A

Devanagari, Transliteration, and Translation

SUTRA 1:1

अथ योगानुशासनम् ॥१॥

atha yogānuśāsanam ॥1॥

Now begins the instruction on the practice of Yoga.

SUTRA 1:2

योगश्चित्तवृत्तिनिरोधः ॥२॥

yogaścittavṛttinirodhaḥ ॥2॥

Complete mastery over the roaming tendencies of the mind is Yoga.

SUTRA 1:3

तदा द्रष्टुः स्वरूपेऽवस्थानम् ।।३।।

tadā draṣṭuḥ svarūpe'vasthānam ॥ 3 ॥

Then the Seer becomes established in its essential nature.

SUTRA 1:4

वृत्तिसारूप्यमितरत्र ।।४।।

vṛttisārūpyamitaratra ॥ 4 ॥

Elsewhere [the Seer] conforms to the roaming tendencies of the mind.

SUTRA 1:5

वृत्तयः पञ्चतय्यः क्लिष्टाक्लिष्टाः ।।५।।

vṛttayaḥ pañcatayyaḥ kliṣṭākliṣṭāḥ ॥ 5 ॥

The tendencies that cause the mind to rotate are fivefold. They are either afflicting or non-afflicting.

SUTRA 1:6

प्रमाणविपर्ययविकल्पनिद्रास्मृतयः ।।६।।

pramāṇaviparyayavikalpanidrāsmṛtayaḥ ॥ 6 ॥

The five mental functions are correct understanding, false understanding, imagination, dreamless sleep, and memory.

SUTRA 1:7

प्रत्यक्षानुमानागमाः प्रमाणानि ॥७॥

pratyakṣānumānāgamāḥ pramāṇāni ॥ 7 ॥

Correct understanding is threefold: sense perception, inference, and revelation documented in the scriptures.

SUTRA 1:8

विपर्ययो मिथ्याज्ञानमतद्रूपप्रतिष्ठम् ॥८॥

viparyayo mithyājñānamatadrūpapratiṣṭham ॥ 8 ॥

Mistaking the unreal for the real is false understanding. False understanding is not grounded in reality; instead it corresponds to that which has no ground.

SUTRA 1:9

शब्दज्ञानानुपाती वस्तुशून्यो विकल्पः ॥९॥

śabdajñānānupātī vastuśūnyo vikalpaḥ ॥ 9 ॥

Imagination is knowledge, which due to the use of words appears to have content but in reality is devoid of content.

SUTRA 1:10

अभावप्रत्ययालम्बना वृत्तिर्निद्रा ॥१०॥

abhāvapratyayālambanā vṛttirnidrā ॥ 10 ॥

Swirling of the mind around the cognition of non-being is dreamless sleep.

SUTRA 1:11

अनुभूतविषयासम्प्रमोषः स्मृतिः ।।११।।

anubhūtaviṣayāsampramoṣaḥ smṛtiḥ ॥ 11 ॥

Not being completely disconnected from the objects of previous experiences is memory.

SUTRA 1:12

अभ्यासवैराग्याभ्यां तन्निरोधः ।।१२।।

abhyāsavairāgyābhyāṁ tannirodhaḥ ॥ 12 ॥

That can be controlled through practice and non-attachment.

SUTRA 1:13

तत्र स्थितौ यत्नोऽभ्यासः ।।१३।।

tatra sthitau yatno'bhyāsaḥ ॥ 13 ॥

Ardent effort to retain the peaceful flow of mind free of roaming tendencies is *abhyasa*.

SUTRA 1:14

स तु दीर्घकालनैरन्तर्यसत्कारासेवितो दृढभूमिः ।।१४।।

sa tu dīrghakālanairantaryasatkārāsevito dṛḍhabhūmiḥ ॥ 14 ॥

That becomes firm only when done for a long period of time, with no interruption, and with reverence.

SUTRA 1:15

दृष्टानुश्रविकविषयवितृष्णस्य वशीकारसंज्ञा वैराग्यम्
॥१५॥

dṛṣṭānuśravikaviṣayavitṛṣṇasya vaśīkārasaṁjñā vairāgyam
॥ 15 ॥

Non-attachment, known as *vashikara samjna*, belongs to the one who is free from the craving for sense objects and objects mentioned in the scriptures.

SUTRA 1:16

तत्परं पुरुषख्यातेर्गुणवैतृष्ण्यम् ॥ १६॥

tatparaṁ puruṣakhyātergunavaitṛṣṇyam ॥ 16 ॥

The highest level of non-attachment, leading to self-realization, takes place when the aspirant is free from all forms of desire, including the desires resulting from the interplay of *sattvic, rajasic,* and *tamasic* forces of nature.

SUTRA 1:17

वितर्कविचारानन्दास्मितारूपानुगमात् सम्प्रज्ञातः
॥१७॥

vitarkavicārānandāsmitārūpānugamāt samprajñātaḥ ॥ 17 ॥

***Samprajnata samadhi* is accompanied either by a gross object, a subtle object, joy, or the feeling of I-am-ness.**

SUTRA 1:18

विरामप्रत्ययाभ्यासपूर्वः संस्कारशेषोऽन्यः ॥१८॥

virāmapratyayābhyāsapūrvaḥ saṁskāraśeṣo'nyaḥ ॥ 18 ॥

The other [higher samadhi] is preceded by *abhyasa*, which brought all cognitions to a complete halt. What remains is the *samskara* [of abhyasa itself].

SUTRA 1:19

भवप्रत्ययो विदेहप्रकृतिलयानाम् ॥१९॥

bhavapratyayo videhaprakṛtilayānām ॥ 19 ॥

The experience of the higher level of samadhi is innate to [extraordinary yogis technically known as] *videha* and *prakritilaya*.

SUTRA 1:20

श्रद्धावीर्यस्मृतिसमाधिप्रज्ञापूर्वक इतरेषाम् ॥२०॥

śraddhāvīryasmṛtisamādhiprajñāpūrvaka itareṣām ॥ 20 ॥

In the case of others, it [samadhi] is preceded by faith, vigor, retentive power, stillness of mind, and intuitive wisdom.

SUTRA 1:21

तीव्रसंवेगानामासन्नः ॥२१॥

tīvrasaṁvegānāmāsannaḥ ॥ 21 ॥

Samadhi is near for those whose aspiration is steadfast.

SUTRA 1:22

मृदुमध्याधिमात्रत्वात् ततोऽपि विशेषः ॥२२॥

mṛdumadhyādhimātratvāt tato'pi viśeṣaḥ ॥ 22 ॥

Depending on whether the seeker's steadfast aspiration is mild, intermediate, or supreme, there are further distinctions.

SUTRA 1:23

ईश्वरप्रणिधानाद्वा ॥२३॥

īśvarapraṇidhānādvā ॥ 23 ॥

From trustful surrender to Ishvara [God], samadhi also comes.

SUTRA 1:24

क्लेशकर्मविपाकाशयैरपरामृष्टः पुरुषविशेष ईश्वरः ॥२४॥

kleśakarmavipākāśayairaparāmṛṣṭaḥ puruṣaviśeṣa īśvaraḥ ॥ 24 ॥

Ishvara [God] is a unique being untouched by afflictions, karmas, the results of karmas, and the repository of karmas.

SUTRA 1:25

तत्र निरतिशयं सर्वज्ञबीजम् ॥२५॥

tatra niratiśayaṁ sarvajñabījam ॥ 25 ॥

Therein [in Ishvara] lies the seed of unsurpassed omniscience.

SUTRA 1:26

स एष पूर्वेषामपि गुरुः कालेनानवच्छेदात् ॥२६॥

sa eṣa pūrveṣāmapi guruḥ kālenānavacchedāt ॥ 26 ॥

He is the one who has been the preceptor of all previous teachers for He is not limited by time.

SUTRA 1:27

तस्य वाचकः प्रणवः ॥२७॥

tasya vācakaḥ praṇavaḥ ॥ 27 ॥

***Pranava* [om] is the denoter of That [Ishvara].**

SUTRA 1:28

तज्जपस्तदर्थभावनम् ।।२८।।

tajjapastadarthabhāvanam ॥ 28 ॥

Repetition of That [pranava] means to reflect on its meaning.

SUTRA 1:29

ततः प्रत्यक्चेतनाधिगमोऽप्यन्तरायाभावश्च ।।२९।।

tataḥ pratyakcetanādhigamo'pyantarāyābhāvaśca ॥ 29 ॥

From that comes the experience of Inner Being as well as the elimination of impediments.

SUTRA 1:30

व्याधिस्त्यानसंशयप्रमादालस्याविरतिभ्रान्तिदर्शनालब्ध-
भूमिकत्वानवस्थितत्वानि चित्तविक्षेपास्तेऽन्तरायाः
।।३०।।

vyādhistyānasaṁśayapramādālasyāvirati-bhrāntidarśana-
alabdhabhūmikatvānavasthitatvāni cittavikṣepāste'ntarāyḥ
॥ 30 ॥

Disease, mental inertia, doubt, carelessness, sloth, inability to withdraw from sense cravings, clinging to misunderstanding, inability to reach the goal [samadhi], and inability to retain it throw our mind outward; they are obstacles.

SUTRA 1:31

दुःखदौर्मनस्याङ्गमेजयत्वश्वासप्रश्वासा
विक्षेपसहभुवः।।३१।।

duḥkhadaurmanasyāṅgamejayatvaśvāsapraśvāsā
vikṣepasahabhuvaḥ ॥ 31 ॥

Pain, mental agitation, unsteadiness or trembling of limbs, [abnormal or disturbed] inhalation and exhalation all arise with the obstacles.

SUTRA 1:32

तत्प्रतिषेधार्थमेकतत्त्वाभ्यासः ।।३२।।

tatpratiṣedhārthamekatattvābhyāsaḥ ॥ 32 ॥

Meditation on one single reality is the way to overcome these obstacles.

SUTRA 1:33

मैत्रीकरुणामुदितोपेक्षाणां सुखदुःखपुण्यापुण्यविषयाणां
भावनातश्चित्तप्रसादनम् ।।३३।।

maitrīkaruṇāmuditopekṣāṇāṁ sukhaduḥkhapuṇyāpuṇya-
viṣayāṇāṁ bhāvanātaścittaprasādanam ॥ 33 ॥

Transparency of mind comes by embracing an attitude of friendliness, compassion, happiness, and non-judgment toward those who are happy, miserable, virtuous, and non-virtuous.

SUTRA 1:34

प्रच्छर्दनविधारणाभ्यां वा प्राणस्य ॥३४॥

pracchardanavidhāraṇābhyāṁ vā prāṇasya ‖ 34 ‖

Transparency of mind also comes by practicing pranayama that involves forceful exhalation and breath retention.

SUTRA 1:35

विषयवती वा प्रवृत्तिरुत्पन्ना मनसः स्थितिनिबन्धिनी ॥३५॥

viṣayavatī vā pravṛttirutpannā manasaḥ sthitinibandhinī ‖ 35 ‖

A unique cognition pertaining to a sense object arising from within also anchors the mind to *sthiti*, the peaceful flow free from all thought constructs.

SUTRA 1:36

विशोका वा ज्योतिष्मती ॥३६॥

viśokā vā jyotiṣmatī ‖ 36 ‖

The state of consciousness free from sorrow and anguish and infused with inner light also anchors the mind to *sthiti*, the peaceful flow free from all thought constructs.

SUTRA 1:37

वीतरागविषयं वा चित्तम् ॥३७॥

vītarāgaviṣayaṁ vā cittam ॥ 37 ॥

Or the ability to retain the peaceful flow of mind comes by focusing on someone who is free from all desire.

SUTRA 1:38

स्वप्ननिद्राज्ञानालम्बनं वा ॥३८॥

svapnanidrājñānālambanaṁ vā ॥ 38 ॥

Or by meditating on the knowledge gained from dreams and sleep, one acquires stability of mind.

SUTRA 1:39

यथाभिमतध्यानाद्वा ॥३९॥

yathābhimatadhyānādvā ॥ 39 ॥

Or by meditating on a well-considered object of one's choice, one attains steadiness of mind.

SUTRA 1:40

परमाणु परममहत्त्वान्तोऽस्य वशीकारः ॥४०॥

paramāṇu paramamahattvānto'sya vaśīkāraḥ ॥ 40 ॥

A yogi's mastery stretches from the smallest particle to the biggest object.

SUTRA 1:41

क्षीणवृत्तेरभिजातस्येव मणेर्ग्रहीतृग्रहणग्राह्येषु
तत्स्थतदञ्जनता समापत्तिः ॥४१॥

kṣīṇavṛtterabhijātasyeva maṇergrahītṛgrahaṇagrāhyeṣu
tatsthatadañjanatā samāpattiḥ ॥ 41 ॥

A mind free from its roaming tendencies is like a crystal. It takes the form of whatever object is in its proximity, whether the object is the perceiver, the process of perceiving, or the object of perception. This is *samapatti*, complete absorption.

SUTRA 1:42

तत्र शब्दार्थज्ञानविकल्पैः संकीर्णा सवितर्का समापत्तिः
॥४२॥

tatra śabdārthajñānavikalpaiḥ saṁkīrṇā savitarkā samāpattiḥ
॥ 42 ॥

Meditation that has an object mingled with the distinct awareness of a word, the meaning of the word, and the awareness of focusing on the word and its meaning leads to a form of absorption known as *savitarka*.

SUTRA 1:43

स्मृतिपरिशुद्धौ स्वरूपशून्येवार्थमात्रनिर्भासा निर्वितर्का ।।४३।।

smṛtipariśuddhau svarūpaśūnyevārthamātranirbhāsā nirvitarkā ॥ 43 ॥

Upon the refinement of memory, there arises mental absorption named *nirvitarka samapatti*, in which the object of meditation seems devoid of its own form and is expressive only of its meaning.

SUTRA 1:44

एतयैव सविचारा निर्विचारा च सूक्ष्मविषया व्याख्याता ।।४४।।

etayaiva savicārā nirvicārā ca sūkṣmaviṣayā vyākhyātā ॥ 44 ॥

Accordingly, the *savichara* and *nirvichara* levels of mental absorption, which have extremely subtle objects as their focus, are explained.

SUTRA 1:45

सूक्ष्मविषयत्वं चालिङ्गपर्यवसानम् ।।४५।।

sūkṣmaviṣayatvaṁ cāliṅgaparyavasānam ॥ 45 ॥

That which ultimately dissolves into irreferable Prakriti is the subtlest of all objects.

SUTRA 1:46

ता एव सबीजः समाधिः ॥४६॥

tā eva sabījaḥ samādhiḥ ॥ 46 ॥

Those are indeed samadhi with seed.

SUTRA 1:47

निर्विचारवैशारद्येऽध्यात्मप्रसादः ॥४७॥

nirvicāravaiśāradye'dhyātmaprasādaḥ ॥ 47 ॥

Spiritual transparency and joy come from the continued purification of *nirvichara samapatti.*

SUTRA 1:48

ऋतम्भरा तत्र प्रज्ञा ॥४८॥

ṛtambharā tatra prajñā ॥ 48 ॥

There that self-luminous field of Consciousness is laden with truth.

SUTRA 1:49

श्रुतानुमानप्रज्ञाभ्यामन्यविषया विशेषार्थत्वात् ॥४९॥

śrutānumānaprajñābhyāmanyaviṣayā viśeṣārthatvāt ॥ 49 ॥

Because intuitive wisdom contains the meaning (or essence) of "the Unique," it has a different scope than the knowledge gained from scriptures and from inference.

SUTRA 1:50

तज्जः संस्कारोऽन्यसंस्कारप्रतिबन्धी ॥५०॥

tajjaḥ saṁskāro'nyasaṁskārapratibandhī ॥ 50 ॥

Samskaras born of intuitive wisdom cancel all other samskaras.

SUTRA 1:51

तस्यापि निरोधे सर्वनिरोधान्निर्बीजः समाधिः ॥५१॥

tasyāpi nirodhe sarvanirodhānnirbījaḥ samādhiḥ ॥ 51 ॥

Upon cancellation of even that, everything else is cancelled. This is *nirbija samadhi*.

APPENDIX B

Detailed Translation (Word by Word)

SUTRA 1:1

अथ योगानुशासनम् ॥१॥

atha yoga-anuśāsanam ॥ 1 ॥

Now begins the instruction on the practice of Yoga.

atha	a term indicating auspicious beginning; it implies there is a right time to undertake a practice, and that time is now. In the Sri Vidya tradition, *atha* is a shortened form of अ (*a*), क (*ka*), and थ (*tha*), the three letters that constitute the guru chakra, also known as *trikuti* and *bhrikuti*. Due to its association with the guru chakra, *atha* is representative of the inner eye, the primordial pool of intuitive wisdom.

yoga-	derived from the verb *yuj*, to unite; thus, *yoga* literally means "union." In different contexts, *yoga* refers to the union of the individual soul with the universal being, the union of *puruṣa* with *prakṛti*, the union of prana and mind, etc. In the *Yoga Sutra*, *yoga* means arresting the roaming tendency of the mind, making it one-pointed and inward, thus gaining total stillness of mind. In this state, consciousness has the opportunity to recognize and become established in its pure, pristine, intrinsic nature. According to Vyasa, *yoga* is *samādhi*.
anu-śāsanam	*nom. sg. n.* instruction; discipline; conforming to established techniques *anu*, that follows; that which is accompanied by; along with; in accordance to; in conformity with; *śāsanam*, discipline; administering; execution; bringing into practice; conforming to an established set of techniques

SUTRA 1:2

योगश्चित्तवृत्तिनिरोधः ॥२॥

yogaḥ citta-vṛtti-nirodhaḥ ॥ 2 ॥

Complete mastery over the roaming tendencies of the mind is Yoga.

yogaḥ	*nom. sg. m.* union, balance; harmonious state of mind. Experientially, *yoga* means arresting the roaming tendencies of the mind, thus enabling the mind to reclaim its innate luminosity, a

condition crucial for letting our consciousness become established in its essential nature.

citta- derived from the verb *citi,* to experience, to feel, to comprehend. Thus, *citta* means the faculty of comprehension, thinking, identification, and discernment. *Citta* is a generic term for all aspects of the mind.

vṛtti- literally, "spinning; revolving." In the context of yoga, *vritti* refers to the roaming tendencies of the mind; thought constructs.

ni-rodhaḥ *nom. sg. m.* confinement; complete control; restraint

ni, completely; in every respect; from every direction; *rodha,* confining; restraining; disciplining; not allowing to roam aimlessly

SUTRA 1:3

तदा द्रष्टुः स्वरूपेऽवस्थानम् ।।३।।

tadā draṣṭuḥ svarūpe avasthānam ॥ 3 ॥

Then the Seer becomes established in its essential nature.

tadā then; only after

draṣṭuḥ *gen. sg. m.* of *draṣṭṛ*; seer; perceiver; pure witness; pure consciousness; pure intelligence; the divine being; the transcendental reality; *puruṣa*; soul

sva-rūpe *loc. sg. n.* one's own form

sva, one's own; essential; intrinsic; natural; *rūpa,* form; state

avasthānam	*nom. sg. m.* establishment; residence; resting ground

SUTRA 1:4

वृत्तिसारूप्यमितरत्र ॥४॥

vṛtti-sārūpyam itaratra ॥ 4 ॥

Elsewhere [the Seer] conforms to the roaming tendencies of the mind.

vṛtti-	literally, "spinning; revolving." In the context of yoga, it refers to the roaming tendencies of the mind; thought constructs.
sārūpyam	*nom. sg. n.* the essence of *sarūpa,* with form; accompanied by an identifiable characteristic *sa,* with; *rūpa,* form
itaratra	elsewhere; everywhere other than in *samādhi;* anytime the mind is not still

SUTRA 1:5

वृत्तयः पञ्चतय्यः क्लिष्टाक्लिष्टाः ॥५॥

vṛttayaḥ pañcatayyaḥ kliṣṭa-akliṣṭāḥ ॥ 5 ॥

The tendencies that cause the mind to rotate are fivefold. They are either afflicting or non-afflicting.

vṛttayaḥ	*nom. pl. m.* of *vṛtti,* spinning; rotating; behaviors; functions; workings of the mind; thought constructs; mental modifications
pañcatayyaḥ	*nom. pl. m.* fivefold; five categories; group of five

kliṣṭa-akliṣṭāḥ *nom. pl. m.* afflicted and not afflicted; derived from *kliśa,* to afflict

kliṣṭa, that which causes afflictions; that which has its source in *avidyā,* ignorance, and inherently contains *avidyā*; or that which is caused by afflictions; harmful; painful; *akliṣṭa,* that which is minimally afflicting; not painful

SUTRA 1:6

प्रमाणविपर्ययविकल्पनिद्रास्मृतयः ॥६॥

pramāṇa-viparyaya-vikalpa-nidrā-smṛtayaḥ ॥ 6 ॥

The five mental functions are correct understanding, false understanding, imagination, dreamless sleep, and memory.

pra-māṇa- thought constructs that can be logically supported by sensory, inferential, or scriptural evidence; that which is taken as valid knowledge

pra, precisely, specifically; *māṇa,* that which can be validated; that which can be supported by evidence

viparyaya- thought constructs containing information or knowledge that is false; contrary to valid knowledge

vikalpa- imaginary; fiction; that which can be communicated through words but in reality is devoid of substance

nidrā- dreamless sleep

smṛtayaḥ *nom. pl. m.* of *smṛti,* memory

SUTRA 1:7

प्रत्यक्षानुमानागमाः प्रमाणानि ॥७॥

pratyakṣa-anumāna-āgamāḥ pramāṇāni ॥ 7 ॥

Correct understanding is threefold: sense perception, inference, and revelation documented in the scriptures.

prati-akṣa- that which is associated with one or more of the senses; sensory perception; information received through seeing, tasting, touching, smelling, and hearing

prati, toward; associated with; belonging to; *akṣa,* sense; sense organ

anu-māna- inference; information or knowledge derived from, or dependent on, valid sensory perception

anu, that which follows; *māna*, valid information; valid knowledge

ā-gamāḥ *nom. pl. m.* information that is regarded as valid knowledge; knowledge that requires no further evidence; information documented in the scriptures; revealed knowledge

ā, previous; before; in every respect; from every direction; *gama*, that which comes; that which is known; that which is confirmed

pramāṇāni *nom. pl. n.* of *pramāṇa*, information that can be validated; that which is supported by evidence

SUTRA 1:8

विपर्ययो मिथ्याज्ञानमतद्रूपप्रतिष्ठम् ॥८॥

viparyayaḥ mithyā-jñānam atadrūpapratiṣṭham ॥ 8 ॥

Mistaking the unreal for the real is false understanding. False understanding is not grounded in reality; instead it corresponds to that which has no ground.

viparyayaḥ — *nom. sg. m.* false comprehension; miscomprehension; false understanding

mithyā- — false; unreal

jñānam — *nom. sg. n.* knowledge

a-tad-rūpa-pratiṣṭham
nom. sg. n. corresponding to that which has no ground
a, not; *tad*, that; *rūpa*, form; state; *pratiṣṭha*, established; residing in; located in

SUTRA 1:9

शब्दज्ञानानुपाती वस्तुशून्यो विकल्पः ॥९॥

śabda-jñāna-anupātī vastu-śūnyaḥ vikalpaḥ ॥ 9 ॥

Imagination is knowledge which due to the use of words appears to have content but in reality is devoid of content.

śabda- — word

jñāna- — knowledge

anupātī	*nom. sg. m.* of *anupātīn,* that which follows
vastu-	content; substance
śūnyaḥ	*nom. sg. m.* void; empty; lacking content; non-existent
vikalpaḥ	*nom. sg. m.* imagination; fiction

SUTRA 1:10

अभावप्रत्ययालम्बना वृत्तिर्निद्रा ॥१०॥

abhāva-pratyaya-ālambanā vṛttiḥ nidrā ॥ 10 ॥

Swirling of the mind around the cognition of non-being is dreamless sleep.

a-bhāva-	non-existence; absence; negation *a*, not; *bhāva*, existence; feeling; emotion; being
pratyaya-	cognition
ālambanā	*nom. sg. f.* support
vṛttiḥ	*nom. sg. f.* modification of mind; operation of mind; thought construct; that which revolves
nidrā	*nom. sg. f.* dreamless sleep

SUTRA 1:11

अनुभूतविषयासम्प्रमोषः स्मृतिः ॥११॥

anubhūta-viṣaya-asampramoṣaḥ smṛtiḥ ॥ 11 ॥

Not being completely disconnected from the objects of previous experiences is memory.

anubhūta- that which has been experienced before

viṣaya- objects

a-sam-pra-moṣaḥ
nom. sg. m. that which is not completely disconnected or that which has not fallen outside the pale of conscious awareness
a, not; *sam*, completely; *pra*, specifically; *moṣaḥ*, stolen; hidden; not available; outside the pale of conscious awareness

smṛtiḥ *nom. sg. f.* memory

SUTRA 1:12

अभ्यासवैराग्याभ्यां तन्निरोधः ॥१२॥

abhyāsa-vairāgyābhyāṁ tan-nirodhaḥ ॥ 12 ॥

That can be controlled through practice and non-attachment.

abhyāsa- practice; the effort involved in retaining the peaceful flow of mind free from roaming tendencies

vairāgyābhyāṁ *ins. du. n.* of *vairāgya*, non-attachment; dispassion; derived from *vi-rāga*: *vi,* devoid of;

	free from; beyond; *rāga,* coloring; attachment; *vairagya,* the essence of *virāga,* the state of mind not tainted by karmic impressions
tat-	that; those
ni-rodhaḥ	*nom. sg. m.* mastery; complete control; discipline; restraint *ni,* completely; in every respect; from every direction; *rodha,* confining; restraining; disciplining; not allowing to roam aimlessly

SUTRA 1:13

तत्र स्थितौ यत्नोऽभ्यासः ॥१३॥

tatra sthitau yatnaḥ abhyāsaḥ ॥ 13 ॥

Ardent effort to retain the peaceful flow of mind free of roaming tendencies is *abhyasa*.

tatra	there
sthitau	*loc. sg. m.* of *sthiti,* state; a stable condition of mind; mental state free from roaming tendencies
yatnaḥ	*nom. sg. m.* ardent effort; vigor; enthusiasm; attending with vigor and enthusiasm
abhyāsaḥ	*nom. sg. m.* practice; the effort involved in retaining the peaceful flow of mind free from roaming tendencies

SUTRA 1:14

स तु दीर्घकालनैरन्तर्यसत्कारासेवितो दृढभूमिः ॥१४॥

saḥ tu dīrgha-kāla-nairantarya-satkāra-āsevitaḥ dṛḍha-bhūmiḥ ॥ 14 ॥

That becomes firm only when done for a long period of time, with no interruption, and with reverence.

saḥ	*nom. sg. m.* that
tu	verily; definitely
dīrgha-	long
kāla-	time
nairantarya-	continuously; without any interruption
satkāra-	respect
āsevitaḥ	*nom. sg. m.* fully attended; completely served
dṛḍha-	firm; strong; unshakeable
bhūmiḥ	*nom. sg. f.* ground

SUTRA 1:15

दृष्टानुश्रविकविषयवितृष्णस्य वशीकारसंज्ञा वैराग्यम् ॥१५॥

dṛṣṭa-ānuśravika-viṣaya-vitṛṣṇasya vaśīkāra-saṁjñā vairāgyam ॥ 15 ॥

Non-attachment, known as *vashikara-samjna*, belongs to the one who is free from the craving for sense objects and objects mentioned in the scriptures.

dṛṣṭa- seen; perceived; object of senses; the experience of sensory objects

ānuśravika- that which has been heard; that which has its source in books; that which is mentioned in the scriptures; that which is passed on in the oral tradition

anu, that which follows; *śravika,* hearing; reading; scriptural; found in texts that document information which has been passed on for generations

viṣaya- object

vitṛṣṇasya *gen. sg. m.* free from sense cravings

vi, devoid of; *tṛṣṇa,* pertaining to thirst; craving; clinging

vaśīkāra-saṁjñā

nom. sg. f. a state characterized by the ability to grant complete self-mastery; that which enables the mind to remain free from the charms and temptations of the world, as well as from the temptations described in books, including revealed scriptures

vaśīkāra, the mind's ability to stay under control; *saṁjñā*, nomenclature; definition

vairāgyam *nom. sg. n.* non-attachment; dispassion; derived from *vi-rāga*: *vi,* devoid of; free from; beyond; *rāga,* coloring; attachment; *vairagya,* the essence of *virāga,* the state of mind not tainted by karmic impressions

SUTRA 1:16

तत्परं पुरुषख्यातेर्गुणवैतृष्ण्यम् ।। १६।।

tat-paraṁ puruṣa-khyāter guṇa-vaitṛṣṇyam ॥ 16 ॥

The highest level of non-attachment, leading to self-realization, takes place when the aspirant is free from all forms of desire, including desires resulting from the interplay of *sattvic*, *rajasic*, and *tamasic* forces of nature.

tat- that

paraṁ beyond; absolute; the highest

puruṣa-khyāteḥ *abl. sg. f.* of *puruṣa-khyāti*, knowledge pertaining to *puruṣa*; the knowledge that clearly distinguishes consciousness from matter; knowledge that reveals the true nature of pure consciousness

puruṣa, consciousness; core being; *khyāti*, knowledge; recognition; revelation

guṇa- qualities; attributes of *prakṛti*

vaitṛṣṇyam *nom. sg. n.* derivative of *vi-tṛṣṇa*, a state of mind which is free from all forms of desire

vi, devoid of; *tṛṣṇa*, clinging; thirst; craving

SUTRA 1:17

वितर्कविचारानन्दास्मितारूपानुगमात् सम्प्रज्ञातः ॥१७॥

vitarka-vicāra-ānanda-asmitā-rūpa-anugamāt samprajñātaḥ ॥ 17 ॥

Samprajnata samadhi **is accompanied by a gross object, a subtle object, joy, or the feeling of I-am-ness.**

vitarka- reasoning; supposition; argument; discussion; in this context, it refers to a tangible object that can be named and can be precisely comprehended; a gross meditative object

vicāra- thinking; contemplation; here it refers to a subtle object; devoid of physical characteristics

ānanda- pleasure; happiness; here it refers to the joy that is derived from inside; joy that is not dependent on the senses contacting their objects

asmitā- I-am-ness; self-identity

rūpa- form; essence

anugamāt *abl. sg. m.* of *anugama*, that which accompanies; that which induces

sam-pra-jñātaḥ

nom. sg. m. the state of *samādhi* in which the yogi is aware of the object being attended by the mind, the process of attending it, and oneself as a witness

sam, completely; in every respect; all around; from every angle; fully; *pra,* precisely; in the most evolved, elevated manner; superbly; *jñātaḥ,* known; understood; cognized

SUTRA 1:18

विरामप्रत्ययाभ्यासपूर्वः संस्कारशेषोऽन्यः ॥१८॥

virāma-pratyaya-abhyāsa-pūrvaḥ saṁskāra-śeṣaḥ anyaḥ ॥ 18 ॥

The other [higher samadhi] is preceded by *abhyasa*, which brought all cognitions to a complete halt. What remains is the *samskara* [of abhyasa itself].

virāma-	cessation; coming to a halt; the end
pratyaya-	cognition; thought construct; modification
abhyāsa-	practice; the effort involved in retaining the peaceful flow of mind, free from roaming tendencies
pūrvaḥ	*nom. sg. m.* preceded by; that which existed before; anterior
saṁskāra-	subtle impressions of past deeds; impressions stored in the form of memories
śeṣaḥ	*nom. sg. m.* residue; remainder
anyaḥ	*nom. sg. m.* the other

SUTRA 1:19

भवप्रत्ययो विदेहप्रकृतिलयानाम् ॥१९॥

bhava-pratyayaḥ videha-prakṛti-layānām ॥ 19 ॥

The experience of the higher level of samadhi is innate to [extraordinary yogis technically known as] *videha* and *prakritilaya*.

bhava-pratyayaḥ

nom. sg. m. the experience that comes with birth; the knowledge that innately accompanies a yogi; an extraordinary yogi with the privilege to be born with his knowledge and experience intact

bhava, to come into being; the process as well as the phenomenon of coming into being; birth; being born; cycle of death and birth; *pratyaya*, experience; cognition; realization; to become aware of

videha-prakṛti-layayānām

gen. pl. m. a special category of yogis who, due to being established in *ānanda anugata samādhi* and *asmitā anugata samādhi,* become absorbed in pure joy and the pristine state of *prakṛti,* respectively, at death

videha, without a body; not confined to the body; beyond bodily consciousness; a special category of yogis who have reached the state of *ānanda anugata samādhi* and after death reside in their pure, intrinsic, self-luminous joy; *prakṛti-laya,* dissolved into *prakṛti*; a special category of yogis who have reached the state of *asmitā anugata samādhi* and after death reside in the pristine state of *prakṛti*

SUTRA 1:20

श्रद्धावीर्यस्मृतिसमाधिप्रज्ञापूर्वक इतरेषाम् ॥२०॥

śraddhā-vīrya-smṛti-samādhi-prajñā-pūrvakaḥ itareṣām ॥ 20 ॥

In the case of others, it [samadhi] is preceded by faith, vigor, retentive power, stillness of mind, and intuitive wisdom.

śraddhā-	faith; conviction; trust
vīrya-	vigor; the essence of body, senses, and mind; core strength; the elixir of life; the energy that makes us shine; sexual energy; inner strength
smṛti-	retentive power; memory; the power to recollect
samadhi-	stillness of mind; all-consuming focus; mind free from all roaming tendencies
prajna-	intuition; discerning wisdom
pūrvakaḥ	*nom. sg. m.* preceded by; accompanied by
itareṣām	*gen. pl. m.* others; in the case of others; yogis other than those belonging to the category of *videha* and *prakṛtilaya*

SUTRA 1:21

तीव्रसंवेगानामासन्नः ॥२१॥

tīvra-saṁvegānām āsannaḥ ॥ 21 ॥

It [samadhi] is near for those whose aspiration is steadfast.

tīvra-	intense; steadfast

saṁ-vegānām *gen. pl. m.* of *saṃ-vega,* thoughts, feelings, aspirations, desire, ambition—all at full speed
saṃ, complete; full; *vega*, speed

āsannaḥ *nom. sg. m.* of *āsanna,* near; close

SUTRA 1:22

मृदुमध्याधिमात्रत्वात् ततोऽपि विशेषः ।।२२।।

mṛdu-madhya-adhimātratvāt tataḥ api vieṣaḥ ॥ 22 ॥

Depending on whether the seeker's steadfast aspiration is mild, intermediate, or supreme, there are further distinctions.

mṛdu- mild; soft; tender

madhya- intermediate

adhi-mātratvāt
abl. sg. n. the highest level; utmost; unprecedented; supreme
adhi, grounded in; serving as a base; on the ground of; *mātratva,* due to the quality of exclusiveness

tataḥ *abl. sg. n.* of *tat,* from that

api also

viśeṣaḥ *nom. sg. m.* special; distinct; outstanding

SUTRA 1:23

ईश्वरप्रणिधानाद्वा ॥२३॥

īśvara-praṇidhānāt vā ॥ 23 ॥

From trustful surrender to Ishvara [God], samadhi also comes.

īśvara- sovereign ruler; inner controller; guide; knower of past, present, and future; total sum of all powers; locus of all powers; almighty; God

praṇidhānāt *abl. sg. n.* trustful surrender

pra, highest; utmost; supreme; *ni*, completely; *dhāna*, the process of holding firmly; becoming established; nurturing

In the aggregate, this term has a fixed meaning: surrender; surrendering oneself uniquely and completely to the divine will

vā option; also; in addition to

SUTRA 1:24

क्लेशकर्मविपाकाशयैरपरामृष्टः पुरुषविशेष ईश्वरः ॥२४॥

kleśa-karma-vipāka-āśayaiḥ aparāmṛṣṭaḥ puruṣa-viśeṣaḥ īśvaraḥ ॥ 24 ॥

Ishvara is a unique being untouched by afflictions, karmas, the results of karmas, and the repository of karmas.

kleśa- affliction; that which causes suffering; technically refers collectively to *avidyā, asmitā, rāga, dveṣa,* and *abhiniveṣa*

karma- action

vipāka- result; fruit; post-digestive effect

āśayaiḥ *ins. pl. n.* of *āśaya,* repository; treasury; resting ground; container

a-parāmṛṣṭaḥ *nom. sg. m.* untouched; unstained; unaffected
a, not; *parāmṛṣṭa*, touched by

puruṣa-viśeṣaḥ *nom. sg. m.* special being; supreme consciousness; the immutable divinity that remains above the cycle of birth and death
puruṣa, one who dwells in the city of life; one who resides in the body; one who pervades and permeates the body; one who is the seer as well as the power of seeing; soul; the source of, and the locus for, pure intelligence; *viśeṣa,* unique; special; extraordinary; outstanding

īśvaraḥ *nom. sg. m.* derived from the verb *īśa,* to be capable of; the capacity to administer, rule, guide, supervise; the divinity with unhindered capacity

SUTRA 1:25

तत्र निरतिशयं सर्वज्ञबीजम् ॥२५॥

tatra niratiśayaṁ sarvajña-bījam ॥ 25 ॥

Therein [in Ishvara] lies the seed of unsurpassed omniscience.

tatra therein

niratiśayaṁ *nom. sg. n.* without limit; that which cannot be surpassed; the highest; absolute

sarvajña-bījam	*nom. sg. n.*	the seed of omniscience; the one with the capacity to know everything and everyone; the omniscient divine being *sarvajña*, all-knowing; *bījam*, seed

SUTRA 1:26

स एष पूर्वेषामपि गुरुः कालेनानवच्छेदात् ।।२६।।

saḥ eṣaḥ pūrveṣām api guruḥ kālena-anavacchedāt ॥ 26 ॥

He is the one who has been the preceptor of all previous teachers for He is not limited by time.

saḥ	*nom. sg. m.* he
eṣaḥ	*nom. sg. m.* this
pūrveṣām	*gen. sg. m.* of *pūrva*, the previous ones
api	even; also
guruḥ	*nom. sg. m.* guide; spiritual preceptor; teacher
kālena-	*ins. sg. m.* of *kāla*, time
anavacchedāt	*abl. sg. m.* not limited

SUTRA 1:27

तस्य वाचकः प्रणवः ।।२७।।

tasya vācakaḥ praṇavaḥ ॥ 27 ॥

***Pranava* [om] is the denoter of That [Ishvara].**

tasya	*gen. sg. m.* of *tat*, of that; here it refers to *īśvara*, the omniscient divine being

vācakaḥ	*nom. sg. m.* denoter; indicator
praṇavaḥ	*nom. sg. m.* that which is imbued with newness; ever-new; the sound *oṁ*

SUTRA 1:28

तज्जपस्तदर्थभावनम् ॥२८॥

tat-japaḥ tat-artha-bhāvanam ॥ 28 ॥

Repetition of That [pranava] means to reflect on its meaning.

tat-	that
japaḥ	*nom. sg. m.* repetition
tat-	that
artha-	meaning; content
bhāvanam	*nom. sg. m.* contemplation; reflection; thinking

SUTRA 1:29

ततः प्रत्यक्चेतनाधिगमोऽप्यन्तरायाभावश्च ॥२९॥

tataḥ pratyak-cetanā-adhigamaḥ api antarāya-abhāvaḥ ca ॥ 29 ॥

From that comes the experience of Inner Being as well as the elimination of impediments.

tataḥ	*abl. sg. m.* of *tat*, from that
pratyak-	inner; inward; inwardly flowing; directly, without any mediator

cetanā-	consciousness; awareness
adhigamaḥ	*nom. sg. m.* attainment; inducement
api	also; in addition to; furthermore
antarāya-	that which creates a gap, causing separation; obstacle
abhāvaḥ	*nom. sg. m.* absence; removal
ca	and

SUTRA 1:30

व्याधिस्त्यानसंशयप्रमादालस्याविरतिभ्रान्तिदर्शनालब्ध-
भूमिकत्वानवस्थितत्वानि चित्तविक्षेपास्तेऽन्तरायाः ॥३०॥

vyādhi-styāna-saṁśaya-pramāda-ālasya-avirati-
bhrāntidarśana-alabdhabhūmikatva-anavasthitatvāni citta-
vikṣepāḥ te antarāyāḥ ॥ 30 ॥

Disease, mental inertia, doubt, carelessness, sloth, inability to withdraw from sense cravings, clinging to misunderstanding, inability to reach the goal [samadhi], and inability to retain it throw our mind outward; they are obstacles.

vyādhi-	disease; imbalanced state of *vata*, *pitta*, and *kapha* *vi,* special; supreme; highest or subtle; *ādhi,* disease; physical ailment
styāna-	mental inertia; inaction of the mind; dullness; inability to put our thoughts into action
saṁśaya-	doubt; skepticism; the mindless tendency to grasp two extreme ends and the failure to grasp what lies in between

pramāda- carelessness; negligence; lacking interest in attending the object of concentration

ālasya- sloth; inability to engage due to heaviness

a-virati- the inability to withdraw from sense cravings; failure to maintain a dispassionate state

a, not; less; lacking; *vi*, devoid of; away from; absence of; free from; untouched by; *rati*, craving; clinging; holding on to; sense pleasure; lust

bhrānti-darśana-

confused understanding; clinging to misunderstanding; insistence on believing in that which is contrary to truth; active attachment to ignorance; unwavering faith in misunderstanding

bhrānti, illusion; distortion; unreal; imaginary; fictitious; *darśana*, seeing; perceiving; grasping

alabdha-bhūmikatva-

inability to reach the goal; inability to comprehend the goal

a, not; *labdha*, achievement; *bhūmikatva*, the essence of the ground; essential foundation; gist of the goal

anavasthitatvāni

nom. pl. n. the mind's inability to stay in *samādhi*, inability to maintain inner stability; inability to maintain the goal; inability to maintain constant awareness; tendency to slide back

citta-vikṣepāḥ *nom. pl. m.* mental distraction
citta, mind; *vikṣepa,* that which throws the mind outward; that which makes the mind become agitated; that which makes the mind run into the external world

te *nom. sg. m.* they

antarāyāḥ *nom. pl. m.* obstacle; impediment

SUTRA 1:31

दुःखदौर्मनस्याङ्गमेजयत्वश्वासप्रश्वासा
विक्षेपसहभुवः।। ३१।।

duḥkha-daurmanasya-aṅgamejayatva-śvāsa-praśvāsāḥ
vikṣepasahabhuvaḥ ॥ 31 ॥

Pain, mental agitation, unsteadiness or trembling of limbs, [abnormal or disturbed] inhalation and exhalation all arise with the obstacles.

duḥkha- pain; sorrow

daurmanasya- associated with or derived from a negative or impure mind; negative frame of mind

aṅgam-ejayatva-
conditions causing limbs to shake; trembling of limbs; racing of organs; hyperactivity of limbs and organs
aṅgam, limbs; *ejayatva,* unsteadiness; shakiness; condition of being shaken; trembling

śvāsa- breathing in; inhalation; inspiration

praśvāsāḥ *nom. pl. m.* breathing out; exhalation; expiration

vikṣepa-saha-bhuvaḥ

nom. sg. m. the conditions that accompany impediments

vikṣepa, distraction; casting off the mind; throwing away or disposing of the mind; letting the mind fall apart; *saha*, with; *bhuva*, to be born; birth

SUTRA 1:32

तत्प्रतिषेधार्थमेकतत्त्वाभ्यासः ॥३२॥

tat-pratiṣedhārtham ekatattva-abhyāsaḥ ॥ 32 ॥

Meditation on one single reality is the way to overcome these obstacles.

tat- that

pratiṣedha-artham

nom. sg. m. to prevent; to negate; to cancel; to overcome

pratiṣedha, prevention; negation; cancellation; *artham*, for the purpose of

eka-tattva- one single reality; pertaining to only one truth

eka, one; *tattva*, truth; element; essence of being

abhyāsaḥ *nom. sg. m.* practice; specifically, ardent effort to retain the peaceful flow of mind free from roaming tendencies

SUTRA 1:33

मैत्रीकरुणामुदितोपेक्षाणां सुखदुःखपुण्यापुण्यविषयाणां भावनातश्चित्तप्रसादनम् ॥३३॥

maitrī-karuṇā-muditā-upekṣāṇāṁ sukha-duḥkha-puṇya-apuṇya-viṣayāṇāṁ bhāvanātaḥ citta-prasādanam ॥ 33 ॥

Transparency of mind comes by embracing an attitude of friendliness, compassion, happiness, and non-judgment toward those who are happy, miserable, virtuous, and non-virtuous.

maitrī-	derived from *mitra,* friend; *maitrī,* the essence of friendship; the essential quality of friendship
karuṇā-	compassion; a genuine desire to give, serve, love, and care
muditā-	the virtue of cheerfulness; a joyful condition of mind
upekṣāṇāṁ	*gen. pl. f.* seeing without judging; uninvolved observation
sukha-	happiness
duḥkha-	pain; sorrow; suffering
puṇya-	virtue; merit; spiritual quality that frees us from the bondage of karma
apuṇya-	lack of virtue; demerit; vice; degrading quality that binds
viṣayāṇāṁ	*gen. pl. m.* object; in this context it means "in relation to"
bhāvanā-taḥ	*abl.* suffix *tan* with *bhāvanā,* from thinking; contemplation

citta-prasādanam
nom. sg. n. transparency of mind; mental refinement; mental purification
citta, mind; *prasādana*, transparency; clarity

SUTRA 1:34

प्रच्छर्दनविधारणाभ्यां वा प्राणस्य ।।३४।।

pracchardana-vidhāraṇābhyāṁ vā prāṇasya ॥ 34 ॥

Transparency of mind also comes by practicing pranayama that involves forceful exhalation and breath retention.

pracchardana- unique method of exhalation
pra, very special; unique; exceptional; *chardana*, peeling off the layers; chiseling; sculpting; forceful exhalation

vidhāraṇābhyāṁ
ins. du. n. a special form of concentration while retaining the breath
vi, unique; special; *dhāraṇa*, to hold; to retain; to confine; to fill; to concentrate

vā also; and; or

prāṇasya *gen. sg. m.* of *prāṇa*, life force

SUTRA 1:35

विषयवती वा प्रवृत्तिरुत्पन्ना मनसः स्थितिनिबन्धिनी ॥३५॥

viṣayavatī vā pravṛttiḥ utpannā manasaḥ sthiti-nibandhinī ‖ 35 ‖

A unique cognition pertaining to a sense object arising from within also anchors the mind to *sthiti*, the peaceful flow free from all thought constructs.

viṣayavatī *nom. sg. f.* comprised of an object; accompanied by the object of the senses

vā also; and; or

pravṛttiḥ *nom. sg. f.* special modification of mind
pra, special; refined; superior; *vṛtti*, modification of mind; thought construct; mental engagement

utpannā *nom. sg. f.* that which is born, manifest, or evolved

manasaḥ *gen. sg. n.* of the mind

sthiti-nibandhinī
nom. sg. f. that which firmly binds the mind to *sthiti*, peaceful inward flow; that which compels the mind to remain concentrated on one object; that which makes the mind one-pointed
sthiti, peaceful inward flow; stability; *nibandhinī*, anchoring with all certainty

SUTRA 1:36

विशोका वा ज्योतिष्मती ।।३६।।

viśokā vā jyotiṣmatī ॥ 36 ॥

The state of consciousness free from sorrow and anguish and infused with inner light also anchors the mind to *sthiti*, the peaceful flow free from all thought constructs.

viśokā *nom. sg. f.* beyond *śoka,* a state of consciousness free from sorrow and anguish; a state of sorrowless joy

vi, beyond; devoid of; lacking; *śoka,* sorrow and anguish; an inner state afflicted with sorrow caused by doubt, fear, anger, grief, regret, guilt, and shame; an inner state that prevents us from experiencing the joy and beauty inherent in life

vā and/or

jyotiṣmatī *nom. sg. f.* made of light; filled with light; accompanied by light; luminous

SUTRA 1:37

वीतरागविषयं वा चित्तम् ।। ३७।।

vīta-rāga-viṣayaṁ vā cittam ॥ 37 ॥

Or [the ability to retain the peaceful flow of mind] comes by focusing on someone who is free from all desire.

vīta-rāga-viṣayaṁ

nom. sg. n. one whose perception is not colored by desire, anger, hatred, greed, and ego; one

	whose mind is not colored by preconceived notions and prejudices; a person of undistorted perception; a person who sees things the way they are; a person whose mind is not under the influence of sense cravings *vīta*, away from; done with; devoid of; *rāga*, attachment; coloring; preoccupation; *viṣaya*, object
vā	and/or
cittam	*nom. sg. n.* mind

SUTRA 1:38

स्वप्ननिद्राज्ञानालम्बनं वा ॥३८॥

svapna-nidrā-jñāna-ālambanaṁ vā ॥ 38 ॥

Or by meditating on the knowledge gained from dreams and sleep [one acquires stability of mind].

svapna-	dream
nidrā-	sleep
jñāna-	knowledge; cognition; experience
ālambanaṁ	*nom. sg. n.* ground for resting; object of focus; support
vā	and/or

SUTRA 1:39

यथाभिमतध्यानाद्वा ॥३९॥

yathā-abhimata-dhyānāt vā ॥ 39 ॥

Or by meditating on a well-considered object of one's choice [one attains steadiness of mind].

yathā- accordingly

abhimata- well thought out; accepted or acceptable without doubt; agreed upon

abhi, in every direction; all around; *mata*, understanding; opinion; choice

dhyānāt *abl. sg. n.* of *dhyāna*, meditation

vā and/or

SUTRA 1:40

परमाणुपरममहत्त्वान्तोऽस्य वशीकारः ॥४०॥

paramāṇu-parama-mahattva-antaḥ asya vaśīkāraḥ ॥ 40 ॥

A yogi's mastery stretches from the smallest particle to the biggest object.

parama-aṇu- the smallest particle imaginable

parama, highest; absolute; *aṇu*, atom

parama-mahattva-antaḥ

nom. sg. m. the biggest entity; the highest expansiveness; the first and the most subtle state of manifest reality; the inner core of the most subtle of all stages of manifestation *parama*, highest; absolute; *mahattva*, the essence of bigness; the first and the foremost category of the manifest world evolving from unmanifest *prakṛti*; the most subtle and pervasive stage of evolution; *antaḥ*, inner; interior; the final end

asya — *gen. sg. m.* of the pronoun *idam*, this, it, he

vaśīkāraḥ — *nom. sg. m.* the particular state of *samādhi* described in sutra 1:15; a fully controlled state of mind; a mind free from all forms of attachment, including the attachment to celestial pleasures

SUTRA 1:41

क्षीणवृत्तेरभिजातस्येव मणेर्ग्रहीतृग्रहणग्राह्येषु
तत्स्थतदञ्जनता समापत्तिः ॥४१॥

kṣīṇavṛtteḥ abhijātasya iva maṇeḥ grahītṛ-grahaṇa-grāhyeṣu
tatstha-tadañjanatā samāpattiḥ ‖ 41 ‖

A mind free from its roaming tendencies is like a crystal. It takes the form of whatever object is in its proximity, whether the object is the perceiver, the process of perceiving, or the object of perception. This is *samapatti*, complete absorption.

kṣīṇa-vṛtteḥ — *gen. sg. f.* of *kṣīṇa-vṛtti,* a mind whose roaming tendencies are extinct

kṣīṇa, extinct; destroyed; erased; cleansed; *vṛtti*, roaming tendency of the mind; thought constructs

abhijātasya — *gen. sg. m.* of *abhijāta,* a totally transparent, high-quality gem; in Indian mythology, a wish-fulfilling gem *iva* like

maṇeḥ *gen. sg. m.* of *maṇi*, jewel

grahītṛ-grahaṇa-grāhyeṣu

loc. pl. m. the perceiver, the process of perceiving, and the object of perception

grahītṛ, perceiver; receiver; witness; *grahaṇa*, perceiving; receiving; *grāhya*, perceivable; receivable

tatstha-tadañjanatā

nom. sg. f. assuming the form of what lies next to it

tat-stha, residing in that; sitting in that; located in that; *tad-añjanatā*, taking on the quality of that; being transformed into that

samāpattiḥ *nom. sg. f.* complete absorption; merging into one

SUTRA 1:42

तत्र शब्दार्थज्ञानविकल्पैः संकीर्णा सवितर्का समापत्तिः ॥४२॥

tatra śabda-arthajñāna-vikalpaiḥ saṁkīrṇā savitarkā samāpattiḥ ॥ 42 ॥

Meditation that has an object mingled with the distinct awareness of a word, the meaning of the word, and the awareness of focusing on the word and its meaning leads to a form of absorption known as *savitarka*.

tatra there

śabda-artha-jñāna-vikalpaiḥ
ins. pl. m. word, its meaning, and cognition of the word and its corresponding meaning
śabda, word; *artha*, meaning; *jñāna*, cognition; awareness; *vikalpa*, distinct

saṁkīrṇā *nom. sg. f.* mingled; mixed

savitarkā *nom. sg. f.* accompanied by inquiries; accompanied by a tangible gross object

samāpattiḥ *nom. sg. f.* complete absorption

SUTRA 1:43

स्मृतिपरिशुद्धौ स्वरूपशून्येवार्थमात्रनिर्भासा निर्वितर्का ॥४३॥

smṛtipariśuddhau svarūpaśūnyā iva arthamātranirbhāsā nirvitarkā ॥ 43 ॥

Upon the refinement of memory, there arises mental absorption named *nirvitarka samapatti*, in which the object of meditation seems devoid of its own form and is expressive only of its meaning.

smṛti-pariśuddhau
loc. sg. m. refinement of memory; purification of memory
smṛti, memory; *pariśuddhi*, purification; refinement; cleansing

svarūpa-śūnyā *nom. sg. f.* devoid of one's own form
svarūpa, one's own form; one's own nature; *śūnyā*, empty; void; devoid of

iva	as if
arthamātranirbhāsā	*nom. sg. f.* where the meaning alone is illumined *artha*, meaning; *mātra*, only; *nirbhāsā*, illumination
nir-vitarkā	*nom. sg. f.* cognition affording no room for options *nir*, devoid of; *vitarkā*, option; alternative; cognition

SUTRA 1:44

एतयैव सविचारा निर्विचारा च सूक्ष्मविषया व्याख्याता ||४४||

etayā-eva savicārā nirvicārā ca sūkṣma-viṣayā vyākhyātā ॥ 44 ॥

Accordingly, the *savichara* and *nirvichara* levels of mental absorption, which have extremely subtle objects as their focus, are explained.

etayā	*ins. sg. f.* accordingly; by the same token; in the same fashion; similarly
eva	only
sa-vicārā	*nom. sg. f.* accompanied by a thought or feeling *sa*, with; *vicārā*, thought; feeling
nir-vicārā	*nom. sg. f.* that which is beyond thinking *nir*, without; *vicārā*, thought; feeling

ca and

sūkṣma viṣayā *nom. sg. f.* that which has a subtle object as its focus
sūkṣma, subtle; *viṣayā,* object

vyākhyātā *nom. sg. f.* described; explained; narrated

SUTRA 1:45

सूक्ष्मविषयत्वं चालिङ्गपर्यवसानम् ।।४५।।

sūkṣma-viṣayatvaṁ ca-aliṅga-paryavasānam ॥ 45 ॥

That which ultimately dissolves into irreferable Prakriti is the subtlest of all objects.

sūkṣma-viṣayatvaṁ
nom. sg. n. meditation on the most subtle object
sūkṣma, subtle; *viṣayatva*, essence of the object; the nature of the object

ca and

aliṅga-paryavasānam
nom. sg. n. that which dissolves into irreferable *prakṛti*; that which rests in primordial nature; *buddhi; mahat tattva*
aliṅga, irreferable; that which cannot be indicated; indescribable; *paryavasānam,* the point of dissolution; the final end

SUTRA 1:46

ता एव सबीजः समाधिः ॥४६॥

tāḥ eva sabījaḥ samādhiḥ ॥ 46 ॥

Those are indeed samadhi with seed.

tāḥ	*nom. pl. f.* those
eva	only; alone; indeed; precisely
sa-bījaḥ	*nom. sg. m.* with seed; along with karmic impressions; accompanied by subtle impressions *sa,* with; accompanied by; embedded in; *bīja,* seed
samādhiḥ	*nom. sg. m.* the experience arising from mental absorption

SUTRA 1:47

निर्विचारवैशारद्येऽध्यात्मप्रसादः ॥४७॥

nir-vicāra-vaiśāradye adhyātma-prasādaḥ ॥ 47 ॥

Spiritual transparency and joy come from the continued purification of *nirvichara samapatti.*

nir-vicāra-	that which is beyond thinking *nir*, without; *vicāra*, thought; feeling
vaiśāradye	*loc. sg. m.* of *vaiśāradya*, continued refinement; ever-increasing purification; expansion of transparency
adhyātma-prasādaḥ	*nom. sg. m.* spiritual joy; clarity and joy

pertaining to our core being

adhyātma, at the center of the soul; the center of consciousness; pertaining to our core being; *prasādaḥ,* illumination; enlightenment; happiness; joy; transparency

SUTRA 1:48

ऋतम्भरा तत्र प्रज्ञा ।।४८।।

ṛtam-bharā tatra prajna ॥ 48 ॥

There that self-luminous field of Consciousness is laden with truth.

ṛtam-bharā — *nom. sg. f.* laden with truth; full of truth; infused with the power that governs the forces of nature

ṛtam, eternal law; law of nature; the fundamental law that governs and guides the dynamics of matter and energy and the world composed by them; the ultimate principle of sustainability; the fundamental principle of reality, which assigns an entity its nature and maintains that nature in all circumstances; this term is used more frequently in Vedic literature; *bharā,* filled with; laden with

tatra — that; there; therein; within

prajñā — *nom. sg. f.* intuitive wisdom; knowledge that transcends the limitations of time and space; the self-luminous field of consciousness; the infinite field of intuition

SUTRA 1:49

श्रुतानुमानप्रज्ञाभ्यामन्यविषया विशेषार्थत्वात् ।।४९।।

śruta-anumāna-prajñābhyām anya-viṣayā viśeṣa-arthatvāt ॥ 49 ॥

Because intuitive wisdom contains the meaning (or essence) of "the Unique," it has a different scope than the knowledge gained from scriptures and from inference.

śruta-anumāna-prajñābhyām

abl. du. f. of *śruta-anumāna-prajñā*, knowledge gained from scriptures and from inference

śruta, that which has been heard; that which has been passed on by the oral tradition; the experiential knowledge documented in the scriptures; the ancient spiritual text popularly known as the *Veda*; *anumāna*, inference; *prajñā,* intuitive wisdom, but here used to mean knowledge, understanding, comprehension

anya-viṣayā *nom. sg. f.* that which is totally different

anya, other; different; *viṣayā*, object

viśeṣa-arthatvāt

abl. sg. n. having *viśeṣa*, "the unique," as its content

viśeṣa, unique; special; extraordinary; extraordinary supreme being; *arthatva,* essential meaning; the essence of the content

SUTRA 1:50

तज्जः संस्कारोऽन्यसंस्कारप्रतिबन्धी ॥५०॥

tat-jaḥ saṁskāraḥ anya-saṁskāra-pratibandhī ॥ 50 ॥

Samskaras born of intuitive wisdom cancel all other samskaras.

tat-jaḥ *nom. sg. m.* born of that; evolving from that

saṁskāraḥ *nom. sg. m.* subtle karmic impression; impressions of the past

anya-saṁskāra-pratibandhī
nom. sg. m. of *anya-saṁskāra-pratibandhin,* that which blocks other impressions; that which cancels or neutralizes karmic impressions
anya, other; different; *saṁskāra,* subtle karmic impression; mental impression; *pratibandhin,* that which blocks, cancels, neutralizes, nullifies

SUTRA 1:51

तस्यापि निरोधे सर्वनिरोधान्निर्बीजः समाधिः ॥५१॥

tasya api nirodhe sarva-nirodhāt nirbījaḥ samādhiḥ ॥ 51 ॥

Upon cancellation of even that, everything else is cancelled. This is *nirbija samadhi.*

tasya *gen. sg. m.* of *tat,* of that

api even; also

nirodhe *loc. sg. m.* restraining; confining; cancelling

sarva-nirodhāt

abl. sg. m. cancellation of everything; dismissal of everything

sarva, all; *nirodha,* cancellation; restraint; dismissal

nir-bījaḥ *nom. sg. n.* without seed; without any karmic impressions, including meditative impressions; a technical term for the highest state of *samādhi*

samādhiḥ *nom. sg. m.* completely still, pristine state of mind

APPENDIX C

The Theory and Practice of Sankhya Yoga

Only the immature, not those who are learned, regard Sankhya and Yoga as two different paths.

The [state of] realization gained through the practice of Sankhya can also be gained through the practice of Yoga. An aspirant fully established in one attains the fruits of both.

—**Bhagavad Gita (5:4 and 5:5)**

For centuries, with little or no regard for the living tradition, scholars have been debating whether Sankhya and Yoga are part of the same system of philosophy or two different systems. According to the living tradition, however, there is no room for debate: Sankhya is the theoretical aspect of Yoga; Yoga is the practical aspect of Sankhya. Sankhya and Yoga form one complete system of philosophy and practice, hence the term *Sankhya Yoga.*

To be clear: The wisdom of Yoga has flourished for thousands of years due to an uninterrupted stream of practicing yogis, not due to the appearance of occasional texts and commentaries. This uninterrupted stream of practitioners constitutes the living tradition of Yoga. In Yoga, as in any other applied science, the value of a tradition far exceeds what appears to be documented in only a few texts or commentaries, which themselves are separated by centuries. I am a product of a living tradition, specifically the Sri Vidya tradition of Yoga sadhana, which is firmly grounded in Sankhya Yoga. This rare privilege prevents me from using my academic training and skill to tear apart an organic body of wisdom, an approach that renders an experiential science like Yoga lifeless.

The scope of Sankhya Yoga is vast. Like all other systems of Indian philosophy, it expounds specific doctrines pertaining to the ultimate truth, the evolution of the universe, the purpose of life, the phenomenon of birth and death, the doctrine of karma and reincarnation, the source of valid knowledge, the concept of vice and virtue, the possibility of attaining immortality, and finally, true fulfillment and freedom. Sankhya Yoga addresses these and many other issues for one purpose and one purpose only: to explore the means of fulfilling our innate desire to be free here and now. Tradition captures this core theme by calling Sankhya Yoga *moksha shastra,* the science and practice leading to ultimate freedom.

Origins of Sankhya Yoga

Sankhya Yoga is the oldest Indian philosophical system. Its concepts and precepts have influenced every school of philosophy, religion, and spirituality on the Indian subcontinent, yet its original writings are the most poorly preserved. The *Sankhya Karika* of Ishvara Krishna is the most complete (and perhaps the most ancient) text on Sankhya Yoga available today. Ishvara Krishna states that the *Sankhya Karika* is a summary of a much longer text, *Shashti Tantra,* which he received from the guru-disciple lineage (SK 71 and 72). He compressed the content of this 60-chapter text into 70 verses in the *Sankhya Karika,* perhaps under the assumption that his readers are as rigorously trained in the wisdom of the tradition as he was. Taken alone, the text is full of internal contradictions. Only in concert with knowledge preserved in the tradition, and information available in other texts, can we resolve these contradictions and formulate a coherent philosophy of Sankhya Yoga. To delineate the doctrines of Sankhya Yoga, therefore, I have taken the liberty of drawing on the training I have received from the living tradition. Further, in addition to the *Sankhya Karika,* I rely heavily on the *Yoga Sutra* and the *Bhagavad Gita,* and occasionally consult the *Tattva Samasa,* a text attributed to the sage Kapila.

According to the tradition, the sage Kapila is the first teacher of the philosophy and practice of Sankhya Yoga. To grasp the scope of his teachings, we must know something about his role in the philosophical and spiritual history of India. The majority of scholars consider Kapila a mythical figure. As proof, they cite Vyasa's statement: "Driven by sheer compassion, the first wise being, the primordial sage [Kapila] assumed a self-created mind (*nirmana chitta*) and imparted the knowledge (*tantra*) to Asuri" (YS 1:25). Another reference to Kapila's extraordinary identity is found in Mathara's commentary on the *Sankhya Karika,* where Asuri, the second teacher in the Sankhya lineage, is said to have undertaken a 3,000-year-long ritualistic practice. Kapila imparts the knowledge of Sankhya to Asuri only after he completed this lengthy practice. These and similar references undermine Kapila's identity as a living human teacher.

Tradition tells a different story, however. In the *Bhagavad Gita*, Krishna reckons Kapila a *siddha* master par excellence (BG 10:26). He is the epitome of knowledge, non-attachment, virtue, and godly powers. These qualities are innate to Kapila (Mathara's commentary on SK 43), yet Kapila is as human as we are. According to the *Srimad Bhagavatam,* the sage Kardama is his father and Devahuti is his mother. When Kapila's father renounced family life, his mother sank into deep sorrow. At that juncture, Kapila taught her the unique system of meditation on the lotus of the heart, thus guiding her to a state of pure luminous joy.

In the tradition of Sri Vidya, Kapila is the first in a line of seventy-one masters (*Sri Vidyarnava* 1:52–60). Although these and similar references may not be useful in establishing Kapila's exact date and place of birth, they demonstrate that he is a master of extraordinary stature. He is recognized as a prominent master across all traditions and sub-traditions of India. Kapila is more than the founding father of Sankhya, Yoga, or Sankhya Yoga. He is also among the highest masters of Tantra, more precisely the Sri Vidya tradition of Tantra. His yogic power and wisdom are beyond compare. The wisdom he transmitted to Asuri reveals (*khya*) the truth completely (*sam*) from every vantage point (*a*), hence the word *sankhya*. He also imparted the techniques for realizing the truth (*yoga*), hence the term *Sankhya Yoga.*

This philosophy begins with a realization common to us all: there is pain and we must attain freedom from it. It explains the nature of our core being and the process that leads to the acquisition of pain. It offers a step-by-step explanation of how to eliminate life's painful conditions and enter a state of consciousness free from want and need—a state of ultimate freedom and joy. In this context, Sankhya Yoga poses four key questions: Who are we? Where do we come from? Why are we here? Where do we go when we die? In response to these questions, this ancient system of philosophy and practice describes the nature of Absolute Reality; the process of the manifestation of the universe; the phenomenon of birth and death; the concept of bondage and liberation; the concepts of God, the individual soul, and the power of the mind; and the technique of meditation to discover our pure, pristine core being.

Our Limitless Grandeur

Each of us is a pure, self-luminous, intelligent being. Pure existence (*sat*), consciousness (*chit*), and bliss (*ananda*) are intrinsic. Our core is pure joy. Due to our self-luminous nature, we have the inherent power to know who we are, where we came from, why we are here, and where we go when we die. We are limited only by eternity. We are soul; the body is our locus. The mind is a tool for discovering and experiencing the vast universe contained deep within us. The body, the mind, and the world inside and outside us all serve a single purpose: they enable us to experience our limitless grandeur—pure existence, consciousness, and bliss. This grandeur can be comprehended only by our self-contained, unalloyed Consciousness.

Our outward journey—the journey toward birth—is propelled by our intrinsic joy, which arises from knowing ourselves as limitless. The essence of our intelligence (*buddhi sattva*) emerges from this spontaneous joy. It is as pure and bright as Consciousness itself. It has the ability to know everything, including the Knower. It has the ability to see everything, including the Seer. It is the very principle of knowing (*buddhi samvit*).

The term Sankhya Yoga uses most frequently for this power of intelligence is *buddhi.*

The range of our intelligence is infinitely vast. For the sake of simplicity, Sankhya Yoga divides it into four parts: the ability to remember, retain, and retrieve (*chitta*); the ability to comprehend, discern, and decide (*buddhi*); the ability to identify, define, and circumscribe (*ahamkara*); and the ability to notice, cognize, and objectify (*manas*). In this account, I am using "mind" to denote all four functions of our intelligence.

In Sankhya Yoga, consciousness in conjunction with the mind is known as *purusha,* the individual self. The fact that we are individuals in no way prevents us from knowing and experiencing the limitless grandeur of our core being, for we are endowed with a powerful mind. The mind is integral to us. Its creative and discerning power is immense. Nothing in the world is beyond its reach. It has the ability to turn imagination into reality. It has the power to give form to the formless. It can infuse matter with intelligence and transform an inanimate object into a living being. With the help of the mind we can discover the mystery of Consciousness that has made the body its locus, as well as the mystery of Consciousness that stretches beyond the domain of our body. We can also discover the mystery of the mind itself.

In other words, we have the innate ability to discover and experience the vast universe within us and outside us. We can also solve the mystery pertaining to the reality that bridges the internal and external worlds. With the help of the mind, we can unravel the mysteries of time, space, and the law of cause and effect. We can solve the mystery of where we come from, why we are here, and where we go after we die. But even though we have this wonderful mind, we suffer. Why?

The Cause of Suffering

According to Sankhya philosophy, suffering is created by the mind. The mind becomes the cause of suffering when it forgets the purpose of its existence. We acquired the mind for the purpose of exploring and experiencing our inherent grandeur (Vyasa on sutra 2:19). With the passage of time, however, we forgot that it is an inner instrument (*antahkarana*). We forgot that the function of the mind is to perceive, identify, discern, and gain a clear understanding of the objective world. The mind's job is to discover the vast world of thoughts and feelings and make them available to Consciousness, so it can express its inherent beauty and joy in the most rewarding manner. Instead of doing its job, however, the mind begins to accumulate experiences for itself. Rather than serving as an agent of Consciousness, the mind begins behaving as the owner of the objects of its experiences. Its strong identification with them causes the mind to forget that it is simply a conduit of experiences, not their owner and master. The mind's clarity, power of comprehension, and confidence is intended for the purpose of gathering experiences and presenting them to Consciousness without distortion. Instead, the mind begins to use its abilities to convince both itself and Consciousness that all experiences belong to the mind. This is how the seed of ignorance (*avidya*) is planted.

The more the mind insists on claiming its experiences, the thicker the veil of ignorance becomes. Without realizing the gravity of its mistake, the mind begins to operate shrouded by this veil. Oblivious to the tremendous loss of clarity, power of comprehension, and confidence, it begins exerting its considerable remaining power to claim the objective world corresponding to its experiences. The mind fails to understand that it has lost an infinitely vast universe and is now only the owner of a small self-created world. In this little world, the mind struggles to maintain its identity as the proprietor of experiences, in the process identifying with their pleasant and unpleasant consequences. This is how a sense of I-am-ness (*asmita*) is born.

The mind latches on to whatever it finds pleasant and repels whatever it finds unpleasant. This is how attachment (*raga*) and aversion (*dvesha*) are born. Likes, dislikes, and the experiences corresponding to them are the mind's own creation; it cannot bear to see them destroyed. It wishes to preserve them forever, but this is impossible because it gained these experiences through the senses, and sensory experiences are short-lived. The mind continues revisiting these experiences until one day the body becomes old and is headed toward death. Losing everything to death is terrifying; thus, fear of death (*abhinivesha*) is born. We cling to life in vain.

It is important to remember that the outward journey of Consciousness begins with the intention of experiencing its own infinite grandeur. It accomplishes this by creating the mind and infusing it with its own infinite intelligence. Consciousness creates the mind by using "material" intrinsic to its own being, known as Prakriti. Prakriti means "creativity par excellence." Prakriti is the intrinsic Power of Consciousness (*Chiti Shakti*). Through its sheer intention, Consciousness brings forward a world of infinite wealth lying in unmanifest form in the vast field of its creative power—and does so while retaining complete mastery over it. Unmanifest Prakriti, creativity par excellence, manifests spontaneously.

The mind is the first recognizable state of this manifestation. It is the perfect blend of Pure Consciousness and its intrinsic Creativity. As said earlier, at this stage the mind is as pure and brilliant as its source—Consciousness and its Intrinsic Creativity. It contains everything its source contains. Propelled by the initial intention of Purusha and Prakriti, the mind brings forward the objective world.

The first thing the mind brings forward is the expanded vision of its own functions—different faculties of the mind evolve. Its power to discern, to identify, to think, and to store the experiences in the form of memory becomes concrete. This is how the mental faculties of discernment (*buddhi*), identification (*ahamkara*), thinking (*manas*), and retention (*chitta*) evolve. From here, the essence of sound, touch, sight, taste, and smell manifest. Similarly, the five cognitive senses of hearing, touching, seeing, tasting, and smelling manifest, along with the five senses of action pertaining to grasping, moving, speaking, procreating, and defecating. These are followed by the manifestation of the five gross elements of space, air, fire, water, and earth. The mind is at the center of this entire manifestation, and the mind is itself a perfect blend of Consciousness and its Intrinsic Creativity. Yet it falls prey to ignorance, setting in motion a long train of sorrow.

In the course of daily life, we are surrounded by pleasant and unpleasant experiences. We are busy acquiring objects of our desire and warding off undesirable objects and experiences. We see the world through the lens of our likes and dislikes and are caught in a complex net of love, compassion, selflessness, forgiveness, and their counterparts—hatred, cruelty, selfishness, anger, and so on. Our actions are primarily motivated by fear and greed. The harsh realities of life occupy so much of our mind that we rarely pause to ponder the purpose behind our actions. We do not have any idea that the mind is an instrument and this instrument is meant to serve the purpose of Consciousness. In fact, we never experience ourselves as separate from our mind.

The scriptures tell us that our core is Consciousness. It is a witness. Consciousness uses the mind, senses, and body to experience the objective world but does not involve itself in action. We are not aware there is a witness (Consciousness) and a doer (the mind) in us, and that they are separate. We have never experienced Consciousness and the mind as two separate entities. All we know is that we are alive. We know we exist. We know we are attracted to pleasure and try to avoid pain. The desire for pleasure and the aversion to pain is the primary motivation for our actions. We are further motivated by our notions of right and wrong, good and bad, loss and gain, honor and insult. When we engage in an action, we do not know who in us is the doer and who or what in us is an instrument. We know only that we are a single, indivisible entity. We witness our actions while we are performing them, and we reap their fruits. We are accountable for our actions, and our conscience justifies our ownership of the fruits.

This perfectly blended duo of mind and consciousness is responsible for all actions. We are aware that we are a thinking being, but we know nothing about Consciousness as a witnessing agent. We know ourselves only as our mind. The mind is us; we are the mind. When the mind is entangled, we are in bondage. With the liberation of the mind comes our liberation. As mind we are born, as mind we live, and as mind we die, only to be born again. Our world of personal pleasure and pain, love and hate, birth and death, bondage and liberation exists only as long as the mind is veiled by ignorance (*avidya*), I-am-ness (*asmita*), attachment (*raga*), aversion (*dvesha*), and fear (*abhinivesha*). That is why the sages call the mind the greatest of all mysteries.

The Wheel of Karma

Nothing we do can be destroyed. This is an immutable law (BG 2:40). The mind upholds this law by storing the essence of our actions, the fruits of our actions, and the experiences pertaining to them. Everything we do is stored in the mind in the form of subtle impressions (*samskaras*). Every action—physical, mental, or verbal—creates an impression in the mind. Every time we repeat an action, the impression makes a deeper groove. Eventually the subtle impressions become so strong that from deep within they begin to influence our thought processes. At this point, we find ourselves acting on impulse.

If not checked, these powerful impulses begin to control our decision-making faculty. They dominate the mind so completely that we begin to perceive, think, and feel in the light of the subtle impressions stored in our mind. At this stage, the impressions are called *vasanas*. *Vasana* means "coloring." A *vasana* is a subtle impression powerful enough to subdue the original radiance of the mind and force it to experience the world in the light of those impressions. Collectively, numberless impressions shape our personality. They mold our thoughts, feelings, and behaviors.

We have been performing actions for untold ages. Our actions are propelled by deeply ingrained impressions of the past and are seasoned with like and dislike, good and bad, right and wrong. Furthermore, they are charged with emotion. Behind every action is a negative emotion, a positive emotion, or a mixture. Elements such as anger, hatred, jealousy, greed, fear, revenge, love, kindness, compassion, generosity, and pity are always present. Consequently, the subtle impressions created by our actions contain these elements.

Eventually, our mind turns into a warehouse of samskaras and vasanas that are pleasant in part and unpleasant in part, a mixture of desirable and undesirable. In Sankhya Yoga, the mind infused with these potent impressions is known as *karmashaya,* the repository of karmas. This mind is our abode—but more than that, this mind *is* us. These powerful subtle impressions are the building blocks of our life. They dictate how we think, feel, and act. They dictate that we no longer know and experience ourselves as Pure Consciousness. We no longer know ourselves as Pure Witness of any of our actions, thoughts, and feelings. We do not perceive ourselves as Pure Being. We find ourselves as happy or sad, peaceful or agitated. We perceive ourselves as rich or poor, good or bad, virtuous or non-virtuous.

We perform our actions under the spell of the subtle impressions stored in the mind and our actions reinforce these subtle impressions. Sankhya Yoga calls this process *vritti samskara chakra,* the wheel made of subtle impressions and the mind's roaming tendencies. Subtle impressions engender roaming tendencies; roaming tendencies strengthen the subtle impressions. Once in motion, this wheel revolves at an ever-increasing velocity. This is the mind we have created for ourselves, and it is with this mind that we are trying to find life's purpose: to discover our grandeur, experience our intrinsic beauty and joy, and bathe in the inner luminosity of our soul. The precious moments of our life fly by quick as a wink. As we age and begin to wane, we find ourselves confronted with purposelessness, anxiety, and fear of death. We attempt to cling to life. Pulled by the forces of life and death, we finally breathe our last. Exhausted by the strains of life, we resolve to rest. We die.

The Cycle of Birth and Death

What happens to us when we die answers the questions of who we are, where we come from, and why we are here. Death is preceded by the process of dying—our bodily functions fail; our organs collapse; sensory feelings, including our self-awareness, dissolve into the mind. The mind resorts to its self-created world—the world of our samskaras and vasanas. It is important to remember that we are the mind and the mind is us. Thus once we die, we are left with the contents of our mind—our long cherished likes and dislikes, loves and hatreds, and an infinitely vast collection of memories. But having lost our body and sense organs to death, we have no means of knowing what we have and do not have. We do not even know whether we exist. We are enveloped by the utter darkness of death. Lacking any self-awareness, we are virtually non-existent.

Primordial Nature is our resting ground. In Sankhya Yoga, the name for Primordial Nature is Prakriti, the creative matrix of the universe. As we have seen, Prakriti is creativity par excellence. It is one and all-pervading. It is eternal and absolute. It is beyond time, space, and the law of cause and effect. It has no form and no name. Philosophers call it Prakriti for it embodies unsurpassed (*pra*) ability to be, to become, and to create (*kriti*). The potential for existence is within the fold of Prakriti; it *is* that potential. The universe in its manifest form evolves from it, exists in it, and dissolves back into it. Our outward journey also evolves from it, exists in it, and dissolves back into it. After death, there is no place but Prakriti for us to rest. The question of how long we rest in Prakriti, along with all our samskaras and vasanas, is irrelevant, for with death comes the death of time itself. Time is regulated by the law of relativity, and death devours both. Thus, the lack of awareness enveloping us is timeless.

When we are dead, we exist in Prakriti with no awareness of who we are, what we are, and where we are. We do not know what destiny holds for us. With the dissolution of the mind, our craving for life and our repulsion for death have also dissolved. Even the thought of praying for our own well-being is dead. We are essentially *asat,* a virtually non-existent entity resting in the vast field of Prakriti. Sankhya Yoga begins with the narration of the step-by-step process of how we come out of this timeless slumber of death, how we begin to pulsate, how we regain our memory, and how we enter the world again.

While resting in the vast field of nameless, formless, all-pervading, eternal Prakriti, we are utterly unaware of who we are, where we are, and what destiny awaits us. The term for this type of entity is *purusha,* a term that describes our inherent condition. Death has rendered us inert. We are sleeping (*sha*) in the city (*puri*) comprised of the potential to manifest the infinitely vast range of the objective world. This is the city of infinite possibilities. Prakriti is inside us, outside us, and all around us, but we are unaware of it.

Next to us, however, is a unique Purusha, which, like Prakriti, is also outside us and all around us. Unlike us, this unique Purusha is beyond death, decay, and destruction. It is untouched by ignorance, I-am-ness, attachment, aversion, and death. It is beyond time, space, and the law of cause and effect. It is never affected by actions, fruits of actions, and karmic vehicles, which keep us caught in the cycle of birth and death (YS 1:24). This unique Purusha is as eternal and all-pervading as Prakriti itself. It is Ishvara, in whom lies the unsurpassed seed of omniscience (YS 1:25). Because it is not limited by time, this unique Purusha is the primordial master, guru, and guide of all previous preceptors (YS 1:26). The watchful eye of this unique Purusha is always on us, even when we are dead. It is this unique Purusha that breathes life into us and pulls us out of the timeless slumber of death.

Two Categories of Purusha

The *Bhagavad Gita* tells us, "In this world there are two kinds of beings: perishable (*kshara*) and imperishable (*akshara*). All those who emerge from the past (*bhutani*) are perishable; the One who remains above the phenomenon of time is imperishable. The Imperishable One is the highest being. It is known as *Paramatma,* the Supreme Being. It is Ishvara. Having penetrated the threefold world, it protects and provides nourishment to all." (BG 15:16–17)

In simpler language, we are perishable and Ishvara is imperishable. We are subject to death, decay, and destruction; Ishvara is not. We are enveloped by the fivefold affliction (*klesha*)—ignorance, distorted sense of I-am-ness, attachment, aversion, and fear of death. Ishvara is not touched by these afflictions. Due to these five kleshas, we identify with our actions and cling to their fruits. Ishvara is untouched by actions and their results (YS 1:24). Due to identification, we reap the fruits of our actions and consume them, whether they are pleasant or unpleasant. In regard to reaping and embracing the fruits of our actions, a sense of helplessness accompanies us. We become *bhokta,* a helpless consumer of the fruits of our actions. Ishvara is the Pure Seer and the Power of Seeing itself. We are many and Ishvara is one. The process of wear and tear is an integral part of us. There is no wear and tear in Ishvara. We are always accompanied by change. Ishvara is constant. These contrasting attributes make us an ordinary purusha; Ishvara is the Special Purusha.

We are *jivatma,* a soul dependent on breath to bring us back to life—a fact indicated by the verb root *jiva,* which means "breathing." We awaken to life when the primordial Seer casts his glance on us and spontaneously becomes aware of our inherent condition. Free of the confinement of time and space, he knows the total truth about us. He knows that, exhausted by the strains of life, we have resorted to death. Enveloped in utter inertia, we are resting in the vast field of Prakriti. Our numberless subtle impressions still fill our mind, and the Divine Being knows we are unaware of them. Ishvara also knows that our lack of awareness does not free us from our impressions—sooner or later, we must attain freedom from the bondage of our dormant samskaras. We must become manifest and we must become aware of our samskaras. Only then can we make a conscious effort to attain freedom from them.

Driven by sheer compassion, so to speak, Ishvara looks at Prakriti, creativity par excellence. The ever-vibrant Prakriti, in response to the intention (*sankalpa*) of Ishvara, instantly resolves to bring forward the infinite wealth of the objective world from her bosom. She begins to pulsate with purpose and meaning, and we awaken from the timeless slumber of death. The luminosity of Ishvara penetrates our being. We become aware of ourselves. We become cognizant beings; our sense of I-am-ness returns. Our samskaras reawaken. Samskaras compel us to achieve fulfillment, but this is possible only if we have instruments with which to express ourselves and to interact with the objects of our experience. This necessitates the evolution of the senses and sensory objects. To comprehend how Prakriti brings forth the objective world and fills it with an infinite number of diversities, we must first understand the relationship between Prakriti and Ishvara.

Two Categories of Prakriti

As we have seen, Sankhya Yoga posits the theory of two categories of purusha: perishable and imperishable. We, the individual souls, are perishable and Ishvara is imperishable. We are ordinary beings; Ishvara is an extraordinary being. We are many and Ishvara is one. Similarly, there are two categories of prakriti: lower (*apara*) and higher (*para*).

Our inherent properties constitute lower prakriti. Apara prakriti consists of our numberless subtle impressions, our likes and dislikes, and our vast range of desires. The fivefold affliction—ignorance, distorted sense of I-am-ness, attachment, aversion, and fear of death—is its defining property. Apara prakriti is our locus. It is as perishable as we are and as potent. This lower prakriti of ours is subject to death, dissolution, and re-emergence.

Para Prakriti—the highest Prakriti—is an intrinsic attribute of Ishvara. It is *aishvarya,* the godly power of the Supreme Being. Para Prakriti is as pure as the Supreme Being. It is beyond samskaras and vasanas, likes and dislikes. It is beyond the reach of the fivefold affliction. It is Ishvara's own creativity par excellence. It is as pervasive, imperishable, and as potent as Ishvara himself. Unlike lower prakriti, it is not subject to death and dissolution. The notion of re-emergence does not apply, for Para Prakriti is the ever-lit intrinsic luminosity of Ishvara. We rest in this highest Prakriti after death. This Prakriti has room for an infinite number of souls, with their infinite universes comprised of an infinite number of lower prakritis. An infinite number of universes are being born from Para Prakriti and are dissolving into it. In other words, Para Prakriti, intrinsic to Ishvara, is the origin of everything that exists and the ground for its dissolution (BG 7:5–6).

The Union of Purusha and Prakriti

Regarding the manifestation and dissolution of the objective world, the Sankhya Yoga texts deliberately switch back and forth between Prakriti and Purusha. The *Bhagavad Gita,* for example, follows this pattern, but prefers attributing the manifestation and dissolution of the universe to Ishvara, whereas the *Sankhya Karika* and the *Yoga Sutra* take the opposite approach. According to the *Bhagavad Gita,* Ishvara is the source of creation. Everything begins from Ishvara (BG 7:7, 9:17, 10:8, and 15:4). According to the *Sankhya Karika,* the manifestation of the universe starts from Prakriti. Prakriti is the source of everything (SK 3, 22, 56, 57, and 58).

The concept of the manifestation of the universe becomes muddy when the scriptures use the terms *purusha* and *prakriti* without specifying how they are using them. It becomes even more complicated (and frankly, bewildering) when the *Sankhya Karika* and its commentators use the analogy of a blind person and a lame person to describe Purusha and Prakriti, and then propose that it is the union of an impaired Purusha and a hobbled Prakriti that brings the universe into existence. These texts do not clarify whether it is the union of prakriti with ordinary, perishable purusha(s) or extraordinary, imperishable Purusha (*Ishvara*) that is the source of the manifestation of the universe. The scriptures are consistent, however, in telling us that this union and what evolves from it is inherently painful, and in order to attain freedom from this pain, Purusha and Prakriti have to be isolated from each other. At the same time, these scriptures tell us that the manifestation of the universe resulting from this union has only one purpose: freedom from pain. A reader who is less than adept in Sankhya Yoga is left in utter confusion.

The traditional approach to the study of Sankhya Yoga is simple and straightforward: First, distinguish the higher self, the imperishable Supreme Being (*Paramatma*), from the lower self, the perishable, ordinary being (*jivatma*). Second, distinguish the higher Prakriti that is paired with the Supreme Being from the lower prakriti associated with an ordinary being. Third, clarify whether the prakriti of these two purushas is intrinsic to them or is an acquired characteristic. If it is intrinsic, it cannot be separated from them; but if it is acquired, it can. Fourth, clarify which kind of union—and the world manifesting from it—embodies pain, and which kind of union grants freedom. A clear understanding of these four points enables us to delineate the entire philosophy of Sankhya Yoga and the practice based on it without ambiguity. Let us examine each of these in turn.

The notable difference between the higher and the lower self is that the former is imperishable (*akshara*) and the latter is perishable (*kshara*). Ishvara is the higher self; we are the lower self. Unlike us, Ishvara is not subject to destruction, decay, and death. Ishvara is unborn (*aja*) and immutable (*avyaya*) (BG 4:6). We are born before (*purvotpanna*) (SK 40) and are born again. Unlike us, Ishvara is not caught in the cycle of samsara. Ishvara allows creation to come forward while retaining mastery over Prakriti, while the world of samskaras manifesting from us is not under our control (BG 9:8).

Ishvara's Prakriti is divine and self-luminous (BG 9:13). Our prakriti, comprised of our samskaras, is stained by the five afflictions, with ignorance as the leader (YS 2:24). Ishvara is self-luminous, and luminosity itself is his Prakriti. His luminosity is intrinsic. Both Ishvara and his luminosity are undiminishing (*avyaya*). We are also luminous beings, but our luminosity is constrained by our prakriti, which is comprised of afflictions and a large range of samskaras. Ishvara is the Seer (*drashta*) and his Seeing

Power—Prakriti—is never compromised. Furthermore, Ishvara's Prakriti is creativity par excellence, and is thus the source of, and ground for, the infinitely vast and diverse universe.

We are also seers, but our power of seeing is compromised. Our creativity is limited, and even that becomes dormant when we die. Our prakriti, the samskaric potentials, are the source of, and ground for, our finite world—the world of our likes and dislikes, pleasure and pain, personal bondage and liberation. We are both blind and lame. Our ability to know the truth and our ability to walk on the path of fulfillment and freedom is marred by ignorance and the four afflictions evolving from it.

Ishvara's Prakriti is intrinsic; ours is acquired. Ishvara's Prakriti is his *svabhava*, his own essential nature. In the case of Ishvara and Prakriti, the question of who influences who is meaningless for they are one. Ishvara is the Seer; Prakriti is the Power of Seeing. Thus, the question of whether the world evolves from Ishvara or from Prakriti is senseless, for Ishvara and Prakriti are an indivisible whole. Just as Ishvara and Prakriti cannot be separated, the world cannot exist apart from Ishvara.

Our prakriti is not intrinsic but acquired. It is different from us. Our personal world evolves from our prakriti, which is comprised of our samskaras. In other words, our samskaras constitute our *svabhava*, our personal nature. Samskaras are our prakriti. The mind mingled with samskaras defines what we are. Our union with this prakriti is caused by ignorance (YS 2:17 and 2:24). Ignorance maintains and nurtures this union, generating a long chain of pain, which comes to an end only when we see the difference between Consciousness and the prakriti within us. In Sankhya Yoga, this process is known as *viveka khyati*, discerning knowledge. This discernment clears away our confusion regarding who we are and what our relationship is with our acquired prakriti (YS 2:25–2:27).

Just as there are two categories of purusha and two categories of prakriti, there are two categories of manifestation: *bhautika sarga*, the manifestation of the material world, and *pratyaya sarga,* the manifestation of our mental world.

Manifestation of the Material World

Bhautika sarga, the manifestation of the material world, begins with Ishvara or with intrinsic Prakriti. To distinguish Ishvara's intrinsic Prakriti from the lower prakriti associated with individual souls, philosophers prefer the terms *Para Prakriti*, the highest Prakriti; or *Mahad Brahma,* the highest, ever-pervasive Reality; or *Pradhana,* the Main. This form of creation is eternal, for Prakriti is intrinsic to Ishvara. Its purpose is to provide complete fulfillment and freedom to the individual soul (YS 2:18). There is no beginning and no end to Purusha and Prakriti (BG 13:19). Similarly, there is no beginning or end to the universe, which exists intrinsically in Purusha/Prakriti. In order to avoid creating the false impression that Purusha and Prakriti are different, the scriptures deliberately switch back and forth when attributing the manifestation of the material world. In this respect, Purusha and Prakriti are one and the same—the difference lies merely in the existence of two different terms. There is dualism in Sankhya Yoga, not because this system posits the theory that Purusha and Prakriti are different from each other, but because there is a difference between the unique Purusha, the imperishable being, and ordinary purusha(s), the perishable beings.

The *Yoga Sutra* (4:32 and 4:33) tells us the manifestation of the material world is of two kinds: *akrama shrishti,* non-linear creation, and *krama shrishti,* linear creation. Non-linear creation is indistinguishable from Prakriti. In this realm, the law of cause and effect does not apply. The principle of time is non-existent. The infinite varieties of attributes and qualities are contained indistinguishably in one homogenous field of intelligence, and these powers are intrinsic to it.

For the sake of discussion, the infinite varieties of powers are lumped into three categories: *sattva,* the force of illumination; *rajas,* the force of animation; and *tamas,* the force of concealment. Numberless forces, qualities, and attributes—known and unknown to us—are derived from, and comprised of, these three forces. In non-linear creation, these forces are contained in each other and do not exert their contrasting influence. In the world of non-linearity, there is no division of time, space, cause, and effect. These three forces and their infinite variants flow indistinguishably within Purusha/Prakriti, the Supreme Being.

Linear creation is the world of matter and energy—an infinite number of universes within the universe, all ever-expanding—which emerges from the non-linear realm. We are part of linear creation. This creation is regulated by time, space, and the law of cause and effect. Here the forces of illumination (*sattva*), pulsation (*rajas*), and concealment (*tamas*) exert their influence on each other. From their mutual interaction, an immense range of energies manifest vividly. Some are known to us; many are unknown.

The linear world manifests when the Supreme Being casts his glance on the individuals lying inert in the vast field of Prakriti and instantly perceives their painful condition. Numberless individuals are in Ishvara's full view. Their samskaras and vasanas, likes and dislikes, cravings and ambitions are fully known to him (YS 4:18). Ishvara also knows their powerful attachment to the world they once created. He knows that these individuals have only two options: either renounce their attachment to the world of their desires or fulfill their desires. They can pursue these options only if they are made aware of the world of their desires and attachments. They have to be awakened—they must see and be reunited with their mental world. Their mental faculties must be reintroduced to them. In other words, they need their mind and their senses. They need a body fitted with the appropriate limbs and organs, and they need a concrete material world where they can use their body, mind, and senses to find their life's purpose.

They must be brought back to their familiar world—a world governed by time and space and the law of cause and effect. They have to be given an identity. They must find their relatives, friends, and enemies, and re-examine themselves in the light of success and failure, gain and loss, honor and insult. They must reclaim what they consider theirs and pay their karmic debts to others. They have to isolate themselves from what they have mistakenly identified as theirs. They need to resolve their conflicts and be at peace with themselves. They must rediscover their true identity and become established in their essential nature (*svarupa-pratishtha*). They must experience their grandeur—their limitless existence, consciousness, beauty, and bliss.

Ishvara sees each one of these individuals. Driven by sheer compassion, he resolves to arouse them from their timeless slumber. The term for this resolution is *sankalpa,* the initial intention laden with an infinite variety of powers, qualities, and attributes capable of bringing forward a world of limitless diversities. With this intention Ishvara looks at his intrinsic Prakriti, and the world of limitless diversity unfolds.

As explained earlier, all the forces, qualities, and attributes of Prakriti are divided into three categories: sattva, rajas, and tamas. In the world of non-linearity, these forces flow peacefully inward within the irreferable realm of Prakriti. But now, when Prakriti resolves to manifest as the objective world, the threefold forces begin to influence each other and interact. From their interaction, limitless diversities evolve.

The world manifesting from Prakriti includes the faculty of comprehension (*buddhi*), the faculty of identification (*ahamkara*), the faculty of thinking (*manas*), the essence of sound, touch, sight, taste, and smell (the five *tanmatras*), the five senses of cognition (hearing, touching, seeing, tasting, and smelling), the five senses of action (grasping, moving, speaking, procreating, and defecating), and the five gross elements (space, air, fire, water, and earth). In Sankhya Yoga, these twenty-three broad categories of our manifest world, along with Prakriti, the twenty-fourth, are called *tattva,* loosely translated as "elements." However, with the exception of the five gross elements, none of the others are elements, strictly speaking. For centuries, this loose translation has been a breeding ground for confusion. The literal meaning of the Sanskrit term *tattva* is "the essence (*tva*) of that (*tat*)." *Tat* refers to irreferable Prakriti (Vyasa on sutra 2:19 and BG 4:6, 7:7, 9:10, 9:13, and 10:8).

It is important to remember that this evolutionary process is spontaneous. The compassion-driven resolve to empower individuals to find fulfillment and freedom arises in the awareness of the Supreme Being, who is beyond time, space, and the law of cause and effect. Prakriti, pulsating with the power of manifestation, is similarly beyond time, space, and the law of cause and effect. The realm where the manifestation is taking place is non-linear. The Seer sees, and the Seeing Power of the Seer is instantaneously transformed into what the Seer sees.

There are texts that, while describing the process of manifestation, give the impression that the twenty-three elements evolve from Prakriti in a particular sequence. But keep in mind that this scheme of describing the entire range of manifestation in twenty-three categories is only from the standpoint of humans, whose capacity to comprehend reality is quite limited. We are rarely aware of knowledge itself, for example; we are aware only of the object of our knowledge. We are not aware of the principle of Intelligence itself, which enables us to understand the objects we perceive. Due to the limitations imposed on the conduits of our comprehension, our understanding of the world is confined to only twenty-three elements. Only when we transcend human limitations are we able to comprehend how infinitely subtle and profound the world is and how far the mystery of Prakriti's manifestation stretches.

The scriptures speak of the different realms of existence and of beings whose knowledge and powers are beyond our comprehension. For this reason, Prakriti is said to be the repository of an infinite number of wonders (*ananta-vaichitrya-nirbhara*) and expert at creating things that have never been created (*aghatita-ghatana-ghatiyasi*). Furthermore, in the realm of Prakriti, the entire universe exists as one indivisible reality. It has no shape and no size. The realm of Prakriti is so subtle that even the concept of subtle vanishes here (YS 1:45). When the scriptures speak of the manifestation of the universe from Prakriti, it means Prakriti unveils her vast potentials in a manner that can be comprehended by us. The design of our mind allows us to experience the objective world only when it is presented to us in linear order. For us to experience an object it must have shape and size, and that shape and size must be compatible with the capacity of our senses and mind. The object cannot be too big or too small, too far away or too close. Furthermore, there cannot be more than one object in the same place at the same time.

Prakriti unveils her vast potential in a linear manner so that we can experience and comprehend the objective world. She does this by manifesting the principles of time (*kala*) and space (*akasha*), and the principle of cause and effect (*karana-karya-bhava*). These three together introduce the notion of number. Together, time, space, cause and effect, and number enable us to comprehend the objective world. The phenomenon of linearity is regulated by these factors, and our mind is designed to comprehend only the linear world. Only when we reach a unique state of samadhi—*dharma megha samadhi*—are we able to comprehend the reality that transcends the linear world (YS 4:32). The doctrine of the manifestation of the universe in twenty-three categories (*tattva*) is for the benefit of those of us not yet established in dharma megha samadhi.

With this in mind, let us return to our discussion of the two categories of manifestation. *Bhautika sarga,* the world comprised of matter and energy, manifests from Ishvara/Prakriti. It is as big as Prakriti herself. It is finite only in the sense that we cannot comprehend it all. Manifestation of this world is for the sake of our fulfillment (*bhoga*) and ultimate freedom (*apavarga*) (SK 36, 42, 56, 57, 58, and 59; YS 2:18). To understand the inherent properties of the manifest world and its role in helping us find our life's purpose, it is important that we learn about *satkarya-vada,* the distinctive doctrine of Sankhya Yoga (SK 9).

According to the doctrine of satkarya-vada, the effect (*karya*) always exists (*sat*) in its cause. An effect cannot grow out of a non-existent cause. All the qualities, properties, and attributes of an effect are always present in its cause. Whatever does not exist in the cause cannot be found in the effect, and whatever exists in the cause must exist in the effect. Put simply, according to this doctrine, the cause is itself transformed into the effect. Philosophers have gone to great lengths to examine, discuss, and prove this doctrine.

In the context of attaining life's purpose, it is important to note that the objective world is an effect; it exists in its cause, Purusha/Prakriti. The world is as real as Prakriti, and vice versa. All of the qualities and attributes of Prakriti are present in the objective world. It is the source of the objective world and the provider. Every aspect of the objective world is infused with the compassionate intention that caused Prakriti to unveil her limitless potentials and bring forth this manifest world.

The objective world manifests from the divinely inspired Prakriti, exists in Prakriti, and operates in conformity with her intention to empower us to find our life's purpose. Every aspect of the objective world is imbued with the primal intention of Purusha: may the one charged with the capacity to see, see; and may the one charged with the capacity to be revealed, be revealed. Individuals have the capacity to see themselves, and the mind has the capacity to reveal. Individuals who, under the sway of ignorance, have lost their capacity to know and see themselves now get their capacity back. The mind that lost its capacity to reveal now gets its power of revelation back. Individual souls are no longer blind and the mind is no longer lame. The mind and Consciousness purposefully embrace.

From this union manifests a world that was dormant and resting in the realm of Ishvara. We awaken to a fresh reality. We begin to feel our own presence; our self-identity returns. Our samskaras, desires, cravings, and ambitions become vivid. We feel the need for fulfillment and freedom. We become fully aware of our condition. We realize that before resorting to death, we were caught in the *vritti samskara chakra,* the cycle of vritti, to samskara, back to vritti, and we realize how unfulfilling was the journey of life (SK 40).

Now the strong urge arises to reverse this cycle, find life's purpose, and free ourselves from the chain of afflictions. In response to this urge, the power of the senses; the subtlest building blocks of our body (*tanmatra*), which are the essence of sound, touch, sight, taste, and smell; and their counterparts, the five gross elements, are drawn to us (SK 41). The purposeful intention of the Supreme Being guides us through the vast field of the manifest world. It transports us to the right place at the right time. We are born with a body and mind compatible with the consequences of our previous karmas (BG 6:43).

Seated in the deepest recesses of our heart, the imperishable Divine Being awakens our memory and revives our knowledge. He ensures that we gain access only to that portion of our memory we need to accomplish our life's purpose; the rest remains concealed (BG 15:15). The unalloyed luminosity of Prakriti is our eternal companion. It is always with us in the form of intuition. The guiding grace of intuitive wisdom is with us in every moment and at every juncture of our life in the form of conscience. The Divine Being brings us back to a beautiful world endowed with this limitless power, privilege, grace, and guidance. Because the Divine Being is moved by unconditional love and pure compassion for us, the sages address her as the Divine Mother.

At the dawn of this awakening, we realize we are in the full view of the Divine Being. Our entire existence is lit by her luminosity. It is thrilling and reassuring to see, through the eyes of our soul, the Lord of Life standing before us. It is empowering to know our relationship with Ishvara, and humbling to know that, without weighing our merits and demerits, she kept this relationship alive and vibrant even when we were dead. The realization that we are always under her protection and guidance fills us with gratitude. We are confident about ourselves and about accomplishing our life's purpose, for we know the Lord of Life is our mother, father, guru, and friend. She is omniscient and omnipotent. We are the fruit of her unconditional love. We are the luminosity of the Luminous Being. When the Lord of Life is inside us, outside us, and all around us, what else do we need? We are effortlessly pulled toward our true source. We are in ecstasy.

Manifestation of the Mental World

The light that awakens us to see the Lord of Life—our eternal guru, god, mother, father, friend, and provider—also awakens us to see ourselves. We become aware of our mind and the vast world contained in it. This is *pratyaya sarga,* the emergence of our personal mental world. We see our family and friends; our possessions come into full view; our conflicts and unresolved issues come to life. We remember how dear this world once was. We remember our passion for creating it, the difficulty in protecting it, and the pain of losing it. At the same time, we are being pulled toward our source, the Lord of Life.

Our self-created world is deeply alluring. Even when we are being bathed in the light of the Divine Being, we want to hold on to it. Our self-identity is the most powerful aspect of our self-created world. It had been the king of the world and its owner. It had been the creator of all the rules and laws, and it kept itself above all the rules and laws. We know self-identity is the breeding ground of misery, yet it is extraordinarily painful to see it dissolving in the luminosity of the Divine Being. To prevent it from being lost, we resort to ignorance (*avidya*). Ignorance is dismissing what we know to be true and replacing it with that which is contrary to truth (YS 2:5 and Vyasa on YS 2:24). We know who is the giver of our identity and the actual protector, guide, and provider. We know true protection lies in Ishvara's guiding grace. We also know that protecting our self-identity and serving the world it owns means embracing a life of sorrow. Yet we fly in the face of this crystal-clear understanding: we hide ourselves from the very light that has awakened us from death and empowered us to see ourselves—and to see both the Seer and the objective world.

We accomplish this by blanketing ourselves with disbelief in higher reality. Huddled under this thick blanket, we strengthen our belief in our self-identity and the world owned by it. This is avidya—ignorance. Hiding under the blanket of avidya, we force ourselves to believe we are protected from the all-consuming light of the Divine Being. In our ignorance, we do not realize that everything in the universe, including our mind and its most prized creation—self-identity—is within the view of the Lord of Life. Even as we are burying ourselves in ignorance, the guiding light of Ishvara is with us. Every nook and cranny of our existence is infused with his presence. Although Ishvara does not abandon us because we repudiate his boundless love and compassion, closing the eyes of our soul to his light cripples our ability to accomplish life's purpose.

Closing our eyes to the light of the imperishable Supreme Being limits our access to her infinite treasure—unsurpassed omniscience, omnipotence, and omnipresence. Our knowledge of reality becomes confined to the world that exists beneath the blanket of ignorance. We now have only as much power as we need to assert our mastery over our little world. Our self-identity is shaped by the space circumscribed by ignorance. In other words, our ability to know and experience reality declines drastically.

As stated earlier, our self-imposed disbelief in higher reality, and our strong belief in the reality of our long-cherished self-identity and the vast world owned by it, is avidya. Avidya is powerful and mysterious. It is powerful because it negates that which is eternal and self-evident and forces us to embrace that which must be eliminated. It is mysterious because it has no substance of its own, yet impairs our ability to embrace the guiding and nurturing grace of God. As soon as we embrace avidya, a unique world ensues. In Sankhya Yoga, the name for this unique world is *pratyaya sarga,* the world of our cognitions.

Pratyaya sarga is our creation. This world of our cognitions, beliefs, and disbeliefs is propelled by avidya and is rife with affliction. The broad categories of affliction—the sense of I-am-ness, attachment, aversion, and fear of death—all have their source in ignorance. They damage our conscience, the very light of our intelligence. They distort our sense of right and wrong, good and bad. Between lasting joy and momentary pleasure, they force us to choose the mere pleasure. Between ultimate freedom and slavery to our karmic bondage, they force us to choose bondage. This avidya-driven inability to withstand the light of higher truth and embrace it is known as *ashakti* (SK 46).

Ashakti means "having little or no power." As soon as we embrace avidya, we lose a significant degree of the power and wisdom bestowed on us by the Divine Being. Our intuitive wisdom becomes dim. Our will is no longer indomitable. Our capacity to sense, feel, and act is compromised. *Ashakti* dulls our power of comprehension—we wind up with a dense mind, and consequently, have little power of discernment. The technical term for this condition is *buddhi-vadha,* the impaired power of discernment. This impairment leads to the impairment of the eleven senses—the mind, the five senses of cognition, and the five senses of action. The healthy condition of our mind deteriorates. Our thought processes become convoluted. Our mind functions in a disturbed, stupefied, and distracted manner. Our power of hearing, touching, seeing, tasting, and smelling becomes limited. Our ability to grasp, move, speak, defecate, and procreate is constrained. In other words, we become a person of limited comprehension and capacities (SK 49). Our sense of satisfaction (*tushti*) becomes circumscribed (SK 50) and our idea of accomplishment (*siddhi*) narrows (SK 51). While living in this small self-created world, we seek our grandeur—a recipe for endless disappointment.

Fulfillment and Freedom

Through her loving and tender touch, Para Prakriti, the intrinsic Shakti of Ishvara, awakens us from the timeless slumber of death. We instantly see the Lord of Life. We also see her ever-present and infinitely vast universe, which, for our sake, is presented to us in an orderly fashion. We are also endowed with the capacity to see ourselves and the objective world. We are infused with the wisdom to select the tools and means to accomplish life's purpose—fulfillment and freedom. We are given the privilege to be the residents of the universe, which is a direct manifestation of Para Prakriti. We are an integral part of it—we are in it and it is all around us. This world of Para Prakriti is replete with everything we need to find our fulfillment and freedom, and yet, through sheer ignorance, we create a parallel world.

The world we create begins with ignorance and is sustained by ignorance. Everything in this avidya-generated world, regardless of how great and glorious it appears, is trivial and inherently painful (YS 2:15). Every object and relationship in this world is stained by our likes and dislikes, attachments and aversions. Everything here has only relative value. And most important, this avidya-generated world is transitory. Yet this is where we hope to find lasting happiness. Our entire life is nothing more than a sustained attempt to preserve this world. One day this whole world, including we ourselves, is put to rest. The idea of death is frightening but we do nothing to avert it. The score of afflictions—fear, doubt, anger, anguish, regret, guilt, shame, feelings of unworthiness, to name only a few—haunt us. We are not born for this.

We are born to attain freedom from the acquired tendencies of our mind, to minimize the influence of avidya, and eventually, to transcend it altogether. There are several ways to achieve this goal. The most straightforward approach is to undertake a practice that consists of methodical meditation and non-attachment, coupled with trustful surrender to God. The purpose of this or any other yogic practice is to purify the mind, make it one-pointed, and train it to flow peacefully inward. A practice is yogic if it helps us recognize our strengths and weaknesses and fills us with the courage to lift the veil of ignorance. A practice is yogic if it gives us both the vision and the strength to isolate our core being from our *apara prakriti,* the lower prakriti comprised of our habits, samskaras, and vasanas.

As soon as our avidya-driven identification with our samskaras and vasanas dissolves, we are once again bathed in the unalloyed light of the Supreme Being. In this light we are able to see the Seer within. We are established in our essential self (*svarupa-pratishtha*). We are thrilled and at the same time humbled by the realization that Chiti Shakti, the Power of the Supreme Being, is in us and is us (YS 4:33).

APPENDIX D

The Sri Vidya Tradition

The tradition of Sri Vidya belongs to the unique school of Tantra—Shaktism—that integrates the experiences of Vedic sages and the philosophical ideas of Sankhya, Yoga, Mimamsa, and Vedanta. There are several subschools within Sri Vidya. We belong to the Samaya school, and more precisely, the Urdhva-Amnaya lineage. The first master of this lineage is the sage Kapila, who is also the first teacher of Sankhya philosophy. According to the *Sri Vidyarnava* by Vidyaranya Yati, there are seventy-one masters in the Urdhva-Amnaya lineage. They are as follows:

1. Kapila
2. Atri
3. Vashishtha
4. Sanaka
5. Sanandana
6. Sanatsujata
7. Bhrigu
8. Vamadeva
9. Narada
10. Gautama
11. Shunaka
12. Shakti
13. Markandeya
14. Kaushika
15. Parashara
16. Shuka
17. Angira
18. Kanava
19. Jabali
20. Bharadvaja
21. Vedavyasa
22. Ishana
23. Ramana
24. Kapardi
25. Bhudhara
26. Subhata
27. Jalaja
28. Bhutesha
29. Parama
30. Vijaya

31. Bharata
32. Padmesha
33. Subhaga
34. Vishuddha
35. Samara
36. Kaivalya
37. Ganeshvara
38. Supadya
39. Vibudha
40. Yoga (Patanjali)
41. Vijnana
42. Ananga
43. Vibhrama
44. Damodara
45. Chidabhasa
46. Chinamaya
47. Kaladhara
48. Vireshvara
49. Mandara
50. Tridasha
51. Sagara
52. Mrida
53. Harasha
54. Simha
55. Gauda
56. Vira
57. Aghora
58. Dhruva
59. Divakara
60. Chakradhara
61. Pramathesha
62. Chaturbhuja
63. Anandabhairava
64. Dhira
65. Gauda
66. Pavaka
67. Parasharya
68. Satyanidhi
69. Ramachandra
70. Govinda
71. Shankaracharya

This list was prepared more than a thousand years ago. Since that time, many more masters have enriched the tradition through their sadhana and their experiences. The names of some of the important masters passed on to me include:

Srinatha
Adinatha
Anadinatha
Anamayanatha
Anantanatha
Dattatreya
Parashurama
Vishnusharma
Pragalbhachaya
Vidyaranya Yati
Gorakhanatha
Minanatha
Dharamadasa (Madhvananda)
Atmarama
Abhayananda
Sadananda
Swami Rama

Note: In our tradition, we are told not to seek the physical identity of these masters or their dates. In recent years, for the sake of simplicity, we refer to our lineage as the Tradition of the Himalayan Masters or the Himalayan Tradition.

APPENDIX E

Pronunciation and Transliteration Guide

Sanskrit letters form an organized arrangement of sounds, beginning with vowels and concluding with consonants. Each letter corresponds to only one sound. The following pronunciations are approximate; it is helpful to listen to a recording of the alphabet for accuracy.

Vowels in Sanskrit are either short or long. In transliteration, a horizontal line placed over the short vowels (a, i, u, and ṛ) indicates lengthening. Diphthongs (e, ai, o, and au) are long and do not require a diacritical mark. When spoken, long vowels and diphthongs sound about twice as long as short vowels.

a — b**u**t
ā — c**o**t
i — p**i**t
ī — k**ee**p
u — s**u**ture
ū — f**oo**d
ṛ — **ri**d

ṝ **ree**d
e l**a**te
ai **ai**sle
o t**o**te
au l**ou**d
aṁ nasalization of the preceding vowel (s**ung**)
aḥ a slight aspiration of the preceding vowel (**aha**)

Consonants fall into five classes, starting at the back of the throat and working forward to the lips. Each class is, in turn, divided into five categories: unaspirated or aspirated, unvoiced or voiced, and a nasal sound.

1. The guttural consonants are pronounced from the back of the throat:
   k **k**id
   kh pac**kh**orse
   g **g**ive
   gh bi**gh**orn
   ṅ ri**ng**

2. The palatal consonants are pronounced from the soft palate:
   c **ch**ip
   ch pin**chh**it
   j **j**ump
   jh lo**dgeh**ouse
   ñ pi**ñ**ata

3. The cerebral consonants are pronounced with the tip of the tongue contacting the roof of the mouth (a retroflex placement signified by a dot under the letter):

ṭ	tar
ṭh	can't handle
ḍ	dart
ḍh	landhunter
ṇ	under

4. The dental consonants are pronounced with the tip of tongue behind the upper row of teeth:

t	tell
th	pothandle
d	dot
dh	headhunter
n	nod

5. The labial consonants are pronounced with the lips:

p	putt
ph	mophead
b	but
bh	labhead
m	mop

Semi-vowels narrow the stream of air, creating friction as the air passes through the mouth:

y	yes
r	rapid
l	lap
v	halfway between wa (wow) and va (vow)

Sibilants include two variants of sh. In practice, they sound about the same:

ś	shove
ṣ	shallow
s	sunny
h	hot

Glossary

abhinivesha Fear of death; the fifth and final affliction, innate to every living being. Fear of death includes fear of losing one's identity and the anger stemming from being unable to prevent losing one's own life.

abhyasa Generally translated as "practice." In the *Yoga Sutra,* it is used precisely to mean making an ardent effort to create and maintain an internal environment in which the mind is allowed to flow peacefully inward. In other words, abhyasa means making an effort to restore and prolong the peaceful, inward flow of mind; thus, at a practical level, abhyasa is freeing the mind of its roaming tendencies and concentrating it peacefully inward.

acharya A person who lives what he teaches; spiritual teacher; preceptor; an authority in a particular field of knowledge.

affliction See *klesha.*

agama Revealed scriptures; more precisely, tantric scriptures.

ahamkara The function of the mind responsible for self-identification. In Sankhya Yoga, ahamkara is one of the categories of manifest prakriti. Ahamkara is the stage of manifestation in which the mind gives definition to consciousness, thus creating a sense of individuation. At this stage, consciousness is conceived of as an individual entity in contradistinction to pure, unalloyed Universal Consciousness.

aishvarya The intrinsic power of Ishvara; godly power; the power and achievement that makes us special.

aklishta Non-afflicting; non-painful *vritti,* thought construct.

akrama Non-sequential; non-linear; a state of creation that transcends the linearity of time, space, and the law of cause and effect.

akshara Imperishable; the Supreme Being, who is not subject to destruction, decay, and death; also a letter, a phoneme.

ananda anugata samadhi Samadhi propelled by or accompanied by the experience of joy.

anumana Inference.

anushasanam Discipline.

anushravika That which has scripture as its source; belief or knowledge that is dependent on the scriptures.

apara vairagya See *vairagya.*

apavarga Ultimate freedom; the highest goal of life; freedom from the cycle of birth and death.

asamprajnata samadhi The highest state of samadhi. In this particular state of samadhi, the trinity of cognition, object of cognition, and cognizer have blended into one. Consciousness, as separate from cognition, no longer exists, hence the term *asamprajnata,* literally, "lacking cognition and beyond cognition"; the state of perfect spiritual absorption beyond duality.

asana Posture; pose of the body characterized by stability and comfort; yogic pose.

asmita The sense of I-am-ness; the second of the five afflictions. In Sankhya Yoga, the terms *asmita* and *ahamkara* are used interchangeably.

asmita anugata samadhi Samadhi propelled by or accompanied by the sense of pure I-am-ness.

atha A Sanskrit term indicating an auspicious beginning; a term indicating something has come before and something is about to unfold. In the tantric tradition of Sri Vidya, *atha* is a shortened version of *a* (अ), *ka* (क), and *tha* (थ), the Sanskrit letters that constitute the guru chakra.

aversion See *dvesha.*

avidya Ignorance; the first of the five afflictions and the mother of all afflictions. In the *Yoga Sutra,* avidya refers to our unwillingness to let go of false understanding. At the practical level, avidya is a strong attachment to our preconceived notions and our unwillingness to even consider the possibility of an alternative to what we believe is true.

bhakti Love and devotion accompanied by trustful surrender to the higher Divinity.

bhautika sarga The manifestation of the universe pertaining to the physical world.

bhava pratyaya A yogi born with extraordinary wisdom; a yogi who before death was fully established in the state of samadhi characterized by mental absorption in self-luminous joy or in the sense of pure I-am-ness, and thus incarnates with all his knowledge and experience intact.

bhoga Fulfillment; one of the two fundamental goals of life.

brahmacharya Walking in Brahman, higher Consciousness; maintaining awareness of the higher purpose of life; celibacy; the practice leading to mastery over sensual urges, particularly the sexual urge; the practice designed to preserve and nurture life-sustaining energy.

Brahman All-pervading Consciousness; the highest state of Consciousness; non-dual reality.

buddhi The faculty of intelligence; the first stage of the manifestation of Prakriti. According to the *Yoga Sutra*, buddhi is innately luminous and endowed with the power of discrimination.

buddhi samvit The state of inner intelligence where reality is experienced in its fullness and purity.

buddhi sattva The essence of pure intelligence.

Chiti Shakti The Power of Consciousness; self-luminous Being; our essential Self.

chitta Usually translated as "mind"; literally, "the mental faculty that makes us feel that we are—that we exist"; the very principle of awareness. In the *Yoga Sutra,* this term is used for all the different faculties of mind, such as *buddhi,* the faculty that discriminates and decides; *ahamkara,* the faculty that identifies (the mind's boundary-making function); and *manas,* the thinking faculty.

dharma megha samadhi Literally, "the samadhi of the cloud of dharma"; the transitional state between lower and higher samadhi. In this transitional state, the mind has regained its innate luminosity and is spontaneously aware of the distinction between real and unreal, right and wrong, good and bad. Its discerning power is thus unshakeable, and it gravitates naturally to what is good and auspicious. This is what gives this state the name *dharma megha,* "the cloud laden with virtues," which implies that from this stage onward the mind has no reason to involve itself in any action that may lead to bondage.

drashta That which is seen; the information gathered from sense perception; the objects perceived by the senses.

drashtri The Seer; Pure Consciousness; the Seeing Power of the Seer; the core being.

dvesha Aversion; the fourth of the five afflictions.

ekagra One-pointed; one-pointed mind.

ekendriya Pertaining to one sense; in this context, attachment pertaining to the experience of one of the senses; the third stage in the development of lower *vairagya.*

higher samadhi See *nirbija samadhi* or *asamprajnata samadhi.*

I-am-ness See *asmita.*

ignorance See *avidya.*

indriya Sense. In a human being there are five senses of cognition and five senses of action.

intuition See *prajna.*

Ishvara Loosely translated as "God." In the *Yoga Sutra*, Ishvara refers precisely to the unique being who, throughout past, present, and future, is totally free of the fivefold affliction, the threefold karma, karmic consequences, and the karmic vehicles, which transport us from one life state to another. In this unique being, who is beyond gender, number, name, form, time, space, and the law of cause and effect, lies the unsurpassed seed of omniscience. Ishvara is an omnipresent, omnipotent, omniscient being, as opposed to ordinary beings, who are subject to time, space, the law of cause and effect, gender, number, name, and form. In the *Yoga Sutra*, Ishvara is considered the inner guide, provider, and protector of all living beings. The Ishvara of the *Yoga Sutra* is not a personified god, goddess, or deity.

iti A term referring to conclusion. In concept and usage, *iti* is juxtaposed with *atha*.

japa Meditation on a mantra while using a *mala*. There are three kinds of japa: *vachika, upanshu,* and *manasika*. Remembering a mantra while articulating it out loud is vachika japa; remembering a mantra while articulating it internally is upanshu japa; and remembering a mantra purely as an object of cognition is manasika japa. According to Yoga, manasika japa, which involves having the thought of a mantra as a meditative object, is the best form of japa because it allows the mind to be absorbed in the purest form of mantra. Mental absorption in a mantra is the gateway to samadhi.

jivatma Individual soul; a soul engaged in *samsara,* the cycle of birth and death.

jyotishmati Inner luminosity; the intrinsic luminosity of our core being. Inner luminosity is invariably accompanied by a joy untainted by sorrow (*vishoka*). Jyotishmati emerges when we meditate on the lotus of the heart, as described in *Yoga Sutra* 1:36.

kala Time.

kama Desire. The primordial intention of the Supreme Being; the son of the goddess Lakshmi and Vidyeshvara, the master sage of the Kadi lineage of the Sri Vidya mantra.

karma Action; refers to the law, "As you sow, so shall you reap."

karmashaya The repository of karma; the mind field where the subtle impressions are stored; the aspect of the mind where our karmas rest and wait for the right time and the right place to manifest.

klesha Affliction; the fundamental source of suffering. Affliction is fivefold: *avidya* (ignorance), *asmita* (sense of I-am-ness), *raga* (attachment), *dvesha* (aversion), and *abhinivesha* (fear of death).

klishta Painful; painful *vritti,* tendency of the mind.

krama shristi Sequential manifestation; the empirical world that is governed by the linearity of time, space, and the law of cause and effect.

kshara Perishable; the individual soul that is subject to destruction, decay, and death.

kshipta Disturbed; a disturbed state of mind.

lower samadhi See *sabija samadhi* or *samprajnata samadhi.*

mahat "Great"; the first evolute of Prakriti; the evolutionary state comprised of total intelligence.

manas The inner faculty of thinking.

mantra shastra The science of mantra.

mishra Mixture; combination. In the tantric tradition of Sri Vidya, mishra refers to the unique path of sadhana that integrates ritual worship and purely meditative techniques.

moksha shastra The science of liberation. In the Indian philosophical context, it refers to the philosophy of Sankhya Yoga.

mudha Dense; inert; stupefied; mental state characterized by stupefaction.

nirbija samadhi Seedless samadhi; the highest state of samadhi; identical to *asamprajnata samadhi.* Nirbija samadhi gets its name from the fact that, in this state, the seed of the subtle impressions stored in our mind has vanished, and the mind is completely free from even the subtlest causes of disturbance.

nirmana chitta A special kind of mind created by a yogi through her sheer *asmita,* I-am-ness; a yogically created mind, untainted by karmic impurities.

niruddha Constrained; controlled; confined; state of mind characterized by complete mastery.

nirvichara A stage in lower samadhi where the mind is absorbed in a subtle object.

nirvitarka A stage in lower samadhi where the mind is absorbed in a gross object.

non-attachment See *vairagya.*

practice See *abhyasa.*

prajna Intuition; the field of intuitive wisdom; the state of samadhi in which the mind has regained its innate luminosity; the experience unique to *dharma megha samadhi*; one of the five crucial ingredients for intensifying one's practice.

Prakriti The primordial cause of the universe; the intrinsic power of Pure Consciousness. In Sankhya Yoga, there are two categories of Prakriti, higher (*Para Prakriti*) and lower (*apara prakriti*), respectively. Higher Prakriti is intrinsic to Ishvara; lower prakriti constitutes our individual being.

prakritilaya Dissolved in Prakriti; a special category of yogi who died while established in *asmita anugata samadhi* and thus reincarnates with his wisdom and experience intact.

pramana Evidence; valid knowledge.

prana Life force.

pranava Supremely new; the sound *om.*

pranayama Expansion of prana; mastery over *prana shakti*; yogic breathing techniques.

pratyaksha Sensory experience; sense perception.

pratyaya sarga The world of mental cognition; the manifestation of our mental world; the world evolving from our *samskaras,* the subtle impressions stored in the mind.

Primordial Nature See *Prakriti.*

purashcharana The first step. In mantra sadhana, purashcharana consists of a time- and number-bound mantra practice.

Pure Consciousness See *Purusha.*

Purusha Pure Consciousness. In Sankhya Yoga, there are two categories of Purusha, higher and lower. The most frequently used terms are *akshara* and *kshara*, the Imperishable Being and perishable beings, respectively. Higher Purusha is Ishvara; lower purusha refers to ordinary beings.

raga Attachment; the fourth of the five afflictions.

rajas One of the three intrinsic attributes of Primordial Nature; the principle of pulsation.

rishi Seer; the seer of a mantra; an accomplished yogi endowed with extraordinary vision; a master who has received revelation; the recipient of revealed knowledge.

sabija samadhi Samadhi with seed; lower samadhi in contradistinction to higher samadhi; identical to *samprajnata samadhi.* Sabija samadhi gets its name from the fact that, in this state, subtle impressions stored in the mind still persist. As the object of meditation is further refined and the mind becomes totally absorbed in the purest form of the meditative object, lower samadhi culminates in *dharma megha samadhi,* the gateway to *nirbija,* seedless samadhi.

sadhana A well-defined, structured method of spiritual practice.

samadhi A perfectly still, pristine state of mind; a state of mind free from all karmic consequences; a state in which we are fully established in our essential nature. The entire range of samadhi is described in two parts, lower samadhi and higher samadhi. Lower samadhi, known as *sabija* or *samprajnata,* refers to the process of meditation, whereas higher samadhi, known as *nirbija* or *asamprajnata*, refers to the ultimate experience of being established in the purest state of Consciousness.

samapatti Mental absorption; a mental state in which the mind is fully absorbed in the object of meditation.

samaya One of the three schools in the tantric tradition of Sri Vidya, in which exclusive emphasis is placed on internal meditative discipline.

samprajnata samadhi Samadhi with cognition; lower samadhi; identical to *sabija samadhi.* In this state of samadhi, the yogi is aware of himself as a meditator, the object of meditation, and the process of meditation. Further, because the subtle impressions still persist in the mind, the potential remains for them to become the ground for the mind's roaming tendency.

samprasada Complete transparency; complete joy; total expansion; manifestation of spiritual wisdom and joy.

samsara The world characterized by continuous coming and going, birth and death.

samskara Subtle karmic impression. Every action we perform—mental, verbal, or physical—makes an impression in the mind, which is stored in the form of memory. The deeper the impression, the more strongly it influences our current thoughts, speech, and actions. In an attempt to attain self-mastery and reach samadhi, it is crucial that we purify and eventually eliminate our karmic impressions.

samyama A technical term referring to the last three rungs of yoga sadhana: *dharana* (concentration), *dhyana* (meditation), and *samadhi.*

sankalpa A resolve; an intention.

sattva One of the three attributes of Primordial Nature; the principle of illumination.

savichara A stage in lower samadhi characterized by mental absorption in the meaning of the word, rather than in the word itself.

savitarka A stage in lower samadhi characterized by mental absorption in the word, rather than in the meaning of the word.

shraddha Faith; one of the five crucial ingredients for intensifying one's practice.

siddhi Accomplishment; unfoldment of mental power.

sthiti Peaceful flow of mind, free from roaming tendencies; a state free from thought constructs.

subtle impression See *samskara.*

svabhava One's own intrinsic attribute; intrinsic nature; the essential characteristic that defines our being.

svarupa pratishtha Established in one's essential nature; full realization of our core being.

tamas One of the three attributes of Primordial Nature; the principle of inertia and darkness.

tanmatra That alone; the subtlest state of the world made of matter and energy; the essence of earth, water, fire, air, and space.

tapas Austerity; heat; a discipline or observance to cleanse the body and purify the mind; a spiritual practice to transcend our physical and mental limitations.

upaya Method; technique; strategy; tools and means.

upaya pratyaya An aspirant whose self-realization depends on his current practice and the accuracy of the practice; an ordinary yogi, in contradistinction to a *bhava pratyaya* yogi, an extraordinary master; an aspirant who must rely on an authentic technique to achieve his goal.

vairagya Loosely translated as "non-attachment"; literally, "non-coloring, non-smearing." Vairagya refers to the process of detaching ourselves from our karmic impressions and the actions propelled by them. The *Yoga Sutra* divides the range of vairagya in two main categories, lower and higher. Lower vairagya refers to the process of practicing non-attachment, while higher vairagya is a state of awareness free from all attachment. At a practical level, vairagya entails purifying our intelligence and embracing our inner wisdom, which is untainted by our dispositions and preoccupations.

vasana Coloring; a stronger, more active term for *samskara,* subtle karmic impression.

vashikara samjna The state of *vairagya* defined by a high degree of wisdom and self-control; the upper limit of lower vairagya. The definitive characteristic (*samjna*) is that a yogi in this state is so fully guided by intuitive wisdom (*prajna*) that she cannot be influenced by any external source, and thus has attained mastery over herself (*vashikara*).

videha Beyond body or transcendence of body; a special category of yogi who died while firmly established in the experience of self-luminous joy, and thus reincarnates with his knowledge and experience intact.

vikshipta Distracted; distracted state of mind.

virya Vigor; vitality; virility; one of the five crucial ingredients for intensifying one's practice.

vishoka Absence of sorrow (*shoka*); beyond sorrow; the state of our intrinsic luminosity manifesting as joy. Vishoka is a joyful state of mind devoid of all sorrow, as well as its cause. Vishoka emerges as we meditate on the lotus of the heart, as described in *Yoga Sutra* 1:36.

viveka Discernment; clearly understanding the difference between truth and untruth.

viveka khyati The state of spiritual unfoldment characterized by clear understanding; the dawn of intuitive wisdom.

vritti Roaming tendency of the mind; thought construct; modification of the mind; a mental condition that makes the mind revolve; a mental cognition that settles in the mind as an impression and later compels us to perform similar actions.

vritti samskara chakra The wheel of thoughts and subtle impressions; the complex cycle of the thought process which creates impressions and propels our thoughts.

vyatireka Isolating the heaviest and most distracting forms of attachment from those that are lighter and relatively less distracting; the second stage in the development of lower *vairagya*.

yatamana Making an effort; acknowledging the bondage created by attachment and making an effort to free oneself from it; the first stage in the development of lower *vairagya*.

yatna Effort; investing vigor and enthusiasm in a system of spiritual discipline; investing everything it takes to achieve a state of *sthiti,* the inward and peaceful flow of mind.

Index to Sutra References

Index

D

E

F

G

H

I

J

K

R

S

T

U

V

W

Y

About the Author

PANDIT RAJMANI TIGUNAIT, PHD, is a modern-day master and living link in the unbroken Himalayan Tradition. He embodies the yogic and tantric wisdom which the Himalayan Tradition has safeguarded for thousands of years. Pandit Tigunait is the successor of Sri Swami Rama of the Himalayas and the spiritual head of the Himalayan Institute. As a young man he committed himself to arduous spiritual practice and studied with renowned adepts of India before being initiated into the lineage of the Himalayan Tradition by his master, Sri Swami Rama, in 1976.

Pandit Tigunait is fluent in Vedic and Classical Sanskrit and holds two doctorates, one from the University of Allahabad (India), and another from the University of Pennsylvania. As a leading voice of YogaInternational.com and the author of 15 books, his teachings span a wide range, from scholarly analysis and scripture translation to practical guidance on applying yogic wisdom to modern life. Over the past 35 years, Pandit Tigunait has touched innumerable lives around the world as a teacher, guide, author, humanitarian, and visionary spiritual leader.

HIMALAYAN INSTITUTE®

The main building of the Institute headquarters near Honesdale, Pennsylvania

The Himalayan Institute

The Himalayan Institute offers educational programs, services, and tools for yoga, meditation, spiritual development, and holistic health. The Institute's mission is spirituality in action, and includes a range of global humanitarian projects in addition to its educational activities. Founded in 1971 by Swami Rama of the Himalayas, the Institute draws on its roots in the ancient tradition of the Himalayan masters to facilitate personal growth and development and service to humanity.

Our international headquarters is located on a beautiful 400-acre campus in the rolling hills of the Pocono Mountains of northeastern Pennsylvania. Our spiritually vibrant community and peaceful setting provide the perfect atmosphere for seminars and retreats, residential programs, and holistic health services. Students from all over the world join us to attend diverse programs on subjects such as hatha yoga, meditation, stress reduction, ayurveda, and yoga and tantra philosophy.

In addition, the Himalayan Institute offers the following products, services, and programs:

Global Humanitarian Projects

The Himalayan Institute's humanitarian projects bring spirituality into action. Our projects offer education, vocational teaching, healthcare, and environmental regeneration, serving impoverished communities in India, Mexico, and Cameroon, West Africa. Through rural empowerment, our humanitarian projects fight poverty and seek to create lasting social transformation.

Yoga International

Yoga International is the educational division of the organization, connecting practitioners of yoga, meditation, and ayurveda to a timeless and authentic source of wisdom. Steeped in a 5,000-year-old tradition, our expert teachers provide systematic instruction at all levels, both in interactive digital learning environments and through immersive retreats.

Visit YogaInternational.com for full-length online seminars, inspiring articles, and delicious recipes, or to register for a retreat or learn about our yoga certification programs. We offer three membership options, and a basic membership is free. Sign up today!

Publications

The Himalayan Institute publishes over 60 titles on yoga, spirituality, and holistic health, including the best-selling *Living with the Himalayan Masters* by Swami Rama, *Power of Mantra and the Mystery of Initiation*, *From Death to Birth* and *Tantra Unveiled* by Pandit Rajmani Tigunait, PhD, and *Yoga: Mastering the Basics* by Sandra Anderson and Rolf Sovik.

Total Health Center

For over 40 years, the Himalayan Institute Total Health Center has combined Eastern philosophy and Western medicine in an integrated approach to holistic health. It offers individualized programs based on these principles, utilizing holistic medical evaluations, massage, yoga therapy, ayurveda, biofeedback, natural medicines, lifestyle education and counseling for a combined approach that facilitates optimal healing and revitalization in both mind and body.

Total Health Products

The Himalayan Institute Total Health product line includes the original Neti Pot™ and includes an assortment of natural, homeopathic, holistic, and ayurvedic products. From non-GMO components, petroleum-free biodegrading plastics, and eco-friendly packaging we create products that have the least impact on the environment. Your patronage is important and appreciated. Part of every purchase supports our Global Humanitarian projects

For further information about our programs, humanitarian projects, and products,

call: 800-822-4547

e-mail: info@HimalayanInstitute.org

write: The Himalayan Institute
952 Bethany Turnpike
Honesdale, PA 18431

or visit: www.HimalayanInstitute.org

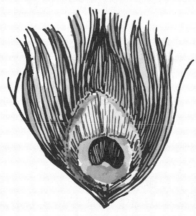

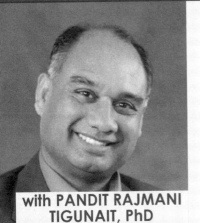

Happiness Is Your Creation

Swami Rama as compiled by
Pandit Rajmani Tigunait, PhD

Did you ever pause for a moment and realize that you are the creator of your destiny? In *Happiness Is Your Creation*, Pandit Tigunait gathered the inspirational teachings of his master, the late Swami Rama, on the yogic prescription for happiness. These enriching passages identify the causes of unhappiness and provide direction to remain centered and joyful in everyday life. Learn how to cultivate a positive mind and charge your body and mind through meditation, allowing you to lead a more active and productive life. This motivational book reveals the ancient teachings of self-discipline, self-mastery, and self-realization through yoga and meditation.

Paperback with flaps, 5½" x 8½" , 136 pages
$12.95, ISBN 978-0-89389-246-3

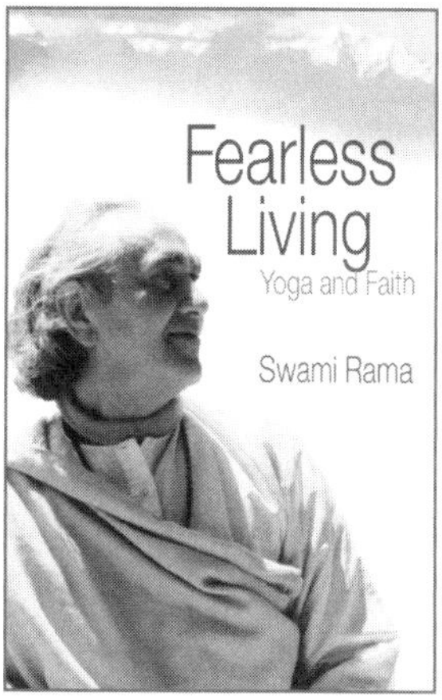

Fearless Living: Yoga and Faith

Swami Rama

Learn to live without fear—to trust a higher power, a divine purpose. In this collection of anecdotes from the astonishing life of Swami Rama, you will understand that there is a way to move beyond mere faith and into the realm of personal revelation. Through his astonishing life experiences we learn about ego and humility, how to overcome fears that inhibit us, discover sacred places and rituals, and learn the importance of a one-pointed, positive mind. Swami Rama teaches us to see with the eyes of faith and move beyond our self imposed limitations.

Paperback with flaps, 5½" x 8½", 160 pages
$12.95, ISBN 978-0-89389-251-7

Touched by Fire

Pandit Rajmani Tigunait, PhD

This vivid autobiography of a remarkable spiritual leader—Pandit Rajmani Tigunait, PhD —reveals his experiences and encounters with numerous teachers, sages, and his mentor, the late Swami Rama of the Himalayas. His well-told journey is filled with years of disciplined study and the struggle to master the lessons and skills passed to him. *Touched by Fire* brings Western culture a glimpse of Eastern philosophies in a clear, understandable fashion, and provides numerous photographs showing a part of the world many will never see for themselves.

Paperback with flaps, 5½" x 8½", 296 pages
$16.95, ISBN 0-89389-239-4

At the Eleventh Hour

Pandit Rajmani Tigunait, PhD

This book is more than the biography of a great sage—it is a revelation of the many astonishing accomplishments Swami Rama achieved in his life. These pages serve as a guide to the more esoteric and advanced practices of yoga and tantra not commonly taught or understood in the West. And they bring you to holy places in India, revealing why these sacred sites are important and how to go about visiting them. The wisdom in these stories penetrates beyond the power of words.

A memorable and impressive picture of a modern-day saint, whose legacy is very much alive in both the East and the West. —Andrew Weil, M.D.

Paperback with flaps, 6" x 9", 448 pages
$18.95, ISBN 0-89389-212-2

To order: 800-822-4547
Email: mailorder@HimalayanInstitute.org
Visit: www.HimalayanInstitute.org

HIMALAYAN INSTITUTE®